THIRD EDITION

# Procedures in Marriage and Family Therapy

**Gregory W. Brock**
*University of Kentucky*

**Charles P. Barnard**
*University of Wisconsin-Stout*

*With a Foreword by*
*Carl Whitaker, M.D.*

Allyn and Bacon
Boston • London • Toronto • Sydney • Tokyo • Singapore

*Series Editor, Social Work and Family Therapy:* Judy Fifer
*Editor in Chief, Social Sciences:* Karen Hanson
*Editorial Assistant:* Susan Hutchinson
*Marketing Manager:* Suzy Spivey
*Production Administrator:* Annette Joseph
*Production Coordinator:* Holly Crawford
*Editorial-Production Service:* Sydney Baily-Gould, Saxon House Productions
*Composition Buyer:* Linda Cox
*Electronic Composition:* Cabot Computer Services
*Manufacturing Buyer:* Megan Cochran
*Cover Administrator:* Jenny Hart
*Cover Designer:* Suzanne Harbison

Copyright © 1999, 1992, 1988 by Allyn and Bacon
A Viacom Company
160 Gould Street
Needham Heights, MA 02194
Internet: www.abacon.com
America Online: keyword: College Online

*Library of Congress Cataloging-in-Publication Data*

Brock, Gregory W.
    Procedures in marriage and family therapy / Gregory W. Brock,
  Charles P. Barnard ; with a foreword by Carl Whitaker. -- 3rd ed.
       p.   cm.
    Includes bibliographical references and index.
    ISBN 0-205-28782-4 (pbk.)
    1. Family psychotherapy.   2. Marital psychotherapy.   I. Barnard,
  Charles P.   II. Title.
  RC488.5.B685   1998
  616.89'156--dc21                                            98-13583
                                                                 CIP

Printed in the United States of America

10  9  8  7  6  5  4  3  2  1        03  02  01  00  99  98

**Permission Acknowledgment:**
Page 215. Gregory W. Brock. "Reducing Vulnerability to Ethics Codes Violations:
An At-Risk Test for Marriage and Family Therapists." Reprinted from Volume (23),
Number (1), of the *Journal of Marital and Family Therapy.* Copyright 1997. American
Association for Marriage and Family Therapy. Reprinted with permission.

*Dedicated to*
*Jeanette, Jessica, Kelly, and Jordan;*
*Marge, Jayne, Matt, and Clare;*
*and*
*Carl Whitaker, M.D.*

# Contents

# Foreword

Most writing in marriage and family therapy presents the reader with an established system of how to change families so as to relieve the symptoms they present or the stress they are suffering. The reader is encouraged to follow a rigid system and adopt one particular theoretical basis for bringing about change.

Brock and Barnard, two hands-on teachers, offer something different. They are sharing a kind of "clinical anthropologist's" view of what happens when a family interacts with an old-timer who has dallied with the fads but finds success in doing what works. There is precious little fluff in these pages. As each of the procedures is described, we capture anecdotal glimpses of family life and the process of family therapy. This is in keeping with the authors' intent, stated early on, that their work is not supposed to replace other texts and extensive study of family and therapy processes but is designed to be used by those familiar with those terrains. The authors have gathered the data and organized it into a multifaceted notebook with value for both the young and the more experienced therapist. The index lists many, many procedures so that the reader can use the book in a bedside-table manner to ponder the procedures along with tomorrow's anxieties.

The casual style makes for easy reading. The usual trappings of hidebound solutions or invasive control of the process of change are avoided. The authors accurately sense and communicate that there is more than one potential solution to various situations but are willing to risk letting their ideas be made known to the professional community. The table of contents sets up a sort of encyclopedia of professional interaction patterns that is a gold mine for the developing therapist and a stimulant to the thinking of even the old hands in our territory.

Hidden behind the descriptions of what to do and when, one can see the message of gentle care offered to families in pain. Hidden also is a respectful awareness of each family as a unique culture that has evolved out of the blending of the parents' families of origin. Finally, I see throughout the book the integrity of the authors and their capacity to be peers with their students and with us, the readers.

*Carl Whitaker, M.D.*
*1992*

# Preface

While teaching courses on marriage and family therapy and supervising casework, we became aware of the need for a resource that defined what we have come to know as procedures in professional marriage and family therapy practice. We asked our students to list what they needed to know and then added our own items. Our intent from the outset was to create a reference for our students and for other professionals who work with families.

Although *Procedures in Marriage and Family Therapy*, Third Edition, will have particular value to therapists new to the field of family therapy, other professionals not trained in family therapy but who see families in the context of their practice will find it useful. We also believe the contents will be provocative and rewarding reading for the open-minded, seasoned clinician. We hope that our ideas will create new insights and new ways of perceiving commonly used approaches to clinical situations.

It is often said that theory provides a map with which to chart a route. As authors, supervisors, and therapists, each of us has a particular theoretical map that influenced the procedures described in this book. Our maps became clearer as we progressed through the writing of this edition and those published earlier. In a similar fashion, we believe the book provides an opportunity for the reader to discern the theoretical map he or she brings to therapy. We encourage you to closely examine those procedures you reject because it is likely that the reasons for rejection will yield more meaning than the reasons for those embraced.

An objection sometimes raised about attempts to define procedure is that the role of the therapist is made trivial. We contend, however, that identifying what works enriches rather than diminishes any activity. By describing the generic ways of handling the most common situations faced by therapists, our goal is to help the field focus on that part of practice beyond the commonplace. Our interest is in freeing the clinician to creatively pursue new approaches. The body of procedure that develops in any field must constantly change, and we hope to aid that process by describing and cataloging standards that are meant to be challenged.

We are not so arrogant as to believe the procedures described here constitute the only way of accomplishing particular therapeutic objectives. We recognize that the field of family therapy has matured to the point of benefiting from many schools of thought, each with seemingly idiosyncratic ways of accomplishing therapeutic tasks. In spite of these supposed differences, we believe there are now some universally agreed ways of accomplishing many therapeutic tasks. We offer the procedures in this book as examples.

## A Note about the Third Edition

Many instructors, students, and clinicians helped us prepare this edition of *Procedures in Marriage and Family Therapy*. Their reviews and comments guided expansion and deletion of material in the book in several important areas and reorganization of the contents. We would like especially to acknowledge the help of reviewers of this edition: William T. Anderson of Texas Women's University, Brian Canfield of Northeast Louisiana University, and Charles C. Hendrix of Oklahoma State University–Stillwater. We are indebted to many people for their support. We would also like to thank the reviewers of previous editions, including Thomas E. Clark, Wake Forest University; Frederick G. Humphrey, University of Connecticut; Harvey Joanning, Texas Tech University; James F. Keller, Virginia Polytechnic Institute and State University; Lynne Kellner, L.U.K., Inc.; Luciano L'Abate, Georgia State University; Eleanor Macklin, Syracuse University; Fred P. Piercy, Purdue University; and Carl Whitaker.

Several important features of this edition differentiate it from earlier ones. Most importantly, we have reorganized the book into sections that enhance it as a teaching resource. Additionally, in keeping with advances in the field, new procedures and whole new groups of procedures are presented. We also have added considerable material to many of the procedures that were described in earlier editions.

One section was reoriented significantly in this edition. Instead of a lamentation about the lack of research, the focus of the commentary about research is on treatment effectiveness. Within the past few years, research of good quality not only has demonstrated the overall effectiveness of marriage and family therapy, but also it has generated a few specific guidelines that all clinicians must know. We have spelled out those guidelines.

As with each previous edition of *Procedures*, this one presents a clinician's resource that is up-to-date and that reflects a pragmatic view of marriage and family therapy. The field is evolving at an ever-increasing rate. Successful practice and training—both of which are becoming more complex activities—depend on authoritative knowledge within easy access. We hope you find what you need here.                                    *G.W.B.*
                                                              *C.P.B.*

# ► 1

# Overview

Clinical procedure in the field of family therapy* traditionally has passed from master to apprentice through live observation and supervision. There are hints at procedure in the family therapy literature, but nowhere has it been collected for easy access and use. Professions that have reached a high level of technical competence, however, have texts and manuals that specify the procedures to be used in specific practice situations. Lawyers, physicians, and ministers all have rich resources—their respective procedural manuals—much to the benefit of their daily practices. The profession and the discipline of family therapy have developed to such a degree that a procedural book for family therapists is an important and necessary addition to the literature.

Authors of family therapy texts have tended to emphasize the conceptual aspects of therapy rather than the procedural. Many texts, especially those with the word *technique* in the title, are so laden with theoretical notions that actual description of what is done to implement theory seems to have been forgotten. Where technique is specified, it is often stated in such a fuzzy manner that its use by the reader is likely to prove difficult at best and even dangerous when the author provides no real decision-making guidance. Many of the technique books are cookbooks that disguise the author's advocacy for a specific brand of family therapy. As a result, readers of the literature are exposed to many maps of theory without the means of traversing the obstacles encountered in therapy.

The purpose of this book is to specify and describe the important and effective procedures that experienced practitioners use in conducting family

---

*Throughout the book the terms *family therapy* and *family therapist* are used rather than the formal titles *marriage and family therapy* and *marriage and family therapist*. Both the field and its practitioners are referred to often and the shortened forms are less awkward.

therapy. This is a how-to book, but it is not a cookbook. The terms *procedure* and *technique* are not synonymous. In this book, *procedure* connotes a refined and time-tested method that is meant to stand alone, outside of any specific family therapy orientation. A group of procedures together might constitute a specific technique or therapeutic approach.

Family system theory, for example, is a valuable tool for assessing family problems and for designing overall treatment goals. The atheoretical, artful aspect of therapy, however, consists of what therapists do to carry out theory-based plans. They implement procedures that have developed out of their experience in attempting to use the various models of family therapy. These procedures are complex behavioral routines that tend to produce the same approximate result in terms of client behavior, and together the procedures define the practice of marriage and family therapy.

This is a record of at least some portion of what we teach our students and what we have found helpful to those who are attempting the difficult task of supplying services to families. In our judgment, practitioners of marriage and family therapy need a greater appreciation for the procedural aspects of practice. The field is fast leaving behind what is called technique and loosely structured treatment. Effective, ethical practice today is the product of highly skilled clinicians who implement procedures having known outcomes.

## ASSUMPTIONS

In writing this text, our assumptions about therapy and the role of the therapist became more apparent. Some assumptions are ordinary and some provocative, and naturally, not all procedures are in keeping with these assumptions; nonetheless, they are stated for your understanding. We believe the following:

1. The task of the family therapist is to change the structure and interaction processes of the client family.
2. The role of the therapist is that of the expert, and the therapist is responsible for the overall structure and process of therapy.
3. Clients are consumers of a service that is most effective when it is familiar to them and follows a format similar to that used by other professionals with whom clients have had prior contact.
4. As long as therapy remains within the bounds of ethical practice, there are no correct or incorrect procedures in family therapy; there are only outcomes which together produce change in family structure and processes.

5. The therapist's skill in using procedure is primarily the result of practice, self-study, and feedback based on observation by other practitioners.

## HOW TO USE THIS BOOK

The book is not designed to be read from cover to cover. To best use it, first recognize the scope of the clinical situations and the procedures it covers. Of course, not all possible clinical situations and procedures are addressed. Nor will you find broad-based treatment strategies for problems such as eating disorders, drug abuse, and so forth. Knowing what situations *are* covered, however, will enable you to use this book as a generic resource, much as a writer uses a style manual.

After becoming familiar with the scope of the book, refer to it when you are faced with a new clinical situation or one that does not seem to be going well. Use the table of contents and the index to locate procedures of interest. If you cannot find your exact situation in the index, try to rephrase it in your mind as you continue to search. If your clinical situation is not addressed, look at a similar one, and you may discover a procedure that can be adapted.

We have attempted to write in a direct and descriptive manner. Early on, we decided that including citations and other means of identifying originators of the procedures would unnecessarily burden the text without any real gain in understanding. That does not mean we wish to claim the procedures as our intellectual property. Nor do we believe that the procedures are the property of anyone else. Procedure is the heritage of a profession and belongs to all its members. It is a labor in common.

# ▶ 2

## First Contact Procedures

The Western tradition of supplying mental health services is based on medical practice in which the first stage of treatment is diagnosis or assessment. Family therapy does not have a strongly developed diagnostic heritage compared to that of the field of psychology or psychiatry, although this area is developing. Even so, to design a treatment plan, each therapist must categorize, judge, and evaluate families.

Besides the actual process of therapy, one of the main distinguishing aspects of family therapy is the group of procedures used when first encountering the client family. The variables examined, the attitude of the therapist, and the cognitive map so often spoken about in family therapy texts all determine the style of treatment that has come to be known as family therapy.

### THE INTAKE TELEPHONE CALL

Clinicians differ on the issue of involvement at the point of the initial phone call. Our preference is to be involved. Studies have demonstrated that the number of family members present at the initial session has definite implications regarding who will be present at future sessions. There is a far greater likelihood of ongoing commitments to therapy coming from those present in the first session than from those not present initially (whom the clinician then attempts to lure in at a later time). For this reason, among others, the family therapist is well advised to take intake calls rather than having a secretary do so. This also places the therapist in a better position to initiate the battle for structure that Whitaker (Napier & Whitaker, 1978) calls essential.

At the point of intake, the therapist can communicate who should attend the first session and begin to establish the tenor and structure of therapy.

For instance, assume the mother of three children calls about a concern regarding one child and states she wants a session alone to discuss this problem with the therapist. If the secretary takes the call and arranges for the requested individual session, the therapist runs the risk of the father and children perceiving the therapist and mother/wife as having an unfair alliance that will be difficult for them to surmount. Their mental set will pose another necessary struggle for the therapist that could have been avoided by having everyone present initially. The task of ensuring an ongoing commitment to the therapeutic alliance is enhanced if all are present from the outset.

The mother in this example may offer many reasons for coming alone, but the therapist should be steadfast in securing the presence of all without offending her. The following example illustrates a way of responding to the mother in this case:

> I realize the problem is primarily with your one child, and that your husband doesn't deal much with the children, but for me to be as helpful to you in this dilemma as I hope to be, I know from past experience it's best to have all present at least for this initial session. Hopefully you can understand and appreciate my desire to be as helpful as I can, and I know this is important. I know the schools will cooperate with allowing the children to be excused, and I would like to have you ask your husband to call me about whatever questions he might have in this regard. [Asking for the husband's phone number and then calling to explain your purpose is often valuable. It is amazing how often fathers cooperate when approached directly and communicated to with a respect that expresses their value and importance to the therapeutic effort.] I certainly could see you alone, and may choose to do that at a later point, but for this initial session I know it's important to have all present. We will need to trust one another, and while I know you don't know me yet, hopefully you can trust me on this count.

With this kind of presentation, it is exceptionally unusual to be met with ongoing apprehensiveness or a refusal to cooperate with the request. It seems that this type of request, while ensuring cooperation and attendance by all, also serves to engage the person on the other end of the phone conversation as they hear the desire to help communicated. It also seems to instill in clients an initial belief in the competence of the therapist. Naturally, these are important and valuable perceptions to have in place prior to the first session.

Once the family is present for the first session, ask the person who called to review what was discussed during the intake call. This serves to communicate that it is important for all to have the benefit of shared understanding, and, hopefully, it eliminates any concerns those not present during the call may have about that initial conversation. Continuing with the case example of the mother, the therapist might say something like: "Mrs. Jones, we spoke together about one week ago, and perhaps you can refresh my memory to make sure I understand what brings you in, and also we can make sure everyone understands the reason for your presence here today." After listening, the therapist might choose to clarify points made in the mother's presentation or add things that seem to have been "forgotten." For instance, perhaps the mother mentioned everything discussed but forgot to mention that she wondered whether or not the father felt he might have anything to contribute to therapy. Perhaps she actually said that she wondered whether the dad cared, but the therapist may choose to frame it as the dad "wondering whether or not he had anything to contribute or if he could be helpful." At these times, reframing or packaging a message can be very helpful.

## ESTABLISHING A RELATIONSHIP WITH CLIENTS

Establishing a relationship, also termed *joining,* is a complicated process that begins the moment either the therapist or the client becomes psychologically aware of the other. From this always sketchy beginning, the therapeutic relationship develops as an adjunct or impediment to family change.

Hans Strupp, one of the most rigorous and well known of all researchers who have investigated the therapist–client relationship, says: "The critical feature of all successful therapy, it seems to me, is the therapist's skillful management of the patient–therapist relationship" (1996, p. 1022). Strupp has been instrumental in orchestrating numerous studies over the past twenty years that have provided powerful evidence regarding the influence of common factors (e.g., empathy, warmth, and respect) on the impact of therapy outcome. Those findings have been substantiated by other researchers as well (Bergin & Garfield, 1994; Lambert, 1992). In fact, it is now commonly believed that as much as 85 percent of therapy outcome variance is attributable to these common factors being demonstrated by the therapist.

It is important to realize that clients who are undertaking therapy for the first time, as well as those with past therapy experience, expect to have the same form of relationship they have developed with other professionals. Unfortunately, most of us have learned to be wary of dentists; we also lie to our physicians and ignore their advice. Unless clients learn that a new sort of relationship is required for family therapy, it may not be successful.

The nature of all therapy demands that the relationship be warm, empathic, and genuine. Carl Rogers (1951) defined these conditions as necessary and sufficient for individual therapy, and training in how to create such relationship conditions has been part of graduate programs for many years. As defined by Minuchin and Fishman (1981) and many others, work with families and married couples requires more, especially in the initial phase of therapy.

Since the client is usually a group of individuals and the problems discussed usually focus on the actions of family members, the awful truth of relationships emerges quickly compared with the pace of disclosure in individual therapy. The relationship needed to support disclosure of family problems is perceived as safe, not confrontative initially, and yet, because clients come to therapy expecting guidance and advice in addition to a sympathetic ear, the therapist needs to be seen as an expert in therapy and not just family life.

Family therapy tends to be action oriented; that is, the therapist introduces new ideas as well as new behavior in the session. Therapists need to redefine and relabel symptoms; thus, persuasion and selling ideas is important. To be persuaded or to accept alternate conceptions of family patterns and symptoms, clients must be confident that going along with their therapist will pay off. Family therapists are familiar with how to act warm and empathic, but very little has been written for us about how to inspire client confidence.

As in any relationship, therapist self-confidence is the best determinant of client confidence in the therapist and is displayed in a number of ways, including diplomas hung on the office wall and the office furnishings. Behaviorally, therapists display confidence through movement, dress, and voice quality. In addition, clients become more confident in their therapist as a result of the authoritative statements made in therapy sessions.

Authoritative statements are those that educate clients about their family and themselves. For example, while listening to a family member describe his or her reactions to a recent death in the family, the therapist might comment, "What you are referring to is a grief reaction to sudden loss. We often go through a series of stages, beginning with denial and then anger, after a sudden loss." In this instance, the therapist is sharing knowledge and expertise with the client. While such statements should not make up the majority of what a therapist says in therapy, statements that are intended to educate the client demonstrate therapist competence and create confidence.

As we enter the domain of discussing procedures to enhance the therapeutic relationship, we wish to give specific attention to what has come to be referred to as the "narrative therapies" (White & Epston, 1990; Neimeyer & Mahoney, 1995). Practitioners of this approach are particularly alert to the client–therapist relationship and acutely sensitive to recognizing clients as the true "experts" regarding their circumstances. The "common factors" of therapy described earlier (Strupp, 1996) as being essential to productive therapeutic outcome are eminently apparent in the narrative approach. These common factors are empathy, warmth, and respect; they are key ingredients to any successful and rewarding relationship.

The narrative approach can perhaps be characterized by a statement attributed to the ancient Greeks: "We are our stories." From the narrative perspective, the psyche is not a fixed, objective entity but rather a fluid social construct or a story that is subject to revision. The therapist's job is to help people "re-author" their stories, or elements of their stories, that are not serving them well.

White and Epston (1990; Cowley & Springen, 1995) the two therapists most closely identified with this approach, maintain that staying cognizant of all of our sensory experiences would overwhelm us. They think that we resolve this potential problem by collapsing our experiences into narrative structures, or stories, to make them intelligible. As individuals and family units forge identities, we give some stories more weight than others. If our "dominant stories" happen to revolve around problems, they can filter out problem-free experiences from our memories, perceptions, and subsequent self-definition. Unfortunately, this then culminates in threads of hope, resourcefulness, and various capabilities otherwise present but not available as we move through our lives.

More conventional therapies tend to assume that problems stem from internal pathologies that need to be identified, scrutinized, and corrected. Narrative therapy does not look for flaws but rather helps people to spot omissions in their stories. According to the narrative therapist, no problem or diagnosis captures or defines the whole of a person's or family's experiences. There are other ways of acting and thinking, but these other ways get overshadowed by the dominant story (e.g., "In a Depressive Disorder," "We are a dysfunctional family"). The therapist is present to assist clients in identifying these "unique outcomes" or in recalling alternative times when they were not dominated by the problem but rather characterized by more growth-enhancing ways of thinking and behaving. The narrative therapist uses questioning as the primary tool for assisting clients to discover these unique outcomes and to reauthor their lives in less problematic ways. Questions serve as accelerators to help move people beyond the brakes that have been applied by their problem-saturated dominant stories. By asking questions, the narrative therapist invites people to ask themselves even more questions that can lead to new doors and pathways.

For instance, the woman who perceives herself as a victim of childhood abuse is helped to understand that she was not, and is not, always as her "dominant story" as victim might suggest. Through the therapist's questions, she is helped to recognize unique outcomes or times when she thinks and behaves contrary to that of victim. She is assisted in beginning to embrace that part of her which is a survivor—competent, capable, and resilient.

To build on this further, the narrative therapist may assist the client in "externalizing the problem." White and Epston (1990) define externalizing the problem as

> *an approach to therapy that encourages persons to objectify and, at times, to personify the problems that they experience as oppressive. In this process, the problem becomes a separate entity and thus external to the person or relationship that was ascribed as the problem. (p. 38)*

In the case just described above, the woman may be helped to perceive the past abuse as an "unwelcome visitor" who periodically enters her life. With the unique outcomes identified, she can now access the resources available to begin to vanquish the unwelcome visitor. She has reauthored her life in a fashion characterized by the rediscovered resources and related possibilities.

White indicates that he initially applied systematic efforts at encouraging people to externalize their problems in the context of family work. He reports that families would present for therapy with problems identified in their children. While the problems were identified as internal to the child, all family members were affected and felt overwhelmed and defeated. They perceived the persistence of the problem and their failed attempts to resolve it as a reflection on themselves, each other, and their relationships. He says the families described the details of what they were seeking therapy for as a "problem-saturated description" of family life. This was their "dominant story of family life." Through externalizing the problem, White was able to help families separate themselves from the problem. The procedure opened up possibilities for them to begin to describe themselves, each other, and their relationships in a new non-problem-saturated way. It enabled the development of another story of family life. He says:

> *From this new perspective, persons were able to locate "facts" about their lives and relationships that could not be even dimly perceived in the problem-saturated account of family life: "Facts" that contradicted this problem-saturated account. Facts that provided the nuclei for the generation of new stories. And, in the process, the child's problem was invariably resolved. (1990, p. 39)*

As mentioned at the outset of this description of narrative therapy, effectiveness is particularly dependent on the development of a positive relationship between therapist and client or clients. The common factors of empathy, warmth, and respect must be conveyed by the therapist's behavior so that clients reveal their stories in the detail necessary to promote more empowered reauthoring. As each of the elements about to be described are considered, we encourage clinicians to reflect on how each might be used to enhance the therapist–client relationship to better insure that clients reveal their stories in the most rapid fashion possible; this, in turn, lends itself to new, less problem-saturated stories being constructed.

## ESTABLISHING A THERAPEUTIC CONTRACT

Family therapists who espouse a brief, problem-specific orientation will inevitably want to develop a contract that specifies therapy goals. Although these therapists promote clear, explicit goal statements, others act in a less defined fashion. Thus far, no research has suggested that one style is superior to the other; thus, each therapist is left to decide the form of the therapeutic contract and what importance to attach to it. Writing down the clients' goals is becoming more common and is an ordinary part of the first session for some clinicians.

For the beginning family therapist, developing more specific and problem-focused therapeutic contracts seems to be valuable. Such contracts provide an opportunity to more clearly assess the movement that is occurring with the family and the effectiveness of various interventions employed. The family also benefits because it has identified criteria to use in determining change. Often, family members seem to work at cross-purposes, using different criteria to assign value to what occurs in therapy. The establishment of a shared set of criteria to assess achievement of goals can be therapeutic by itself for some of these families. Also, in the process of negotiating an initial contract with the family, the therapist is provided with a rich opportunity to observe how the family is organized and how it operates. Many questions may be answered during the negotiation of a contract such as: Who speaks to whom and about what? What affect seems evident as various concerns are discussed? How do various members exercise influence in the family?

Issues such as the frequency and length of meetings and the family's expectations about therapy and the therapist should be determined during contract negotiation. The negotiation of these issues can quickly address the battle for initiative, or the question of who is to do what work to induce change in the family. The family members may believe that all they need to do is to make their scheduled appearances and the therapist/therapy will somehow magically resolve their issues. They may be entering therapy tentatively, because the last two therapists they were engaged with were inappropriately confrontational. One contract used often is to meet one to three times to assess and develop an understanding, realizing that at the end of this agreed-upon time, all members decide whether therapy should proceed. Naturally, the therapist has a vote in proceeding or not, just as the family members do. At the end of a few initial sessions an agreement is arrived at regarding whether to proceed or not, and if so, for what purposes or goals, how long sessions should continue to address these goals before another evaluation, and, what everyone's expectations are in this process.

This type of minimal contract provides all with some clarity of purpose and promotes commitment to the therapy. Working in a contractual framework, or within chunks of time, also provides everyone with a sense of increased freedom to end by choice, rather than a feeling that termination is arrived at in some cumbersome fashion or by simply not appearing for appointments. This sense of freedom to terminate can be particularly valuable for those families or family members who are uneasy and tentative about committing themselves to therapy. For such clients, addressing the element of time seems particularly important, because then their preconceived notions of therapy being endless (or lasting for years, at best) can be dispelled. Also, by specifying issues to be addressed, the therapist can resolve the clients' notion that therapy is magical or something done to them. While negotiating a contract, the family therapist can describe what might be expected of clients in the way of out-of-session work; any paper-and-pencil assessment tasks that may be employed; types of in-session tasks the family may be asked to engage in; whether all members will be present at all sessions or if various subsystems will be seen in isolation; the role of consultants or aids such as videotaping and one-way mirrors; and so on. This type of information often promotes a sense of comfort for the family members, so that they more quickly invest in therapy. Often included in today's therapy contracts are statements about duty to warn, secrets, prearranged information release, and others. The trend is toward more complex and legalistic therapy contracts as a means of reducing liability risk and as a sincere effort to inform clients about the risks they undertake in beginning therapy.

Explaining the risks of treatment has never been common among family therapists. We are not unique among mental health disciplines in that regard. The facts are that we know very little about the risks of family therapy. Gurman and Kniskern (1986) estimated that 5 to 15 percent of couples and families got worse as a direct result of family or marital therapy. Their analysis is now dated, but their lesson remains valuable. Family therapy itself can harm. We should tell clients in the most clear and truthful way we can that while family therapy is not a high-risk intervention, they do undertake some risk nonetheless. At some point in the future, perhaps, we can be more exact. For now, we should at least mention that there is no guarantee of success in therapy and there is some small risk that the problems will worsen despite a good faith effort on everyone's part.

## EXPLAINING THE PURPOSE OF THERAPY

Most clients enter family therapy without a clear idea of what will happen or what they are to do. They are usually anxious and unsure how to act. As a result, many clients may seem defensive or actively resist the therapy. The initial session is a good time to put client fears to rest by describing the process and goals of family therapy.

The description should not be long or complicated. It should also be stated in language that children as well as adults can understand. The following is an example:

> I'd like to take a few minutes to talk about family therapy so that we all understand what we are doing and where we are going. Families are very important to each of you, and to me, and to all of us. All families have rules that tell us what is OK and not OK. They also have roles to help get things done so that everyone in the family understands who they are and what they are to do. When a family is not working well or one family member has problems, we have found that the rules and roles need to be changed so the family helps everyone grow as a person.
>
> Family therapy usually has two parts. First, I need to get to know your family, its history, its rules, its roles, and how you do things together. Then we will all talk about what needs changing. In the second part of therapy, we will work together to make changes. I want to emphasize that in family therapy we don't blame any one person for the problems you are having. Also, we will need everyone's help in making changes.

The objective of describing family therapy to clients is to provide them with an overview so therapy has structure and meaning.

## THERAPY WITH CULTURALLY DISTINCT FAMILIES

A number of authors—McGoldrick, Pearce, and Giordano (1982) and Boyd-Franklin (1989) being the better known—have written about the implications of culture and race on marriage and family therapy and the need to tailor therapy to the needs of families from cultures different from that of the therapist. Their position is that culture makes a difference and that if therapy is to be successful it must be carried out in a manner that is consonant with cultural values and heritage.

Therapy benefits if the therapist has personal experience living in the clients' culture. Without the shared meaning of symbols produced by this living experience, errors and misunderstandings inevitably occur. But simple misunderstanding of verbal and nonverbal messages is not the major concern in working with families from cultures different from that of the therapist. If that were the only concern, a multilanguage dictionary in every consulting room would suffice. Different power and role structures are also not principal issues that influence therapy with culturally different families. A variety of family structures is present within any culture or subculture. In fact, the range of unique family role and power structures within a culture is probably greater than that between different cultures. As Boyd-Franklin (1989) points out, there is no such thing as *the* African American family. The same applies to *the* Mexican American family or even *the* WASP family. All families differ, yet they are more similar than different.

Recognizing the differences permits the therapist to pace the therapy or direct it for the benefit of the family. Families with strong multigenerational ties and allegiances, for example, may need more session time allocated to trust building before the members risk disclosing what they experience. Among families in which the male role is authoritarian, family violence may be described obliquely. The therapist must be sensitive to subtleties of language to pick up what is being disclosed. In cultures in which the status of men and women is traditionally unequal, confronting the family homeostasis by interviewing the wife or husband alone during the initial phase of therapy may prompt the family to terminate. Any good therapist adjusts to the family norms and rules.

As is clear from the foregoing examples, some aspects of some cultures are not easily grasped merely by our being sensitive. Ignorance and blind spots, the products of socialization, create barriers to effective therapy with some families. These can be addressed by the therapist's learning about the needs of those families as they relate to their cultural background. Most self-taught therapists who work effectively with African American and Mexican American families would agree that they could have benefited from specialized training.

As an example of the issues that might make up that training, therapists might consider what Boyd-Franklin (1989) says regarding the characteristics of the African American experience that influence marriage and family life and therapy. She posits that the African American culture is unique as a result of a history that includes an African legacy, slavery, racism, and discrimination and the existing context for such families she terms the *victim system*. Another important issue is how African American families are perceived. She says that the deficit portrayed as being characteristic of these families is maintained in the social science literature and that not enough emphasis is placed on their strengths. Appreciating the strengths of a family is most important, because strengths are what most therapy builds on. Recognizing the strengths of African American and Mexican American families requires that the therapist assess dimensions of family functioning accurately, without prejudice. The tools and procedures described in Chapter 3 can help a therapist gain a clearer picture of family strengths.

Closely related to an appreciation of strengths and designing therapy to build on strengths is the concept of empowerment. Boyd-Franklin says empowering a family should be part of any treatment plan. By *empowerment*, she means the mobilizing of power within a family system to enhance its ability to interact successfully with external systems. Among African American families, she points out, the compounding influences of slavery and victimization have made empowerment an essential component of effective therapy. For example, empowering a family might consist of helping a single-parent mother regain custody of her children despite the reservations of social service agencies. Empowerment means that families feel in control of their own destiny so they can make changes. In Carl Whitaker's terms, empowering families is helping them win the battle for initiative.

While it is important to consider cultural differences in conducting therapy, it is equally important to recognize that the basic processes governing family life and individual behavior are the same regardless of a family's socioeconomic status or cultural heritage. Believing otherwise, that each family is so unique that no generalizing is possible, challenges the validity of family system theory and, for that matter, eliminates the possibility of family theory altogether. Theory must apply to all families regardless of their structure, cultural heritage, financial condition, religion, etc. Attaching too much significance to the differences among families whether in diagnosis or treatment diminishes the benefits of theory. At the simplest level, theory gives us a direction to take when working with families. Without theory we retreat to a less sophisticated, less effective style of intervention.

## GENDER ISSUES IN THERAPY

The field of marriage and family therapy has long promoted awareness that gender is an important aspect of effective therapy with couples and families. Years ago, it was marital therapists who broke with the analyst ranks and brought spouses together in the consulting room. Expressly stated or not, this change in the structure of marital treatment identified gender consideration as integral to treatment. Family therapy was slower to respond until the feminist movement focused attention on the political forces in family life that play out in the gender roles held by family members.

Today therapists know that they must monitor their own behavior to eliminate sexism. At the same time, they must understand clients' problems within the context of both genders. To provide therapists with assistance in these tasks, Good, Gilbert, and Scher (1990) developed what they call Gender Aware Therapy (GAT). GAT is a collection of principles that can guide a therapist away from insensitive practices that limit the effectiveness of therapy or harm clients outright. GAT is described as:

> *integrating the personal and political so that personal problems are understood within the broader political and social context. For example, the fear of a married woman about her ability to financially support herself after divorce or the fear her husband feels that divorce may result in loss of his children are personal concerns arising out of political and economic conditions at the societal level. To fully understand these feelings, a therapist needs to know the context in which they exist.*
>
> *This principle applies to many gender related issues. Spouse abuse, for example, is best understood and best treated if the socio-political status of the genders is integrated with assessment of the spouses' behavior. Otherwise, the therapist may end up blaming the victim.*
>
> *Respecting clients' freedom to make choices is another important principle of GAT. Despite the restrictions of gender roles, therapists must value clients' rights to act according to their own desires. Many times spouses are so trapped by their roles, and they have such a limited sense of self, that they have no clear desires or wants and only experience a vague discomfort or broadly generalized anger. They need permission to explore options. If, through either overt or subtle means, a therapist does not support a client's interest in exploration, little will change. What's worse, a client who has met with resistance from a therapist will likely decide it is their own fault. Unfortunately, such clients can easily come to believe they are flawed in some fundamental, irreparable way because they have tried therapy and failed.*
>
> *A third principle calls for a de-emphasis on the expert role of the therapist. A collaborative, egalitarian relationship is an easier way to practice gender aware therapy. An authoritative role places the therapist in charge of the clients' destiny. Some clients whose primary concerns involve their gender socialization may not be able to grow in such context. They may need to experience an adult, egalitarian relationship that encourages differentiation and personal responsibility. (p. 376)*

Because therapists are of one gender or the other, they struggle with the same gender issues their clients present. Like their clients, becoming aware of their blind spots related to gender requires personal growth. A supervisor can help. Reading can help. Workshops on gender issues are commonplace. Important, too, are conversations with close colleagues who willingly share their dilemmas and insights.

Confronting our hidden agendas so our clients are not abused is a process, not a one-time event. Therapists are not objective or valueless. Our notions about gender-appropriate behavior are the product of our constantly evolving history. Remaining aware of our own selves is most important to minimize the potential harm clients may experience as a result of our prejudices.

## RESEARCH-BASED TREATMENT GUIDELINES

Over the past decade or so, efficacy research literature has been developing in marriage and family therapy, and it is now clear that family therapy works. That is, it is better than doing nothing, and it is at least as good or better than other psychotherapeutic approaches (Shadish, Ragsdale, Glaser, & Montgomery, 1995). More currently, the research has focused on whether results in the research lab generalize to the consulting room—the so-called effectiveness question. Researchers also are addressing which particular client problems are best addressed by family therapy.

For any thriving discipline, answers to these questions are always changing. This is true of family therapy especially at this stage of its development as a professional discipline. The fact that there are many competing modalities of family therapy further complicates treatment decisions. Nonetheless, the practitioner must make treatment decisions based on the best information available at a particular point in time. The question is, where does the best information come from? Is published research the best source? How about the many personal testimonials from the family therapy gurus or the workshop circuit personalities; are they credible resources? What about a clinician's own judgment and experience? Can practitioners correctly gauge the effectiveness of their own work?

In the past, treatment guidelines were largely the product of clinical lore. With no alternatives, personal experience and collected wisdom passed from supervisor to supervisee has done a reasonably good job of protecting clients and designing treatments. Today, however, therapy is a more exacting art. Treatment decisions must be able to withstand the scrutiny of new and old watch dogs. In the end, research gives us the most reliable and valid information for decision making.

What does the research tell us? At present, the behavioral treatments appear to be the treatments of choice. There is more research on these methods of family intervention than on all the others combined. The results of behavioral marital treatments and behavioral family treatments show that they are reliable and effective. This is not to say that other modalities are not equally or more effective, just that the behavioral treatments have established a record of success. That record of research should weigh heavily in treatment decisions.

Beyond this one generalization about behavioral treatments, which is apparent now but will likely change, the following are examples of what may be thought of as treatment guidelines based on what we currently know. Of course, these guidelines should be tempered with currently available published research:

> Psychoeducational treatments for chronic mental and physical diseases appear to be effective for helping clients cope with debilitating diseases and minimize relapse especially when combined with managed drug treatment.

> Marriage and family therapy is an effective treatment for depressed clients who are experiencing family and marital problems.

> Marriage and family therapy is not the treatment of choice for hospitalized unipolar depressed clients.

> For families presenting with autism and conduct disorders, family therapy appears to improve child and parent functioning, and the gains appear to last.

> Family therapy appears to help alcoholics enter treatment but not to reduce drinking.

Another important issue related to treatment effectiveness is the likelihood that certain clients will worsen as a result of family therapy even if the therapy is provided in a competent manner. We have too few studies of client deterioration, but the research is clear that it does happen. Based on what some consider flawed reasoning, Gurman and Kniskern (1986) asserted that individual treatment for marital problems was unethical because research showed the rate of effectiveness for that method of working with marital problems was lower than conjoint treatment and the deterioration rate was much higher.

Gurman and Kniskern's conclusion was the product of careful review of the literature. Quite a controversy occurred at the time, which has since died down. The lesson though is that evaluation of multiple studies is an effective way to develop treatment guidelines that can result in safer and more effective therapy for our clients. Keeping abreast of the literature is key to knowing what works and what can harm.

# ▶ 3

## Assessment Procedures

Assessment, or the taking in of information to make informed decisions, occurs throughout the course of therapy. Good clinicians are always monitoring, probing, testing, and hypothesizing regardless of the stage of therapy. In fact, one might say that when assessment ceases so does therapy.

Another, more commonly attributed meaning to assessment is the group of procedures used at the outset of therapy to design an initial treatment plan. Assessment as part of initial diagnosis is the focus of this chapter, although, as is stated throughout, assessment serves multiple functions. It is an important, necessary part of therapy that is either done well or badly but never not at all.

### ASSESSING THE FAMILY

From the clinician's point of view, assessment is the process of getting to know enough about a family to make informed treatment decisions. More specifically, the procedure of assessment is the sequence of actions taken by the therapist designed to yield information about how the family operates and the function(s) of the presenting problems in the family organization. Whether assessment is therapeutic or not is a moot question in the psychotherapeutic context; it can be, depending on the skills and orientation of the clinician. The time spent in assessment, no matter how brief, should serve the dual purposes of diagnosis and therapy.

The steps in conducting an assessment are several. On first meeting with clients, social chitchat is common and necessary. Human relationships and social encounters tend to begin with small talk. It is nonthreatening and provides an opportunity to check out the other party. From the time the first meeting begins, the therapist collects information about how the family and its members function together. The small talk can be allowed to continue for as long a time as it produces important information.

While gathering this information, and throughout the assessment phase, the family therapist must *think*, not necessarily behave, in terms of family structure and family process. Delving too deeply into the intrapersonal functioning of one or more family members tends to misdirect the clinician's attention toward individuals and away from their social system. Forcing yourself to think in family-system terms is the key element in helping you to conduct family therapy rather than individual therapy in a group. This is not to say that the family therapist should not let individuals talk about their own problems, but that while they are talking and the therapist is attending, the therapist is also thinking about the family structure and the role individual problems play in the family system.

Some sort of executive remark is typically delivered by the therapist to make the transition from small talk to a focus on why the family is in therapy. "What brings you here?" might be one such remark. More typically, though, the therapist conducts the transition from chitchat to the task at hand by referring to the appointment phone call. This statement signals the family to begin talking about its problem(s), and that is what most families believe they are to do. Clinicians need to remember that clients who have not been in family therapy before tend to conduct themselves in accordance with stereotyped therapy sessions they have seen on TV or behave as they might in a physician's office. When families present themselves for therapy, they expect to be asked why they are there and to describe the problem(s) they are experiencing.

While the problem is being presented, the clinician attends to the processes revealed: Who talks first? Do family members talk for one another? Do they interrupt? Where are the alliances? Where is the seat of power? Who is the identified patient (IP)? The answers to all these questions and more are revealed during the problem presentation phase of the assessment. The clinician's questions serve the dual purpose of continuing the discussion and checking out hypotheses regarding the structure and function of the family and its symptoms. More experienced therapists tend to limit the amount of time devoted to describing the problem because experience allows them to make treatment decisions with less data. Less experienced therapists may need to devote more than one session to the assessment process.

## BUILDING CLIENT CONFIDENCE
## IN THERAPIST ABILITY

The best way to establish rapport with clients is to be helpful. For too long therapists have thought that rapport needs to be established prior to being helpful, rather than recognizing that being effective and helpful is the best means of establishing rapport. An important initial step in being helpful is to project an image of confidence and competence. The business world has attended to this issue through various publications on how to dress, shake hands, maintain eye contact, and decorate an office correctly. While all these factors likely play a role in projecting competence and facilitating development of the client's sense of confidence, the therapist can also engage in specific behaviors that further this development.

The therapist can make statements such as the following to facilitate confidence development. After a couple has initially described their circumstances, the therapist can say, "Your situation is one I am very familiar with. I have seen many couples, particularly in the recent past, with almost identical situations, and they have been very successful in securing the change they wanted." This statement communicates that their circumstance is not a new one for the therapist and also conveys a sense of hope. Naturally, the therapist needs to be careful of overdoing this to a point that the couple feels misunderstood because their "uniqueness" is disqualified.

Another way of inspiring confidence is to anticipate what clients are thinking but have not yet spoken, and then say it for them. For instance, consider the couple in which the wife is disturbed about her husband's drinking and identifies herself as the adult child of an alcoholic, abusive father. She has just finished a detailed explanation of her disturbance secondary to the husband's drinking. The therapist might anticipate what the husband is thinking and address him by saying, "Bill, I imagine as you listen to your wife you find yourself wondering how much of Betty's concern is really attributable to you and how much of her concern is the residual of having been raised with her alcoholic father. You wonder about the fairness of it all." He will likely be quick to agree and attribute some degree of competence to the therapist for understanding his situation. Further, similar anticipations can be stated about Betty's thoughts in response to Bill's agreement. For instance, a therapist might say to her, "And Betty, I would suppose you perceive his agreement with what I'm suggesting as further evidence of how he is just like your father with all the denial and projection of responsibility." These efforts at speculating about what spouses are thinking or feeling in the initial stages of therapy can quickly foster clients' sense of confidence in the therapist.

Accepting what clients present without overt signs of being shocked or overwhelmed is another way of developing client confidence in the therapist. Being visibly overwhelmed or aghast by what is presented will likely promote alarm for the couple or family as they wonder if their therapist is up to the task of working with them. Although some families may benefit from the therapist's dramatizing his or her affect (Minuchin, 1974), particularly in the early stages of therapy, most families benefit from perceiving their therapist as calmly accepting and attempting to understand completely what is presented.

There is considerable evidence available that documents the importance of clients' perceiving their therapist as caring for them. This "test of caring" is indeed a valuable component of the therapeutic process. We are suggesting the "test of competence" is of at least equal importance. In fact, work by Goldman and Milman (1978) has suggested that the beginning or joining phase of therapy ends and the middle phase of treatment begins when clients come to perceive their therapist as competent. While the therapist can communicate in ways that enhance the clients' perception of therapist competence, there is evidence that suggests the therapist's belief that change can occur is also conveyed to clients and can further enhance a sense of competence in the provider.

In 1993, Hans Strupp offered a synopsis of his over forty years of studying psychotherapy process and outcome. Among other things, he believes that his four decades of study suggest that the therapist's initial attitude toward the patient might give rise to a self-fulfilling prophecy. For instance, the therapist who does not feel confident and competent will convey this to the client unit in a fashion that promotes greater despair and hopelessness by the clients. This decreased client hopefulness then decreases the therapist's sense of confidence and competence, which then fuels even greater hopelessness by the client and so on. Strupp states that his research suggests therapists can convey a decreased sense of confidence and competence in themselves and their clients by uttering communications such as ". . . interpretations advanced in a subtly blaming manner or 'supportive' messages that simultaneously conveyed a criticism of the patient" (1993, p. 432). For this reason, therapists are well advised to monitor both their attitude and behavior in a fashion to insure that they do not unwittingly prompt greater hopelessness on the part of their clients and then wonder why so many of their clients appear to be so "under-motivated."

Related to this notion of confidence and competence in one's therapist, Howard, Lueger, Maling, and Martinovich (1993) have advanced a three-phase model to describe the process of psychotherapy. The phases are remoralization, remediation, and rehabilitation. They propose that movement into a later phase of treatment depends on whether or not progress is made in an earlier phase. They postulate that many clients have experienced painful symptomatology resulting in perceptions of powerlessness and hopelessness, or the state of being demoralized. Remoralization, the first of their three phases, consists of enhancing the clients' sense of hopefulness and sense of subjective well-being. In fact, Howard and his cohorts suggest that addressing and resolving only the phenomena of hopefulness with clients may ". . . allow them to mobilize their own coping resources in a way that facilitates resolution of the triggering events that led to help seeking in the first place, and they will require no further formal treatment" (1993, p. 679). Neither the second phase of this proposed model, remediation (resolution of symptoms, life problems, or both), nor the third, rehabilitation (the unlearning of troublesome, maladaptive, longstanding patterns and then establishing new ways of dealing with various aspects of self and life), may occur if remoralization of the client(s) is not successfully addressed.

We maintain that the clinician who is unable to convey a sense of competence and confidence to their clients is not likely to advance a sense of what Howard and his colleagues refer to as remoralization. This could lead to a long period of frustrating therapy or abrupt termination. If clinicians find themselves experiencing what they believe are excessive numbers of clients prematurely terminating therapy, they may find it helpful to seek out supervision and address the possibility that they are not communicating a sense of hopefulness and resultant remoralization.

## CLARIFYING THE PRESENTING PROBLEM

Couples and families seen in clinical practice are frequently fragmented in many ways. They can present considerable disagreement over problem areas and differences in the intensity of their feelings about them. The clinician who does not make an extensive effort to clarify the presenting problem(s) is doomed to operating in as disoriented and fragmented a fashion as the dysfunctional family.

You have probably heard the old dictum: "A problem well defined is half solved." Although the literal meaning of this saying may be an exaggeration, there is no doubt that clarifying the presenting problem is a significant clinical step. A reading of most of the original luminaries in the field of family therapy shows that fairly uniform agreement exists on the value of clarifying the presenting problem.

The clinician may find that there are as many presenting problems as there are individuals in the client group, and then some. For example, the individuals in the group may have their own respective ideas about what the problem is and what needs change. The clinician may also observe various problems not mentioned by the family members; for example, the fact that there is no shared agreement; there is little, if any, effective listening; some strong silencing mechanisms are quite evident; or one or more family members evidence significant affect, which is not even presented as a problem.

The act of delineating the problems of a dysfunctional and chaotic family can often be the first therapeutic intervention. Simply clarifying the family members' issues can prove helpful as they begin to understand what has been contributing to the chaos they experience. Frequently it is helpful to label the various identified problems as clutter that prevents the clients from securing the kind of family/marital life they hope for. Once the clutter is identified, you can determine where to initially direct efforts to eliminate it from the family operation. It is important to be sensitive to addressing problems that are reasonably defined and lend themselves to easy resolution. Further, initially intervening with the problems most likely to be resolved will provide family members with the sense of success and mastery that likely has been absent from their lives.

"I want him to love me more." This type of problem statement is more likely to be resolved when the problem is defined in more specific behavioral terms such as: "I would like him to talk with me for five minutes after dinner, or sometime before we go to bed, rather than just watch TV." "I would like him to help me put the two youngest children to bed three nights a week." Initially breaking problems down into manageable pieces makes it far more likely that everyone will realize what is necessary for success. In selecting those pieces of a problem that are most likely to ensure a sense of accomplishment, it is often wise to negotiate which one seems most reasonable to focus on initially. This process of clients negotiating which piece to address first can provide further evaluative data to the clinician, and it also frequently provides an opportunity to do some effective therapeutic management of communication/negotiation processes and skills.

The process of clarifying the problem also provides the couple/family with a sense of the clinician's competence and capacity for appropriately managing their destructive process. Although the client's perception that care emanates from the therapist has been extensively acknowledged to be important, the test of competence seems just as important, if not more so, in work with families. In fact, if this sense of competence is not perceived by clients, why should they extend the effort and money necessary to keep future appointments?

Each person present should be afforded the opportunity to express what the problem is or what needs to be changed. Framing or defining the problem as "what needs to be changed" conveys the valuable metamessage that the focus of therapy is change. Each succeeding session can then be initiated with a statement such as "What have you changed since we were last together?" This statement also underscores the notion that the family is responsible for the process of change and keeps the initiative for change with them.

Another point to consider regarding clarification of the problem is "Why now?" In most cases the problems presented are not acute in nature but have been present for some considerable period of time. Determining what brings the family members in at *this* time can provide valuable information to the clinician about their attempts to resolve the problem(s) on their own. A good sense of just how creative the group members are will become evident. Also, the clinician will learn what approach not to attempt because the family implemented a solution and it failed.

Clinicians working from a solution-oriented perspective have offered very helpful ideas regarding the initial process of defining the problem(s) and establishing the therapeutic contract (deShazer, 1991; Berg & Miller, 1992). For instance the "miracle question" is a quick way of orienting clients to tell their story and to identify desired changes. This question will be posed as follows, or in a similar fashion depending on the client's language and general worldview:

> Suppose that while you are sleeping tonight a miracle happens. The miracle is that the problems that brought you here today are solved! But you don't know this miracle has happened because you were asleep. When you wake up tomorrow morning, what will be some of the first things that you will notice that will be different that will tell you the miracle has happened?

This sort of question is designed to specify what clients want different, while also beginning to shift their perception from problems to possible solutions. The impact of the miracle question can be further enhanced by follow-up questions, such as "What else will be different after the miracle?" "What would your (spouse, child, parent, friend, etc.) say will be different after the miracle?"

Further questions can then be used to shape what is being described into more specific, behavioral, interactional, and realistic terms. Examples of questions designed to provoke greater specificity that more clearly identify potential solutions are:

> What will be the smallest sign that this (outcome/change) is happening?
>
> What will be the first sign that this (outcome/change) is happening?
>
> If I were a mouse in the corner, what would I see/hear you doing/saying that would suggest to me the problem had been solved?
>
> What exactly will others (spouse, child, parent, friend, etc.) notice that is different about you/the situation that will tell them this has happened?

To further encourage clients to recognize they are already in possession of many necessary ingredients for change, there is value in then asking them about those times when they already experienced the desired outcome just described. These examples are referred to as "instances" or "unique outcomes." It is not uncommon for clients to spontaneously report instances of the desired outcome already appearing while responding to the miracle question and related follow-ups. If not offered voluntarily, questions such as the following can often elicit these examples:

> Tell me about those times when pieces of the miracle you have been describing are already happening?
>
> What is different about those times?
>
> What contributes to this happening at those times?

Questions such as these help to underscore for the client(s) the fact that solutions may not be as far removed or difficult to attain as their problem-oriented thinking may result in them believing.

During this time it is also appropriate to ask about possible "pretreatment changes." As the name implies, this is change that clients experience prior to coming for their first session. Research has demonstrated that as many as 66 percent of clients begin to experience changes even prior to arriving for their first session (Talmon, 1990). To capitalize on this likelihood, there typically is value in asking questions such as the following:

> Many times people notice that in between the time they make the appointment for therapy and the first session, things start to improve. What have you noticed in this regard?
>
> What has allowed/prompted these changes?
>
> What can you do to maintain and build upon these changes?

Attending to this likelihood is a way of capitalizing on the widely heralded thinking of Howard, Lueger, Mating, and Martinovich (1993) mentioned earlier that suggests the crucial first phase of therapy is the "remoralization process." They suggest that prior to treatment clients feel frantic, hopeless, or desperate, which disrupts a person's ability to mobilize their coping resources. Deciding to initiate therapy and making the call for an appointment is the start of the remoralization process. The questions just described are designed to enhance the impact of this process, which is already started for the client:

Another helpful procedure for clarifying and defining the problem from the solution-oriented perspective is the asking of scaling questions. These questions are typically used in three different ways toward the end of the first session. By initially asking clients to rate where they currently are in relation to the problem, a baseline is established against which future progress may be assessed. For instance, the therapist can ask, "On a scale from one to ten, where one is when this situation was at its worst and ten represents the day after the miracle, where would you say you are today?"

The second way scaling questions are used assists in identifying a realistic and achievable goal. For example, if a client responded to the initial scaling question with a two, the therapist could follow with, "On that one-to-ten scale, if you are currently at a two what will be different when things are just slightly different, such as a two and a half or three on the scale?"

Lastly, scaling questions are used to assess the client's willingness to change or motivation. The therapist can ask, "From a slightly different perspective, where ten indicates you will do almost anything to solve this problem and one represents you are not willing to invest to secure change, where would you say you are at this moment?"

A last point for consideration involves determining and changing the family's perceptual context of the problem. To assess this area, think along the lines of a "bad-sad" continuum. If a family member identifies another member's problem in terms that might be called "bad"—angry, mean, bitchy, vindictive—framing the problem as possibly being stimulated by "sad" factors—hurt, depressed, lonely, isolated—can be beneficial. This shift in perception of the problem's basis often proves extremely valuable in introducing greater flexibility and increasing the likelihood of problem resolution as therapy progresses. Certainly great sensitivity must be exercised in this area so that a person with a heavy investment in perceiving a problem in a particular way does not end up feeling abused by the therapist.

## CIRCULAR QUESTIONING

The technique of circular questioning, used as an assessment tool, has the unique value of placing clients in a metaposition, outside of the system they are currently embroiled in. As the family members listen to another member respond to circular questioning, they also may learn for the first time other members' perceptions of the family operation.

Circular questioning also tends to elicit information in a nonthreatening way and especially can help clients who have difficulty expressing themselves directly. For instance, rather than asking someone who is reluctant to respond, such as an adolescent, a sister can be asked to respond as she believes her adolescent brother would. While this provides the information requested, at least from the sister's perspective, it also serves as a stimulus for the brother to respond by correcting his sister or agreeing with her.

O'Brian and Bruggen (1985) have offered a helpful means of categorizing types of circular questioning. One of the types they identify focuses on relationships in the family and is divided into questions that are about two other people in the family and those that are about people in relation to events in family life. For instance, in reference to two other people in the family, the therapist may ask one member, "How do your mother and sister get along?" or "How do your mother and father show that they care for one another?" Regarding people in relation to events in family life, the therapist might ask, "When your sister says she's not going to bed at night, what might your mother do?" or "When your wife drinks as you just described, what will your daughter do? What will she be feeling?"

O'Brian and Bruggen suggest another category of circular questioning designed to help people engage in ranking behavior. Ranking can occur in relation to actual or hypothetical circumstances. For instance, a question about an actual circumstance might be, "Who does the most disciplining of you, your mother or your father?" or "Among your brothers and sisters, who would you say is most disturbed by this situation?" Ranking questions that refer to hypothetical situations might take a form such as this: "When all of your children have grown and gone, who will have the most contact with you, then who, and so on?" or "Let's assume the drinking doesn't change; who will be most disturbed and in what ways, and then who?"

Another category of circular questioning relates to time. These questions may focus on a specific event or project forward or backward in time. Examples of questions regarding a specific event are "How was John different before mother's death?" or "How do you think Suzy felt differently before mom and dad's divorce?" Examples that project forward or backward in time are "How do you remember things being between mom and dad six months ago? How do you think your mother was different then?" or "What do you think Suzy will be most fearful of one year from now if things don't change?"

The last category identifies questioning which refers specifically to a person who does not answer questions presented. This may be someone present who chooses not to respond or someone not present in the session; for instance: "If John answered the question I just asked him as honestly as he could, what would he say?" or "If Jack were here today, what do you believe he would say about that?"

Circular questioning can be a powerful tool to employ during the assessment phase of therapy and at other times also. Besides generating valuable information for the therapist, it can also begin to expose the family to itself in new ways that promote new understanding. Further, it can speed the gathering of information, overcoming the problems of various family members' feeling too shy to talk and of family rules that do not allow family members to directly share the information another member offers about them in response to circular questioning.

## CONDUCTING A GENOGRAM

The genogram as an assessment tool has been around for a long time. Its symbol and mapping tools were popularized by Murray Bowen, and the genogram procedure is endorsed and described in nearly every family therapy text. Consequently, many clinicians use the genogram in the initial stage of therapy to assess family history and as a way to get acquainted.

The structure of a genogram is relatively straightforward. The therapist can best begin the process by spending several minutes explaining (1) the rationale for the genogram (a means of getting acquainted that involves gathering information about families of origin in order to better understand how family background influences current family issues), (2) what clients will be asked to do (answer questions and share insights about one another's families), (3) how long the genogram will last (thirty to forty-five minutes), and (4) the sequence of events (who goes first).

Typically, unless the therapist selects someone to begin, the person who made the appointment will do so. From a relationship-building point of view, however, it is often better if the spouse less interested in therapy is asked to go first. Hopefully, through increased client–therapist interaction during the relatively nonthreatening task of the genogram, the less interested spouse will become more interested in and committed to therapy. The spouse more willing to begin can be chosen if the therapist believes that requesting the less interested spouse to begin will harm the therapeutic relationship at this initial stage. In either case, the less interested spouse cannot be allowed to merely sit by while his or her partner works with the therapist. All family members, especially children, are to be fully involved at all times and enlisted as consultants to the therapist.

The genogram process usually consists of mapping out one family of origin at a time. A large drawing area such as a blackboard or newsprint tablet is very helpful. Clients and therapists alike retain more interest in the experience of the families they are talking about. In addition, diagramming the family structures is the primary method of keeping an entire family involved. It provides a focal point for those members not talking at a given time and allows them to think about someone else's family.

In some styles of therapy, a great amount of detail is gathered during the genogram. Dates of marriages, deaths, divorces, births, and ages of family members across as many generations as possible are dutifully written down. For the genogram commonly used in the initial phase of therapy, however, less is more might be the guiding dictum. A more efficient procedure is to concentrate on the current and immediately previous generations, asking everyone to help map out all the current and past members of the system and obtaining their current ages and the approximate dates of important events such as deaths, marriages, and divorces. This need not take more than a few minutes, and it should not be the therapist's primary focus. The most useful information produced by the genogram is not the family structure but the nature of the relationships making up the structure.

The therapist must direct the spouses to consider the influences from their families of origin that affect the style of their marriage. For example, to gain understanding of the model of marriage displayed to a couple by their parents, ask each person questions such as "How did your parents show affection?" "What was their social life like?" and "What did they do when they disagreed with each other?" To assess the parental model ask: "With which parent did you spend the most time?" "What was the emotional climate of the relationship?" "How did you show irritation toward one another?" and "How was affection displayed?" Questions about the closest parent are especially important, because it is reasonable to assume that the style of relationship developed with the closest parent or caretaker will be the style of relationship sought with a marital partner. Other areas to assess could include role rigidity, power allocation, communication of warmth and empathy, alliances, techniques of adaptation, and major illnesses.

There are several points to keep in mind while conducting a genogram. Because it is often an initial task of therapy, the clinician needs to maintain the involvement of all the family members throughout the experience. Typically, one branch of the family tree is dealt with at a time, and it is easy to spend too much time following the unnecessary strategy of asking questions of one spouse or family member to the exclusion of the others present. After a minute or so spent talking with one person, you can ask another person to agree, disagree, or share a comment about the other's family. Questions such as "Is that your perception?" or "How do you see her (his) family?" can serve this purpose. All members of a family need to be kept involved and can be, as everyone is asked to participate.

Second, because the genogram is usually an introduction to therapy, the experience can be light and even humorous, depending on the wit of the therapist. The material generated by clients needs to be taken seriously, of course, but a little humor can help avoid a dull, question-and-answer grilling that frustrates therapists and clients alike. Third, and most important, the genogram presents an excellent opportunity for the therapist to demonstrate professional competence. At least one study (Brock & Sanderson, 1984) has suggested that clients determine the competence of their therapist in the first session in part by how much they learn about themselves, their family, and family dynamics in general. The genogram presents an ideal opportunity for the therapist to make statements with this point in mind.

For example, if both spouses are firstborn children, a therapist could remark, "We tend to find that firstborn children are more ambitious than later siblings and as a result, I would guess that you two are not only ambitious but also fairly competitive with one another." Or, if one spouse's family of orientation is large and the other spouse is an only child, the therapist could remark, "I imagine you, John, were attracted to the stimulation and activity of her larger family while you, Mary, were attracted to the simplicity and quiet of his family." These remarks or interpretations need not be earth-shaking, brilliant insights into the psyche of either spouse.

It is important for therapists to share their thoughts and conclusions about the families described by their clients. Clients are hungry to learn, and such comments not only allow therapists to investigate perceptions, but also often produce insight about the family, benefiting both the therapist and the family members. During a genogram that is illuminating to clients, a therapist will often hear one client state to another, "So, that's why you are like that" or "I never knew that." Comments such as these bring clients back for the second session.

Teaching clients about themselves, their family, and about families in general has the equally important goal of maintaining a balance of social exchange during the initial phase of therapy. The therapy relationship, like other interpersonal relationships, proceeds through several phases, the first of which is a getting-acquainted period. In this phase, the participants (therapist and client) exchange information about themselves verbally and nonverbally. The exchanges occur on a rapid and short-term basis, and the balance of debits and credits in the relationship is kept carefully balanced. Deferred gratification or exchange imbalance in the early stage of a relationship often produces emotional withdrawal by one participant. For example, the person sitting next to you on a long bus ride over-discloses and you feel more and more emotionally distant as the imbalance in self-disclosure increases.

Such a social exchange imbalance does not usually play a role in healthy relationships until the participants have established a foundation of trust produced by short-term, balanced exchange. Therefore, in the initial phase of therapy, the therapist needs to attend to the balance of exchange, and one good way to maintain the balance is to share observations and insights that come to mind during the genogram with the family. Many therapists merely ask clients questions without giving back information that will help to maintain the balance of social exchange during the initial interview. The full potential of the genogram is not achieved by limiting its purpose to merely collecting information.

Recently the genogram has been blended with both solution-oriented (deShazer, 1985; O'Hanlon & Weiner-Davis, 1989) and narrative (White & Epston, 1990) therapies. These orientations share the belief that change involves helping people reinvent or reauthor their lives. Perception is the key. Preoccupied with their problems, living in problem-saturated stories, clients lose sight of their resources and what is going well. The job of the therapist is to help clients notice exceptions to the identified problems or the belief systems around the problems, reframe meanings, identify what is working, and proceed to create realistic images of what can be achieved.

In these therapies, the question is the therapist's main tool (White & Epston, 1990). The therapist and clients' curiosity are heightened as people are asked what they know about the problem, how they know this, and what new possibilities for solutions might emerge as the problem is examined from different perspectives. Questions bring to the foreground what is already happening or what has happened in the past (in the families of origin) that leads toward a preferred future; the clients' own responses provide evidence that the desired outcome is not only possible but is indeed very accessible, if not already becoming reality.

The genogram as a procedure lends itself nicely to accomplishing the above. The genogram helps all involved to understand how they ended up with the stories or perceptions they operate from, and also provides fertile ground for identifying exceptions or solutions. For instance, as the therapist and couple work the genogram and learn how they came to be hobbled by a particularly debilitating perception, the genogram also contains exceptions or solutions. The full range of the family's responses may have been lost in the transmission of the storied beliefs; "functional" responses may have been "forgotten." Questions to ask include:

How did this uncle's family apparently avoid incorporating that notion and instead seems to perceive themselves differently with outcomes that are also different?

How did this sibling avoid ending up at the same place? What did/ do they do differently?

What were you doing differently back then that resulted in the problem not being present?

The genogram serves as a map that can cast light on the past, present, and future. Questions asked by the therapist prompt new information that casts the problem and its context in a new light, which facilitates viewing the past, present, and future in new and less problem-saturated ways. With the renewed hopes and dreams stimulated, clients often initiate rapid and meaningful change. For instance, what White and Epston (1990) refer to as externalizing the problem across generations can be powerfully applied with the genogram. Assume a genogram reveals that alcoholism has riddled a family for the past three generations and created considerable havoc and destruction. The therapist may then ask, "Did you realize how much alcohol has betrayed and vanquished your family for three generations?" This question externalizes the problem from being perceived as solely isolated to an individual or family, and frames it as an external enemy to be vigilant of and prepared to vanquish. Further questions can then be asked regarding how those who avoided the scourge of alcohol were able to do so. The client may even be encouraged to do some research and determine from other family members how they avoided the ravages of alcohol. In these ways, the genogram becomes much more than just a tool for understanding the past. It becomes a springboard for creating new perceptions and possibilities as well as a rich resource for identifying solutions.

## COLLECTING RELATIONSHIP HISTORY

A number of authors have written excellent descriptions of the ways to conduct the relationship history portion of the initial phase of therapy. Stahmann and Heibert (1977) have presented the Structured Initial Interview for married couples in which the areas to ask about are detailed. Weber, McKeever, and McDaniel (1985) have defined a model for family interviews. The comments below are meant as additions to history taking/assessment models presented in the literature.

### *Initial Attraction*

Couples who are in the midst of turmoil focus intensely on what is wrong with their relationship and each other. By initiating a discussion of how they met and what attracted them, a break in such negative attention is forced. Most often, they will cooperate fully, and the resulting discussion is a pleasant one. Since they have been asked similar questions many times in the past, however, the therapist must help the partners get past their ritualized answers to questions such as "How did you meet?" When they are permitted to answer only with their ritualized answers, little is accomplished.

The initial phase of therapy, which usually involves asking such questions, is the best time to make it understood that therapy will consist of more than the same old disclosures. Asking for detail is one way to get past the ritualized answers. For example, the therapist might say something like, "Surely, there was more to it than that." Through this type of encouragement, partners can receive the specific guidance needed to disclose their feelings and thoughts about each other that they have not shared previously.

## Expectations of a Marital Partner

Some therapists place great emphasis on discovering the expectations each partner had about a marital partner prior to marriage. Unfortunately, these expectations probably were not at all well articulated at that time. Consequently, clients usually have difficulty responding to the question, "What expectations did you have of a wife (husband) when you married?" It is often easier to identify such expectations using the material generated by a genogram than to ask clients to state them. If a genogram is not conducted as part of the assessment process, clients can be asked to compare their parents' marital roles with how they expected their spouse to behave. Such comparisons help the discussion of expectations to be less abstract. Some clients will honestly state that they had no expectations, and they will need help to understand that although they may not have sat down and drawn up a list, they did want a spouse to behave in a certain manner.

## Courtship History

The courtship phase of the relationship is best discussed by referring to major events—such as first intercourse, first item purchased together, major fights and the like—that both spouses probably remember. The events discussed should be restricted to those that both remember. Otherwise, the topic may shift to "Why don't you remember that?" and create hurt feelings, and at this phase of therapy, the emphasis should be on helping a couple remember the positive reasons they chose to marry.

## Significant Events during Marriage

In the same manner, the history of the marriage can be discussed. It is helpful to use a blackboard to create a time line of events to give couples perspective on how much they have been through together. These discussions can become labored and lengthy unless the therapist helps prevent the spouses from telling story after story. Usually, one spouse tells a story while the other listens. The key to maintaining control of the session is to stay actively involved by asking questions of both spouses regarding the event. Their stories will become abbreviated and the nonparticipating spouse will not be able to disengage from the session. Also, when the therapist has heard enough about an event, the couple or family should be encouraged to move on and not be allowed to ramble; for example, saying "Let's go on to the next event" or asking "What was the next major event?" is appropriate.

## FAMILY STRUCTURE AND FUNCTION INDICATORS

One of the goals of the assessment process is to determine the health of the family system. The process demands that the therapist make value judgments in which the client family, its structure, and interaction processes are compared to a model family or against some standard familiar to the therapist. Like it or not, all therapists use such a standard, and all therapists make value judgments about the functioning of their clients. The primary issue here is the makeup of the standard used to define the optimally functioning family. We suggest one that fits with the cultural milieu of the place where the family resides or one that the family identifies with.

The healthy, optimally functioning family has been ignored, to a large extent, in the family therapy literature, but it has received attention from family scientists such as Walsh (1982). If the research on healthy families is distilled into primary functions and indicators of those functions (an onerous task conducted by Lee Walker [1978]), we arrive at six general areas of functioning and a set of descriptive guidelines. These can be used to compare the health of a client family with that of the optimally functioning family by observing and rating client families in each of the six areas. This helps to maintain the focus of therapy on family functioning and to segment family processes into parts easier to observe and evaluate. The six areas of functioning are: (1) roles, (2) emotional expression, (3) interdependence/individuation, (4) power, (5) communication, and (6) subsystems.

Roles are repetitive patterns of individual behavior and serve functional purposes in day-to-day family life. Roles delineate the family's structure and maintain the family's interactional processes.

### *Optimal Family Roles*

1. Clear differentiation exists between the roles of parent, child, and spouse.
2. Roles may be shared, reversed, or changed, depending on the situation.
3. New roles can be tried out or old ones modified.
4. The roles taken by family members complement one another.
5. These roles are also similar across situations and members.
6. Parents share child care.

Emotional expression refers to the notion that each family has an emotional tone that is based on the degree of emotional expressiveness, sensitivity, and responsiveness family members share with each other. Families also create norms of reciprocity that govern reflexive patterns of emotional expression.

### Optimal Family Emotional Expression

1. The overall emotional tone of the family is positive.
2. Family members are sensitive to one another's feelings.
3. The rules for expressing emotion are clear, and the expression of emotion tends to be spontaneous.
4. Expression of negative emotions is allowed as well as sensitivity toward others.
5. The amount of expressiveness is high, with laughter, humor, and warmth evident.
6. Open and unresolved hostility is absent.
7. The family tolerates and encourages the expression of a wide range of feelings.

Interdependence/individuation refers to the amount of autonomy or individuation granted to the individual by the family.

### Optimal Family Individuation

1. Each individual has separate recreational and social activities.
2. Family members discuss individual problems and understand and support one another.
3. Different value systems are tolerated in the family; however, central values concerning sexuality, money, religion, work ethics, and family loyalty are jointly held.
4. Cooperation rather than competition is a family value.
5. Interpersonal relationships with nonfamily members are approved of as long as family routine is not disturbed.
6. The family members take responsibility for their individual behavior and feelings.
7. Differences of opinion are tolerated, and mutual agreement is frequently the product of discussions.

Power can be defined as the degree of influence or control family members have over each other. The use of power and its distribution among family members is very important to the understanding and changing of dysfunctional interaction patterns.

### Optimal Family Power Distribution

1. Everyone has input into family decisions.
2. Family members seek and take leadership in different aspects of family life, and other family members willingly follow such leadership.
3. Power in the family is centralized within the parental dyad.

4. Family rules are enforced through persuasion rather than through intimidation or force. Violence is not tolerated.
5. There is little hostile, angry, acting-out behavior. Conflicts tend to be open, and they are resolved quickly.
6. Except for the parental dyad, coalitions among family members are open and short-term.

Communication is concerned with the delivery and reception of verbal and nonverbal information between family members. It includes skills in exchanging patterns of information within the family system.

### Optimal Family Communication

1. A high volume of information seeking and sharing occurs between family members.
2. Nonverbal and verbal messages are congruent, and the intent of each message is clear and open.
3. Silence is infrequent, and the family deals with a wide range of topics.
4. Conflicts are resolved through discussion.
5. Most family communication is positive in tone.
6. All family members are capable of using problem-solving statements that encourage the efficient resolution of conflicts.

Also important are the subsystems (or subgroupings) within the family and how they maintain the family system. The types of subsystems include the parent, spouse, and sibling groups, and the alliances between and among the members of the groups.

### Optimal Family Subsystems

1. The boundaries between the parental, spousal, and sibling subsystems are clear.
2. Each subsystem performs its functions adequately.
3. There are strong emotional bonds between subsystems and between the individuals within subsystems.
4. The parental subsystem leads the family and holds most of the power.
5. Individuals within subsystems participate in shared activities.
6. Coalitions across subsystems occur but are short-term.

Naturally, families with sources of identity and cultural heritage differing from that of middle- and upper-income North Americans must be evaluated with guidelines somewhat different from those stated here. However, one basic assumption of family therapy is that all families work approximately the same way. The therapist should not stray wildly from the general guidelines for optimal family functioning.

## ASSESSMENT TOOLS

As the field of marriage and family therapy has developed, objective instruments for assessing and cataloging problems have evolved. These instruments are employed for both research and clinical purposes. Although their use in gathering research data is obvious, their use in clinical practice seems less well understood.

As couples and families enter therapy, they are frequently confused by the morass of accumulated emotions they have experienced. Unless issues to be addressed are specified, the therapy can become as fragmented as the clients' emotions appear to be. The advantages of using self-report instruments with couples or families include: (1) they can help to objectify and organize the treatment effort while establishing an atmosphere of purposeful direction to replace family chaos; (2) they provide family members an opportunity to systematically understand what the other members' concerns are (perhaps for the first time, the confusing cloud of emotionality is somewhat dispelled), and (3) individuals are provided with the opportunity to self-disclose through paper and pencil rather than their usual method, which has failed. Frequently, people will find it easier to respond to a checklist of potential problems or specified questions than to describe their concerns verbally. After reviewing a list of marital problems, such as those found in the Marital Diagnostic Inventory (Navran, 1973), couples often report a new perception of their difficulties as they discover that they checked relatively few of the many possible problems. This insight, by itself, can often have great therapeutic value, not to mention the specificity now available to the spouses and the clinician.

The clinician can derive benefits from self-report tests as well. As with any journey, therapy can be expedited with the aid of a map. By using self-report instruments, the clinician can organize the interview data and construct a valuable cognitive map which describes the type and nature of problems being presented. Without this map, the therapeutic journey can become a series of rambling, unsuccessful side trips, unproductive for all involved. Further, gathering this type of information at the outset facilitates evaluation of treatment outcomes; many clinicians administer the same instruments at a later phase in therapy to get feedback on the nature and extent of client changes.

Although many objective instruments are available, clinicians are wise to review them and select the ones most consonant with their style and practice; test publishers are eager to share information about their available instruments. Also, reviewing books such as Straus and Brown's (1978) *Family Measurement Techniques* and the more recent *Handbook of Family Measurement Techniques* (Touliatos, Perlmutter, & Straus, 1990) can prove valuable. Although the marriage and family therapy literature of the 1970s is replete with polemics about this or that correct method or instrument for measuring presenting problems, clinicians do best by selecting those tools that best suit their practice.

In selecting instrumentation, keep in mind the relative complexity of intervening with the family unit as compared to the individual. Ackerman (1958), more than four decades ago, stated that a complete family assessment should take into account the individual family members, roles, the marital dyad, the family as a group, and family members' interrelationships. Fortunately, objective instruments now exist with which to assess these areas, should the clinician so choose.

Clinical use of any assessment tool requires that it possess at least two characteristics in addition to documented validity and reliability. It must be easy to administer, score, and interpret, and it must yield information that the clinician can use. When no testing on system characteristics is conducted, the therapist is more easily seduced to focus on stories and pathology. The therapy resembles individual therapy in a group when this happens, and the impact and promise of system treatment is lost.

One excellent reason, possibly the best one to use tests when treating couples and families, is to stay oriented to systems-based treatment. Assessment of system functioning directs the therapist's attention to the organizational and interactional characteristics of the couple or family. Since the structure and interaction are what we seek to change in marriage and family therapy, that's where our attention belongs.

## ASSESSING READINESS FOR THERAPY

Recognizing that families are composed of individuals, it is important to acknowledge that family readiness for change, in varying degrees, lies within each member. Consequently, the clinician needs to assess the level of readiness or motivation of each member in order to avoid making therapeutic moves that would alienate those least motivated. Along with each member's level of readiness, the clinician needs to be alert to the individual's power or potency within the family organization.

The clinician who is unaware of individuals' levels of readiness and power could easily end up not only being unsuccessful in drawing families into therapy, but may actually push them out. For example, the clinician who does not adequately assess that the father is minimally invested in therapy but is very powerful in the family's organization may prematurely take the mother's side on an issue and provoke the father into sabotaging any return to "that damn therapist." While the clinician's professional ego may be temporarily bruised, the real loser is the family that sought help in the tenuous and uncertain way that most families enter therapy.

The clinician needs to direct more intensive engagement procedures toward family members who seem least ready for therapy and toward those who are most powerful and influential in the family. Continuing the above example, it would be important to direct engagement efforts toward the father, who appears to be the least ready or committed to the treatment effort, but is a powerful decision maker with regard to influencing the family's behavior. To quickly take sides with the mother may be too dramatic a change for the father to adapt to and may also be an affront to his belief about how his role should be regarded: Father is most important. For these reasons, the clinician would probably best engage father by initially being responsive to his perception of the family structure and rules. By doing so, the clinician can also begin to create shock absorbers in the relationship with the father that will facilitate confrontations with him that may later become important. Without the development of these shock absorbers, the dad may never evidence any more than the minimal readiness already displayed, and the clinician, then, will never experience the benefit of having firmer therapeutic leverage than that present initially. Of course, power could be centralized in the mother's role as readily as the father's role. Working with awareness to either possibility is necessary.

Readiness can be assessed by asking questions such as "How did you decide to come here?" "What do you hope will change by being here?" "Recognizing how uncomfortable it can be to come to therapy, what motivates you to be here?" Often it can prove very valuable to ask several family members to answer these questions as though they were someone else in the family. For instance, the clinician may ask the youngest daughter, "Do you think mom really wants to be here?" Assuming the daughter responds affirmatively, a natural follow-up would be, "And what do you think mom hopes can be changed by coming here?" This type of questioning can provide much insight to the family members present, as well as to the clinician. Frequently, such a discussion is the first opportunity family members have had to learn how they are perceived by each other and what beliefs are harbored by each member.

Along with responses to questions such as these, the clinician can assess readiness by observing behaviors such as an apparent eagerness to talk, an authentic and pleasant self-presentation, the presence of tears that seem to communicate a sense of hopefulness or desperation, a warm greeting at the outset or a sincere "thank you" at the end of a session, and comments that convey an individual's readiness to accept personal responsibility for family difficulties rather than to project all blame on others. Although clinicians are frequently heard making statements such as "I can just sense they are ready," it is likely that specific observed behaviors, such as those just identified, are the source of the clinician's sense of family readiness for therapy.

## ASSESSING FAMILY RULES

Rules are part of every relationship, and family rules are the dynamic components of the family's organization. The obvious rules govern who takes out the garbage, who mows the lawn, who does which housecleaning task, and the like, but numerous rules of a more subtle nature also exist. They are the internalized implicit regulations that maintain a family's systemic functioning, valuable to know in developing a therapeutic plan.

Ideally, this plan, though responsive to the family's present rules, will facilitate the development of more functional ones. Ignoring the family's rules could provoke premature termination. For example, the family that functions with the rule of not acknowledging or responding to mother's intense, depressive behaviors may abruptly terminate if the undiscerning clinician comments on it without first having established a relationship of trust and confidence with the family. By identifying the rule, however, the therapist is able to begin formulating a way to introduce a contrary rule in the family's organizational schema to make a more functional organization possible. Mother's depression can be openly acknowledged, increasing the potential for its resolution.

Although hundreds of rule possibilities may apply to a family at any given time, one rule always seems present in the more dysfunctional families—the no-talk rule. This rule is especially destructive, because it forbids any comment on family rules and, consequently, diminishes the potential for changing problematic rules. The therapist can begin to address some of the more problematic rules and demonstrate to the "no-talk family" that it can do this without falling to pieces, and, in fact, can do so with positive consequences.

As an example, assume that a particular family seems to operate with the rule, "You can interrupt anybody who is speaking except dad." The therapist could introduce a new, contrary rule, saying something like:

It is difficult for me to follow the different trains of thought I hear, as all of you seem to talk at the same time. Because of that, I'd like your help, and want to ask you to speak one at a time so that I can hear everything that each of you has to say. I believe all of you have valuable contributions to make here that will be helpful in their own way.

This new rule will probably have to be reinforced before it becomes part of a new interactional pattern. Remember, the old rule has existed for a long while, and interactional patterns are not changed easily.

The following constitute examples of areas around which every family has constructed rules, and questions that can be asked to elicit family rules. How can caring be expressed in this family? How can it be received? By whom? Under what circumstances? And the same can be asked or observed regarding other emotions such as anger, hurt, and so on. How can someone let wants and needs be known in this family? Who can talk to whom, and about what? How can someone be different in this family (if that is even allowed)? When and how can a family member secure space (emotional or physical) to be alone? How can someone secure attention or concern in this family, or show or receive affirmation? How can disagreement be shown? Can anyone comment on what appear to be rules that operate in this family and create a concern for one or more members?

With many families, rules governing these areas can be determined by simply asking questions. With other families, they may need to be deduced by observing interaction. Assessment and determination of a family's operational rules can often be made by interacting with and/or observing the family. What one does not observe can be as valuable as what is directly observed. For instance, if the clinician does not observe any displays of affection despite many opportunities, a working hypothesis would be in order that a rule against displays of affection exists. A way to test this hypothesis is to ask something along the lines of, "How do you know you are cared for as a member of this family?" This question may be posed to the family as a group, or directed to a particular member. Frequently, it is best posed to the entire group, with each member having an opportunity to respond. Just asking this question will often introduce the family to a new rule that says each family member has a perception that is equally valuable. The introduction of a new and more productive rule can also initiate the process of change.

Rules can also be deduced by observing nonverbal behaviors in response to the therapist's questions. If the father, or someone else, becomes restless and seems uneasy when a particular topic or question is broached, it would be reasonable to hypothesize that a rule is being confronted or addressed that has been taboo and/or out of awareness. Or if mother and father are asked to briefly engage in an exchange about a particular issue and a flurry of acting-out by a child occurs, perhaps a family rule has been transgressed. As families become more stressed, or particular areas of their functioning become more stressed, the rules also become more evident.

Often the clinician changes family rules regardless of the particular orientation or strategy employed. When any of the following are engaged in, rules are introduced that likely replace some old, counterproductive family rule: coaching parents on management of children, regulating privacy, establishing an appropriate age hierarchy in the family, promoting open communication, eliciting feelings, providing personal feedback and interpretations to the family, and assigning tasks to be completed outside of the session. Little is done with families that either does not influence family rules or is not influenced by them. For this reason, it is extremely valuable to continually assess family rules.

## ASSESSING FAMILY MYTHS

A family myth is part of the pervasive ideology of the family that evolves from the interaction of the family's rituals, roles, and rules. The therapist should comprehend this ideology, or the family's definition or framing of reality, before developing interventions. Without this understanding, there is a great risk that various interventions will be rejected by the family as not being in accord with "how it is." Naturally, when the family members are not responsive, the therapist can then project blame and define them as resistant rather than acknowledging an error in not being responsive to the family's important myths and framing of reality. For example, a family myth might be: "We are a nice family and, therefore, never openly communicate aggression." In working with this family, it would be contraindicated to ask them to engage in behavior that is directly contrary to this myth. To do so would catapult the family into a contrary position regarding a component of their definition of reality, and resistant behavior would be the predictable result. Remember, myths serve the vital function of maintaining family homeostasis, or equilibrium. The therapist who prematurely and directly confronts the family's myths invites the dissolution of a relationship with them. With an understanding of these operational myths, however, the therapist can develop interventions that the family will most likely receive and respond to. To identify these myths, the therapist, in most situations, need only listen and watch the family interact, guided by the internal question: "What do these people attribute to one another, and to the family as a whole?" As the therapist observes these attributions, the prevailing myths of the family become apparent.

The process of assessing the prominent myths can also be facilitated by structured activities such as asking the family to complete sentence items; for example:

"In crisis, we as a family . . . ."
"As a family, we . . . ."
"In this family, it is easy to . . . ."
"In this family, disagreements are . . . ."
"Closeness in this family is . . . ."

Another activity that can uncover family myths is to ask the family to construct an ad listing them as "a family for sale." Related activities include asking a family to develop a symbolic family crest that conveys the essence of the family or developing a consensus family drawing that portrays them as a group.

Along with assessing the myths about the family as a whole, it is equally important to assess myths regarding individuals in the family. Remember that myths about an individual will usually convey myths about an entire family. For example, consider this statement (by the wife) about one family member (the husband): "He is just not a good manager of finances." Statements about individuals are made in reference to one or more of the other family members, for instance, the speaker. The attribution, "He is not a good manager of finances," implies the existence of a counter or complementary myth: "but, I am (or somebody else is) a good manager of finances." In this respect, a myth about the family's organization can be deduced and used as a working hypothesis until disproved or validated by further information. In this example, it would be foolish to immediately assign financial responsibility to the husband. Knowing that the family myth functions for the family the way defenses do for the individual, it is naive to assume that the myth can be immediately confronted without preparing the family for a shift in perception and the alteration of this buffer.

To prepare the family for a shift in the myths most counterproductive to its organization and operation, the therapist must determine whether it is best to work at eliminating the family's need to maintain the myth or to gradually change the myth until the family realizes it can function without it at least as effectively as it did before. For instance, using the previous example, the therapist might help the wife feel competent enough in other areas of the family's operation so that she can more easily afford to promote the husband's financial competence, or the therapist might gradually increase the husband's competence by encouraging the wife to help him develop financial acumen. With her encouragement and direct assistance, his increasing competence is not as likely to be threatening to her, and consequently, she is less likely to sabotage the change. As the wife assists the husband in securing this new financial competence, the therapist can work with their communication style and foster a new level of trust and understanding between them that goes beyond the issue of the husband's financial management abilities.

As you can see, the determination of family myths is vital to both developing treatment goals and establishing the path of least resistance in achieving them. The therapist who is not sensitive to family myths is probably destined to experience many apparently unexplained roadblocks during the therapeutic process and to excessively attribute resistance to the family. In this sense, the unknowing therapist may fall victim to the myth that the world is populated mostly by resistant families.

## ASSESSING FAMILY RITUALS

Assessing the ritualistic aspects of family life has long played a role in family therapy and in family therapy theory. Unfortunately, attention has been directed toward only one type of family ritual: that composed of routine interaction patterns which occur in conjunction with dysfunctional family structure and process. The type of family ritual that has been ignored and might be termed traditional is made up of activities such as holiday celebrations, birthdays, church ceremonies, and the like.

The reasons for this neglect are several, the most important being the almost complete lack of research demonstrating a connection between the problems families bring to therapy and the quality of traditional rituals. In one study, however, the disruption of traditional family ritual was found to be a principal factor in the intergenerational transmission of alcoholism (Wolin, Bennett, Noonan, & Teitelbaum, 1980). This study, as well as clinical experience, lends credence to the notion that assessing the quality of family ritual is a relevant component of family therapy.

The traditional family ritual is defined as a prescribed procedure of family interaction that involves a pattern of defined behavior which is directed toward some specific end or purpose and acquires rigidity and a sense of rightness as a result of its continuing history (Bossard & Boll, 1950). The ritual is a central component of family culture. Rituals provide intergenerational continuity and serve as developmental links in the process of family life (Schvaneveldt & Lee, 1983).

Assessing the quality of family rituals is not a complex task. When family identity seems to be well defined (meaning, when the therapist can think of a socially desirable label that describes the family), questions such as "What does the family do on your birthday?" or "What happens on Thanksgiving?" will serve to index the quality of traditional rituals. It is important for the therapist to determine who knows the rituals and how clearly the rituals can be described by family members. These questions can be directed to and answered by children as well as teenagers and adults. The most important rituals are usually spoken of first. If family identity seems well defined and yet the family members cannot describe their rituals clearly, or there does not seem to be an established routine, then the therapist should wonder whether a thorough assessment has been carried out. A negative correlation between the reported strength of rituals and a clear family identity is an indicator of inaccurate assessment.

When the family identity is not clear and a singular label cannot be applied, a more thorough process must follow. Most often, with families lacking identity, the traditional rituals cannot be described or they have lost value. Clients will often say, "We used to do _____ , but over the last few years no one has been at home," or "The last time we tried to have a Thanksgiving dinner, he got drunk and pulled a knife on my sister-in-law." It is important to determine when an established ritual was abandoned. The onset of family dysfunction can be presumed to predate the abandonment of a ritual.

A second area of assessment involves the reaction of the family to its disrupted or abandoned rituals. Do the clients feel sad, resentful, or empty because this important aspect of family life is absent or awkward? Asking questions that will draw out these feelings is one way to assess the impact of lost rituals. In the process, the family can mobilize by reestablishing emotional connections and rituals. The events making up disrupted rituals are important to catalog. In the study mentioned before (Wolin et al., 1980), disrupted rituals were not found to be a factor in the intergenerational transmission of alcoholism if the family ignored the disruptive behavior of a family member and continued the ritual. Questions such as "What does this family do when she [disruption] during church or at a birthday party?" A description of events will show how the family copes with disruption of ritual and with disruption of its everyday processes. The absence of coping strategies might suggest the value of helping the family to enhance its repertoire of coping strategies.

Assessing family ritual should play some role in the overall assessment conducted by a therapist during the initial phase of therapy. Rituals are frequently related to the richness and extent of the family support network. They provide a means of preserving family myths, especially those founded on pseudomutuality. Assessing family rituals is also a quick way to determine family roles, the structure of alliances, and subsystem boundaries. Ignoring this symbolic and binding aspect of family life can hamper the therapist's understanding of the family, and, therefore, the treatment options that may be available.

## ASSESSING DISENGAGEMENT

The concept of disengagement in families was introduced by Minuchin (1974) to describe a system in which the boundaries between individuals and/or subsystems are rigid and strongly drawn. As such, the concept can be understood either as a *trait* of a family or as a *state* of current family functioning. More typically, *disengagement* is used to describe the traits of a family.

The concept is used in assessment in several ways. It is a helpful tool to use when attempting to label the interpersonal involvement of a family. Disengaged families are often silent, withdrawn, and sullen, and the members feel isolated from one another even though they may hunger for intimacy. Recognizable signs of such isolation include one-word answers to questions, ignorance of others' feelings and actions, puzzlement about why the family is in therapy, an emphasis on personal financial autonomy (teenagers working, both parents working), lack of shared family interests, low family interaction quality or quantity, lack of family secret keeping, and other signs that communicate the absence of a strong connection between family members and a generalized concept of family.

When the clinician senses that disengagement is part of the family's ritual interaction process (trait), the clarity of family identity can be questioned, or the frequent exercise and misuse of power by all family members might be assumed. Pseudomutuality (in which claims of closeness are made, but no behavioral indicators support such a statement) may also be observed as an important family myth. When a disengaged style appears to be an unusual interaction style for a family (state), then the family may be experiencing a developmental crisis—for example, a teenager may be about to leave home and sever ties with the family.

Disengagement is an important concept in differentiating among families as to the family's level of intimacy and the strength of family members' personal identities. As with all system analysis, knowledge of the purpose served by a given level of disengagement is integral to effective treatment. For example, among families in developmental crisis (state), disengagement often serves to block channels of painful communication. Among families in which disengagement is a rigid style of organization (trait), the low self-concepts of the parental figures can be protected, the absence of a parental coalition can be maintained, and the presence of other strong coalitions can remain hidden; any number of dysfunctional patterns can be in operation. Disengagement is like a fog that distorts clinical perception, a fog that can be lifted by carefully raising a family's emotional temperature.

## ASSESSING PARENTIFICATION

*Parentification* is a concept frequently used in the assessment of families. It is most often applied to a child who has taken on the role of parent or spouse in his or her family, although it could just as easily be used to describe any family member in another role (e.g., aunt, uncle, cousin) who assumes an adult role in a family of procreation.

The term is easy to misuse, because, in healthy family systems, we expect to see children try out adult roles. Since the parent role is the one most frequently observed by children, it is the adult role most likely to be tried out first. Naturally, therefore, we expect to see the teenage son directing the younger siblings in some chore, or the oldest daughter asking her sister and mother to quiet down during a heated discussion. Unfortunately, these natural explorations on the part of children can be mistaken for parentification.

For correct application of the label a number of conditions must exist. First and foremost is the quid-pro-quo context of inappropriate role taking. For example, a nine-year-old daughter taking charge of caring for a much younger sibling would not be parentified unless her mother or father had abdicated the parent role of primary caretaker. In this instance, parentification exists in the context of childification, in which the parent takes on some facet of the child or some other nonparent role.

A second condition involves the cost of the inappropriate role taking to all family members. The parentified child assumes role behavior and responsibility, without being emotionally, intellectually, or, perhaps, physically ready to do so. As a result, stress is created, and other developmental tasks are displaced. For example, a nine-year-old who assumes the primary caretaker role for a younger sibling may not be able to spend time interacting with peers and, thus, may lose an opportunity to develop socially. The costs to other family members, mainly parents, include loss of self-esteem, because a child is seen performing what should be adult tasks, and a lowered stress coping ability, because the pressures to perform as an adult are assumed by someone else. The results of parentification should be evident throughout the system, and if there appear to be no harmful consequences, perhaps the child is in the early stages of inappropriate role taking or the role taking is incidental.

In its most severe form, parentification involves the child taking on much or most of an adult role, not just parts of it, and showing the resultant stress. The son who drops out of school and provides most of the income for his family, a behavior which the father abdicated to him along with other important aspects of the paternal role, might exemplify severe parentification. Likewise, among single-parent families in which children are asked to take on adult roles, perhaps earlier and more frequently than in dual-parent families, severe parentification would be an appropriate label when the child has taken on a number of role-related behaviors (e.g., confidant, sex partner) which are adult in nature.

In assessing parentification, the clinician pays attention to the frequency, duration, system context, and impact on child development of inappropriate role taking. Frequency and duration are assessed through the typical questions of when and how often. System context refers to how the inappropriate role taking affects all system members. Direct questions such as "How do you feel about yourself when you see Mary Jane making the decision of which bill will be paid first?" will sometimes elicit the necessary information. With families in which parentification occurs, however, directly asking for such information may not prove successful. Inappropriate development in a child can be inferred from direct observation of the child interacting with the therapist and with family members. The presence of intense sibling rivalry, incest, or physical abuse may indicate the presence of parentification. More often, the clinician will have to infer the existence of parentification based on answers to questions unrelated to child and adult roles in the family.

## ASSESSING SEXUAL FUNCTIONING

Even though sexuality plays an important role in marital life, family therapists have tended to believe that sexual problems result from relationship dysfunction and to refer clients with such problems to sex therapists. We have never really decided whether to assess marital sexuality during the initial phase of therapy and how much time to devote to it. This is unfortunate because, for many couples with relationship problems, lack of sexual sophistication has given rise to those problems, and, even though treatment of those problems should not typically begin with sex therapy, exploring a couple's sexual history can be very helpful in understanding how and why current relationship dynamics came about.

Several questionnaires have been developed. A good example is the Sexual Performance Evaluation developed by the Marriage Council of Philadelphia. This questionnaire and the sex history interview protocols help make sure all the appropriate questions are asked. They also pace the disclosure about sexuality at a rate that helps most clients remain comfortable. The topics covered typically include:

Childhood Sexuality

Adolescent Sexuality

Orgasm Experiences

Feelings about Gender

Fantasies and Dreams

Dating

Engagement

Marriage

Extramarital Sex

Sex after Widowhood, Separation, Divorce

Sexual Deviations

Venereal Disease

Therapists must consider carefully how they will structure the history taking with couples. This procedure is most beneficial to relationships when partners learn about one another at the same pace. To reduce the chance of surprises, a short meeting with each spouse alone can serve to determine whether a conjoint interview will have a positive outcome. If either spouse holds significant secrets that if disclosed will burden the partner, they should be encouraged to examine the cost-benefit of revealing the secret(s).

Once the partners agree to complete the history, both should be involved at all times. Related questions should be asked of both. For example, both would describe their adolescent sexual experiences before either would be asked their feelings about their gender. By asking both partners to answer the same questions at the same time, both remain involved in the process, feelings can be aired quickly, and resentment will have less of an opportunity to grow.

Another excellent procedure that helps couples talk about their sexual life is the Sexual Genogram. Developed by Hof and Berman (1986), it combines the traditional genogram with the traditional sex history. Emphasis is placed on understanding sexual dysfunction in a multigenerational, family context.

The procedure has several stages. Initially, clients learn the goals of the process and the role of early learning and intergenerational influences on family and individual functioning. Then clients complete a traditional, three-generation genogram. After the genogram is mapped out and explored, each partner is asked to reconsider it over the next week, focusing on:

the family messages about sexuality/intimacy and masculinity/femininity,

who carried these messages and who said nothing,

what were the family secrets related to sexuality/intimacy, and

how each would change the genogram so it reflected what he or she wishes would have occurred regarding messages about sexuality/intimacy.

Answers to these questions and others are written out and shared the following week with the therapist and the partner. Over the course of several weeks this material is discussed by the couple. The resulting insight commonly provides high motivation to work on the couple's sexual problems. In some cases the genogram changes the context for sexual dysfunction so much that the presenting sexual problems need limited attention using traditional sex therapy.

Because marital therapy is not sex therapy, the procedures and questionnaires used by sex therapists are not appropriate. Most important is the therapist's communication that sex will be talked about and that the therapist is comfortable with the topic. The therapist must frankly ask questions such as "When did you first have intercourse?" "What were the circumstances?" "Who initiated?" "What influence did that first experience have on your relationship?" and "How frequently did you have intercourse prior to and after marriage or living together?" Using clinical terms when referring to genitalia is appropriate, and so are questions about satisfaction and orgasm. To help clients feel more comfortable, therapists often interview the couple together and then separately. Paying attention to a couple's sexual history is something a couple expects a good therapist to do.

## ASSESSING FAMILY VIOLENCE

Violence is very common in family life. Siblings are notoriously violent, and parents abuse children and each other. In fact, the family might be considered an inherently violent social institution. As it pertains to clinical practice, this fact of life means that family therapists should *assume* the presence of violence instead of wondering *whether* it is occurring. Focus on learning how pervasive and severe it is. With this sort of attitude—notwithstanding the notion that you will find what you go looking for—fewer victims of violence will suffer in silence and fewer perpetrators will escape notice. Victims especially should feel confident that family therapists will remedy their situation.

Even a therapist who is sensitive to the possibilities of violence can still be caught off guard or blindsided. One reason is our understanding of the behaviors that can constitute family violence. Overt attempts to control a partner or child are easy to identify; this category includes hitting, slapping, punching, pinching, biting, shooting, among others. However, spanking, swatting, shoving, poking, squeezing, even hard tickling, and many other seemingly less harmful behaviors can also be considered violent. A third class of behaviors are designed to intimidate and so accomplish the same goal as overt violence *without* touching. Slamming doors, punching walls, yelling, slamming tables, breaking glass, and throwing household objects can be considered violent acts designed to control others. Alongside these intimidating acts directed at family members are acts that imply that a family member is dangerous. For instance, fighting with strangers or acquaintances can directly influence the behavior of family members. So, the range of violent behavior is quite large, and accordingly, assessment should catalogue the full range of intimidating behavior and intimidating messages.

One trap to avoid in assessing violence is to focus on the perpetrator's intent. If asked why they behave as they do, perpetrators often will assert an intent that rationalizes their violent act or acts. Power struggles can emerge very easily when a therapist feels compelled to argue about the perpetrator's intent. It is much easier to avoid that question by defining intent from the victim's perspective, regardless of what the perpetrator says. For instance, John may assert that when he "shoved" Alice, he was trying to stop her from nagging him about his drinking. From Alice's point of view, however, he not only shoved her but punched her repeatedly. One question is who is correct; another is whether John had a right to defend himself. Since bias is more likely on John's part, we should assume that Alice is more nearly correct. Also, we should see John's behavior as an attempt to hurt Alice and not permit his rationalization to fog our thinking about who is responsible for being violent. A rough guide is to believe victims and to recognize violence as an attempt to inflict pain.

Intimidation behavior can also become confusing. For example, John might say that Alice became frightened when he punched the wall, but that he wasn't trying to scare her. He was just expressing himself in his house. In response, a therapist might say:

> Regardless of what you intended, John, if Alice says she was frightened, then she was. When you punch the wall or yell at her, she feels intimidated. When you come home talking about kicking someone's ass out in the alley behind Joe's Bar, that's related to everyone in your family tiptoeing around you. It isn't necessary to hit someone to have the same effect.

In assessing violence, it is important to understand that overt violence usually occurs within an atmosphere of chronic intimidation. Violence is like an iceberg with one-eighth showing above the water while seven-eighths of its mass is hidden below the surface. Ask questions about yelling, threats, and derogative remarks such as "You are stupid or lazy or just plain no good." Assume that life in a violent family consists of a steady barrage of such comments leveled at the victim. Identifying these comments is necessary. Early researchers described a stage cycle (tension, explosion, honeymoon) of violence. Our understanding today is that while a cycle of violence can occur, a stable and chronic condition of intimidation with violent flare-ups more accurately describes the situation in most violent families.

Our experience is that there are several types of violent relationships. Among some couples for example, *small violence*—for the lack of a better term—in the form of shoving, pinching, throwing objects, yelling, and passive aggressive acts is performed by both men and women. For some of these couples, violence is pervasive, an habituated part of their interaction with one another. Violence carries important messages in that sort of relationship system. Among other couples where instances of small violence by both partners occur infrequently, stressor pileup may be the culprit. The bulk of violent couples fit into this small violence category. They can be assessed from a systemic framework and treated conjointly. Partners can be questioned about violent incidents conjointly, but each should be given time alone with their therapist.

A second category of violence, where battery occurs, must be assessed differently. In almost all cases the perpetrator is male. Even in instances where a woman commits battery, it can usually be shown that she preempted his attack to protect herself. Battery often results in hospitalization of the victim. Other signs include black eyes, broken noses, lacerations, burns, broken limbs, and bruises. Difficulty sitting or painful breathing may signify battery. In this category of violence, attacks can be prolonged episodes with multiple beatings over an extended time.

Usually the perpetrator is defensive and can be highly aggressive in the therapy session itself. Clinicians should pay attention to their own safety perhaps by not seeing such individuals alone. Some clinicians carry communicators to call for help if the need should arise. (Note: With every case, not just with violent clients, therapists should position themselves between the client and an exit door so they cannot be trapped in the consulting room.)

Below is a list of descriptors that can help in identifying potentially violent men:

Believes in the traditional home, family, and gender stereotypes

Has low self-esteem and may use violence to demonstrate power or adequacy

May be sadistic, pathologically jealous, or passive-aggressive

Has a Jekyll and Hyde personality, capable of great charm

May use sex as an act of aggression

Believes in the moral rightness of his violent behavior even though he may go too far at times

Has perpetrated past violent behavior, which includes witnessing, receiving, and committing violent acts, violent acts during childhood; violent acts toward pets or inanimate objects; and has criminal record, long military service, or temper tantrums

Indicates alcohol abuse

Where battery has occurred or there is any question about the safety of either partner being compromised by therapy, partners should be seen alone. Usually, the perpetrator will be under a restraining order to stay away from the victim. Therapy should not countermand that order. Where therapy is court ordered, the victim may or may not be required to attend sessions. If not, therapists should weigh carefully the potential for harm by inviting the victim to pursue therapy. Complications can arise out of fee payment, disclosure of secrets, or accidental meetings at the therapist's office that may breech safety.

If a victim is seen, she should be helped to prepare a safety plan in the first session. A plan consists of preparations ahead of time for leaving a dangerous situation at home—an escape route. Money, legal documents and records, keys, and clothes are gathered and held by a friend. A method of calling for transportation to a shelter or safe place for the victim and children is developed. By the end of the session, the victim should know how to stay safe and should have the confidence to enact the plan. Assessment would include a full description of violent incidents with the current partner and with other partners as well.

Assessing child abuse presents a different spectrum of concerns. As with all families where violence is suspected, children should be given time alone with their therapist. More time may need to be invested in developing a relationship before seeking information indirectly. For instance a therapist might use puppet play to ask a child to describe what happens when someone is mad at them. Follow-up could consist of more direct questions on violence first to the child then to the parents.

Assessment of violence should occur in the context of broader systemic assessment. Exploring relationship history for instance can lighten the sense of failure a couple may feel. A genogram can spot long-standing, violent child-guidance patterns that parents can recognize and then want to change because those patterns are not theirs by choice. Assessment of drug and alcohol abuse can reduce the contributions both make to family violence. Assessment commonly includes a written or verbal no-violence contract. Such contracts are described in Chapter 7.

## ASSESSING DRUG AND ALCOHOL USE

Alcohol and other drugs have come to be recognized as a major problem within families. A 1983 Gallup poll indicated that one-third of all respondents reported that at least one person in their family had what they regarded as a significant drug problem. Because of the pervasive nature of this problem, it is important for the clinician to know how to identify a problem and what to do once it is recognized.

If one or more family members is troubled by another's use of drugs, it is at least an interpersonal problem which signifies a schism between two people that, if not addressed, will likely intensify antagonisms. Although acknowledging these tensions is one obvious way of identifying a problem, more objective means are available to the clinician. The Michigan Alcoholism Screening Test, or MAST (Selzer, 1971) consists of twenty-five questions that are answered with yes or no and yields a weighted score with a demonstrated capacity for objectively identifying the intensity of a drug problem. Similarly, the MacAndrew Alcoholism Scale of the Minnesota Multiphasic

Personality Inventory (MacAndrew, 1965) has forty-nine items and objectively identifies the probability of an alcohol problem existing. Both of these instruments are completed by the person with a suspected drug problem and can help to identify the problem objectively and, in this sense, lift it out of the realm of the family's perceptions. Characteristically, the family with a drug problem is pervaded by distrust, projections, and denial. For this reason, an outside and seemingly objective source can be critical in assisting the family to more productively catalog and address the problem. If family members are left only to their respective perceptions, it is most reasonable to expect tensions in the family to escalate, as reactive accusations are communicated.

Procedures that are more brief and less intrusive are also available to the clinician as a means of introducing some objectivity to an otherwise potentially emotional and reactive situation. One such procedure is referred to as the CAGE questions (Ewing & Rouse, 1970; and Ewing, 1984). The acronym CAGE is derived from the first letter of a key word extracted from each of the four questions. The four questions that constitute this screening procedure, with the key word that contributes to the CAGE acronym underlined are as follows:

Have you ever felt you ought to <u>c</u>ut down on your drinking?

Have people <u>annoyed</u> you by criticizing your drinking?

Have you ever felt bad or <u>guilty</u> about your drinking?

Have you ever had a drink first thing in the morning to steady your nerves or get rid of a hangover (<u>eye opener</u>)?

Ewing found in his original research that all known alcoholics screened with these four questions responded affirmatively to at least two of the questions. Mayfield, McLeod, and Hall (1974), in their validating study of Ewing's work, determined that using two or three positive responses as criteria for minimally identifying abusive drinkers, if not alcoholics, yielded an impressive correlation coefficient of .89. Research such as this has resulted in the CAGE questions coming to be recognized as one of the most efficient and effective screening devices available to clinicians. These questions are easy to administer and reliable in distinguishing alcoholics, and much less intimidating than some of the other available tools and instruments that are more intrusive and obvious.

Another unobtrusive procedure available to clinicians is the knowledge and application of eight symptoms of alcoholism developed by Richard Heilman (Heilman, 1973). Heilman, a psychiatrist and long time consultant to the Hazelden Institute, believes that the presence of four or more of the following eight symptoms should result in a diagnosis of alcoholism "... because they reflect a predominantly nonsocial use of alcohol, the aim of which is to 'get high,' and consequently the obvious manifestation of psychic dependency on alcohol" (1973, p. 11). He maintains that the pattern of drinking reflected in these eight symptoms is characteristic of alcoholics whether they are eighteen or sixty years of age. Heilman's eight symptoms are:

1. *Preoccupation.* Alcoholics think about or talk about drinking when they should instead be concerned with other elements of living. Preoccupation with drinking, or "getting high," is the initial and continuing hallmark of any kind of drug dependency.
2. *Increased tolerance.* Research has documented that early on in the abusive pattern, alcoholics are able to drink considerably more than a social drinker and remain efficient mentally and physically—they can drink others "under the table." Unfortunately, many interpret this ability as a sign of special health of some kind.
3. *Gulping drinks.* As with other kinds of drug dependency, the person takes the drug in a fashion such that it will create its effect quickly. "Doubles," or drinking quickly, is characteristic of the dependent person in order to achieve "the high."
4. *Drinking alone.* Sociability is not the important factor in their drug use. Using at home alone, or stopping and drinking in a bar by themselves under the guise of social drinking because other people are "around," comes to be the norm.
5. *Using as a medicine.* Alcoholics come to recognize the exceptionally rewarding effects of alcohol, thinking of alcohol as a panacea. They use it as a tranquilizer for tension or perhaps as a nightcap to help them sleep. It oftentimes comes to be their first thought for resolution of whatever disagreeable symptom they may be suffering.
6. *Blackout.* This is the experience of amnesia. Alcoholics are unable to recall events of the night before. For instance, the alcoholic is unable to remember how they got home the previous night.
7. *Protecting the supply.* Preoccupation with having a sufficient supply on hand is a trait of any kind of drug dependency.
8. *Non-premeditated use.* This symptom addresses the issue of loss of control. They plan on having just one or two, and instead find themselves once again drinking to the point of intoxication. Heilman contends that anyone who responds positively to the question, "Is your drinking ever different from what you would like it to be?" is probably alcoholic.

The CAGE questions and Heilman symptoms can be extremely helpful to clinicians and to those with whom they work. Because there is no clear standard of normal drinking in our society, alcoholics often simply do not know that their drinking is abnormal or significantly different from that of others. Clinicians can use these procedures as a means of providing a gauge for suspected alcoholics to use like a mirror to help them more clearly understand their circumstance. These relatively objective procedures are far more helpful than judgmental generalizations that they are typically exposed to.

Objective instruments are also available that can be completed by concerned family members to help objectify a problem. Most of these instruments are similar to the one developed by Reddy (1973), in that they consist of about twenty questions responded to by family members and have a norm-based cutoff score, which is used to identify the problem's significance. As with the instruments designed for use with the person who has the suspected problem, these tools can introduce a note of scientific objectivity that replaces the highly charged emotions that have probably been rampant among family members.

In conjunction with tools such as these, the wise clinician will also have a working relationship with a chemical dependency counselor who conducts more extensive drug assessments. Such a referral source can be used when the means mentioned previously are not sufficient to facilitate a productive identification and resolution of drug-related concerns. The outcome of this outside assessment can then be integrated into the family therapy process and become part of the more complete information upon which decisions can be based.

In recent years, a great increase in understanding the concept of alcoholism as a family illness and how all members are affected by it has developed. In light of this development, the clinician should determine if either of the spouses are products of a home in which one or both parents were alcoholic, because there are specific interpersonal behaviors that can reasonably be expected from adult children of alcoholics (Wegscheider, 1981), which can be readily treated, once identified. Without treatment, these behavioral problems are likely to be transmitted to their children and to succeeding generations. In this respect, the clinician engages in truly preventive work.

The clinician should also be aware of the intervention process. This process has been described by Johnson (1973) and is designed to help the family successfully intervene and increase the potential for positive change. Although chemical dependency is a psychological/behavioral problem, physiological addiction can evolve eventually, and a major intervention is frequently then required to effect change. Johnson's widely accepted notion of an intervention consists of gathering together people who are significant to the dependent individual (family members, friends, employers, etc.) and coaching them on what to relate to the person they are concerned about, and how to relate in a fashion most likely to result in the person's making a positive decision for treatment. Without this intervention, it is most reasonable to expect that a reactive and defensive cycle of behavior will become entrenched, and that no change will occur other than problem intensification and further destruction. Interventions have now been successfully used for several years with drug problems, and it is important for these families to have clinicians available who are knowledgeable about this process.

## ASSESSING STRESS

In the last twenty-five years, extensive research and attention has been given to the hypothesis that the stress of life's accumulated events is an important factor in the etiology of somatic and psychiatric disorders. As the body attempts to maintain a state of homeostasis or equilibrium, any life event that upsets that steady state demands adaptation. Similarly, families whose steady states are upset by life events must adapt. Holmes and Rahe (1967) have identified life events as stressors, and the response to these stressors (physiological or psychological) is labeled stress. The instrument they developed to quantify stressors is currently used by many clinicians as a routine screening tool at the point of intake.

Some have also applied these ideas to work with families. Hill (1958) advanced the ABCX family crisis model, which states that A (the stressor event) interacts with B (the family's crisis-meeting resources), which in turn interacts with C (the definition the family makes of the event), and the sequence culminates in the production of X (the crisis). McCubbin and Patterson (1982) advanced Hill's work by developing the Double ABCX model. In their model, the double A includes not only the original stressor, but also the pileup of life events experienced by the family. This work acknowledges the potential cumulative or additive effect of life events.

Recent years have brought the development of a standardized instrument called the Family Inventory of Life Events (FILE) (Olson and McCubbin, 1982). While this seventy-two-item instrument can be a valuable and quick screening tool, the clinician should be sensitive to the family's verbal presentation of various recent life events. Although the FILE can quickly ascertain the number of stressing life events experienced, it is unable to yield an understanding of the effect of these events on the family, something clinicians must determine as they ask family members about their experience of the stressors. Routinely, each family member is asked about significant events in the family's recent history; however, it is also valuable to ask them about their thoughts on how various events affected other family members. It is amazing how frequently the mother, for example, will be surprised as she hears her child vividly and accurately describe her mother's internal experience of an event. This not only provides the clinician with valuable information for assessment but can have therapeutic value by itself. For example, this may be the first time that mother realizes anyone in her family has an understanding of her world.

Just as it is valuable to routinely assess the presence of stressors in a family, it is always appropriate to explore the presence of stressors or changes that preceded the development of a specific problem presented in therapy. This assessment is important to determine whether the problem is evidence of or is worsened by a faulty adaptation to a particular stressor. As an example, let us assume that a family's primary presenting problem is the absence of talking among family members. Assessment suggests this has been a problem for about five years, and it is also determined that it began about the time grandfather died. It well may be that the pain, real and imagined, was projected onto others and was too intense for family members to adequately talk about. They may have resolved the problem by adopting a pattern of elective mutism among themselves. The discussion of this event in therapy may well result in a more adaptive completion of the mourning process and rekindle a sense of concern and connection long absent. Intervention of this sort effectively serves to dislodge the family from the problematic solution (that it originally perceived as a problem). In this sense, the solution to the problem became the problem, which is often the case in a family's attempts to adapt to various stressors.

For these reasons, the clinician is wise to routinely inquire about recent stressors to determine the existence of a correlation between stressors and onset of problems. Not doing so prevents important information from surfacing and may significantly delay responsiveness to treatment.

## ASSESSING WORK PROBLEMS

Although most marriage and family therapists do not receive many referrals to resolve specific work problems, work-related behaviors certainly influence family dynamics and vice versa. That work is significant to personal happiness has been long recognized, and clinicians should remain aware of this fact. Unemployment, supervisor–employee stress, dual careers, children home alone, relocations, job dissatisfaction, and retirement are all examples of work-related issues that affect families. These types of issues can provoke a variety of behaviors in families that, if not accurately related to the work issue, can seem impossible to resolve. Work also involves many "leaving-home" issues such as children going to school, adolescents to their first job, mothers to work, and fathers to new positions or jobs. Each of these changes affect the family and may exacerbate dysfunction in a family already at risk.

Work and its interaction in the family is directly related to important family constructs such as rules, roles, and morphogenic mechanisms. Rules influence the family members' perceptions of what is expected, what is appropriate, and what is possible. They have direct bearing on career selection and issues such as a homemaker taking a job outside of the home, the adolescent preferring a job or technical school to a university, and the young person yearning to move in the direction of some nontraditional occupation. Certainly, the impact of family rules will influence significantly the roles occupied by various family members and the members' subsequent sense of perceived satisfaction. Morphogenic mechanisms are those forces that promote each member of the system to develop according to complex individual needs while remaining a part of the functioning whole and not upsetting the homeostasis or equilibrium of the unit. These mechanisms affect behaviors that influence a person's career development, such as choosing a job to maintain the family name versus choosing according to individual preference (i.e., making independent choices versus choices made to satisfy others' vicarious needs).

As couples and families first present themselves, the clinician is wise to routinely assess the impact of work-related issues on the relationships represented. Often couples/families are oblivious to the subtle, but intense, impact that work-related problems have on their relationships. By inquiring about satisfaction with work and the interaction of work and marriage/family, the therapist can more clearly establish the relationship of these two important life forces. During the initial phase of therapy, there is also value in attempting to discern what can be manipulated in either the family or work environment to ameliorate troublesome behaviors. This discernment can often be used to help a husband and wife move from interpersonal conflict to a sense of cooperation and mastery over their environment.

Typically, this information will need to be extracted as part of an intake or history, because the family is often unaware of the subtle influence that work-related issues have on family dynamics. This information is particularly appropriate and important when working with families that seem unable to specifically describe the locus of their tensions. Also, the clinician can use it to begin to develop various working hypotheses about the family. For example, it is now widely accepted that alcohol problems are more frequently observed among those who work in settings characterized by frequent layoffs, long periods of unemployment, and/or frequent and long absences from the home.

## ASSESSING SEXUAL OR PHYSICAL ABUSE

Sexual and physical abuse are frequently found to coexist. Their long-term destructive effects are obvious. Although relationship problems sometimes promote and maintain these problems, these behaviors themselves often confound and entrench family difficulties. Therefore, astute therapists should be sensitive to detecting abuse in order to ensure that they provide appropriate treatment.

To determine if sexual/physical abuse is present in the family, therapists need to be comfortable enough with their own values and attitudes to
approach families in a matter-of-fact, but sensitive, fashion. Calm and direct
questioning of the family can provide an atmosphere of permission absent
from the family before therapy. Such an approach communicates to the family members that the therapist is not intimidated by abuse problems, and it
also establishes a counter-rule to the no-talk rule frequently observed in
these families. The therapist needs to convey a sense of competence and
strength, while simultaneously establishing the important counter-rule.

Finkelhor (1979) has stated, based upon his research, that 1 percent of all
females are sexually abused by a father or stepfather. Also, certain characteristics of families, such as the presence of an alcoholic parent, seem to increase this probability. Research has identified other correlates to the
existence of sexual and physical abuse in families, and the presence of any of
them should increase the therapist's need to inquire about this type of
abuse. In addition to the presence of an alcoholic parent, other indicators are
as follows:

The family with poor mother–daughter connections/bonds

A mother who is very dependent either psychologically or physically as the result of illness or accident

A father who appears to be very controlling and possessive of his
daughter(s)

An acting-out adolescent girl engaging in sexual promiscuity or
suicidal gestures who is a frequent runaway or drug abuser

A child who appears to be very overresponsible and parentified in
the family context

Although it would be inappropriate to assume that physical/sexual abuse is
present in any family manifesting any of these indicators, it seems just as
inappropriate to neglect further exploration when they are present.

If sexual abuse is disclosed, therapists must be aware of their legal responsibility to report such information to the proper authorities. All states
now have reporting laws, and although there is some variance about who is
to be reported to, there are strict consequences for the professional who has
access to information about abuse and does not follow through with a report. Being aware of the very low incidence of falsely reported incest by
children, therapists must not delude themselves into thinking that child-
reported abuse is just a prank. Remember, not reporting and allowing abuse
to continue is no favor to the victim or the family.

Having made a report, the therapist must be concerned about promoting the best interests of the children and ensuring their safety. Although
geographic variance exists as to the handling of these incidents, the recent

trend is that children are not immediately removed from the house. Professionals now recognize that removal of the child tends to have the following effects:

Intensify the child's sense of guilt

Decrease the potential for strengthening the mother–daughter bond that is so crucial to preventing future incidents

Increase the likelihood of the daughter's being scapegoated and excluded from the family

Promote the likelihood of the father's seducing the mother into an alliance with him

Create the problem of having to find a good placement for the child in the meantime

Instead, fathers are usually asked to leave the home while the investigation proceeds. During this period, the family will be in need of much support and assistance, along with intensive treatment. The nature of the treatment required is beyond the scope of this section, but therapists are reminded of the importance of exploring the presence of these behaviors in the family, and then acting, if they hope to be of help to these people. Granted, it can appear to be very disruptive and temporarily destructive to the family, and likely will be, but without disruption, the hope for productive change is minimal.

Key to accurate assessment of sexual and physical abuse is the individual interview. Most therapists now recognize that without interviewing alone each member of a couple or family system, they simply cannot say with confidence that they have made disclosure of abuse easy for the victim or possibly for the perpetrator.

A good strategy for these interviews is to conduct them early in therapy, certainly within the first session or two. Be straightforward in asking about abusive behaviors. If the individual interview is in the first session, ask a few tangential questions then ask about being hit or touched. When no abuse has been suspected and therapy has gone on for several sessions, but then the therapist notes the possibility of abuse, there is no need to avoid direct questioning right from the outset of the subsequent individual interview.

## ASSESSING POST-TRAUMATIC STRESS DISORDER (PTSD)

Historically, PTSD was considered a problem only experienced by military personnel stemming from their war experiences. Over the past fifteen years, the same problem has been noted among people in nonmilitary, life-threatening situations as well. More recently, PTSD is diagnosed when family members experience high-level stress (e.g., sex abuse, violence, even giving birth). A particularly good overview of PTSD treatment is provided by Dr. Jonathon Shay. Much of the material below comes from his website (jshay@world.std.com). Dr. Charles Figley (1988) has also been a leader in developing PTSD treatment for both individuals and families.

Family therapists learn of their clients' trauma in two circumstances: clients either report the events in the initial session (a child or adult is beaten) or disclose it later as a result of therapy uncovering forgotten or ignored events (an adult recalls being sexually or physically abused as a child). The latter is the so-called recovered memory phenomenon that received a good bit of media attention in the recent past. Media reports have focused on therapists who wittingly, or otherwise, used their influencing ability to persuade clients that they had been abused in some way (usually sexually). Later, when legal action was taken, the clients recanted or the accused proved the recovered memories were false. Whether these recovered memories are real or constructed, the client loses. When a client reports recovered memories, the therapist should proceed with sensitivity and may want to seek immediate supervision. Recording sessions and playing them for a supervisor can help prevent leading the client.

Regardless of whether the traumatic events occurred in the past or are an immediate cause of the presenting problem, the following are warning signs of PTSD as described by the American Psychological Association at its website (www.APA.org):

*Individuals who have experienced a traumatic event often times suffer psychological stress related to the incident. In most instances, these are normal reactions to abnormal situations. Individuals who feel they are unable to regain control of their lives, or who experience the following symptoms for more than a month, should consider seeking outside professional mental health assistance . . . :*

> *Recurring thoughts or nightmares about the event*
>
> *Having trouble sleeping or changes in appetite*
>
> *Experiencing anxiety and fear, especially when exposed to events or situations reminiscent of the trauma*
>
> *Being on edge, being easily startled, or becoming overly alert*
>
> *Feeling depressed or sad and having low energy*
>
> *Experiencing memory problems including difficulty in remembering aspects of the trauma*
>
> *Feeling "scattered" and unable to focus on work or daily activities. Having difficulty making decisions*

*Feeling irritable, easily agitated, or angry and resentful*

*Feeling emotionally "numb," withdrawn, disconnected, or different from others*

*Spontaneously crying, feeling a sense of despair and hopelessness*

*Feeling extremely protective of, or fearful for, the safety of loved ones*

*Not being able to face certain aspects of the trauma, and avoiding activities, places, or even people that remind you of the event*

*Re-experiencing the event through vivid memories or flash backs (APA, 1997)*

Additional items from other sets of guidelines include:

Isolating oneself from family and friends and avoiding social situations

Relying increasingly on alcohol or drugs to get through the day

Feeling guilty about surviving the event or being unable to solve the problem, change the event, or prevent the disaster

Treating PTSD in a family context has elements of several therapy modalities (Shay, 1997). Both the victim and the family need to understand that the symptoms are normal reactions to trauma and therefore are not to be feared or hidden. Educating the family about PTSD so they understand its causes and adjustment pattern is an effective first step.

A second component of treatment consists of support for a diminished sense of self caused by the indignity of the event. Mugging, rape, or other assault are degrading crimes. One feels smaller as a person afterward. Through impatience, frustration, and exasperation, family support may be at low ebb. Refocusing the family on supporting the victim can benefit from modeling by the therapist. Support from both the family and the therapist are needed to empower the victim.

Lastly, it is important to individualize the treatment because the pathway to adjustment is unique for each victim. While some retreat into drugs and alcohol, others drop into depression or violence. Resuming normal habits, focusing on successes, and reestablishing a healthy lifestyle are all important. Associated with these different means of coping with traumatic stress are the different and usual treatment procedures for each one. What works with one PTSD victim may not meet the needs of another. When normal individuals meet abnormal circumstances, adjustment can take strange twists and turns. So can therapy with PTSD victims and their families.

# ▶ 4

# Initial Stage Treatment Procedures

In addition to assessing the family system, several tasks are commonly included in the initial stage of therapy. Unless the clinician practices only one mode of therapy, he or she must decide about an overall strategy for treating the client (whether family or couple). At this time in the development of the field, the wise practitioner is expert at several modalities.

Also in this stage, the family will commonly be told the results of the assessment procedures. Relabeling and/or reframing the presenting symptoms often are carried out in keeping with a treatment plan. If the family cannot redefine their problem, then crisis intervention and trauma resolution may be required. Treatment decisions made in this stage of therapy are not irrevocable, but the therapeutic system is defined, and pace and tenor of therapy are established.

## ESTABLISHING THERAPEUTIC GOALS

Establishing goals is every bit as important for the therapist as it is for the family. For the therapist, goal establishment helps achieve feedback about the impact of interventions. Such feedback can be significant in preventing the burnout that stems from a sense of aimlessness. Without some specific direction and focus, it is easy for a therapist to question effectiveness, especially if a family or couple questions the value of therapy. Typically, this type of questioning and doubt is unproductive, harming the therapist's sense of well-being and purpose, not to mention the family's confidence. A lack of specificity helps the family keep the therapist off balance so that no change is effected, and an undertone of anger and resentment that benefits no one is engendered.

Establishing goals also serves to better ensure a clear understanding by all involved of such parameters as what might be necessary to effect desired change and how long it might take. This focus proves very therapeutic to many families who are fragmented and feeling diffuse regarding their own understanding. Naturally, a sense of diffusion can be a part of the problem itself.

In the first session, it is important to establish the tone of purposefulness by having the family identify what they hope to change/accomplish in therapy. It is important at this time to encourage as much specificity as possible, recognizing that it will probably be difficult because of the masking related to present and past emotions that occurs. For instance, when a wife claims through her tears that she wants her husband to "love me more," it is important to help her define her needs operationally. An effective way of doing this is to ask her, "What would you see or hear from him that is different from how things currently are that would result in your believing he does love you more?" Vague responses, such as "If only he wouldn't look at me with that look he gets on his face," need greater specificity: "Would you describe his look to me now?" "When does that look appear?" "All right, now what else would be different that would help you believe in his love for you?" Pursuing this type of information might provoke anxiety and/or anger in the client, and it is often helpful to diminish this potential by inserting a statement, such as "I realize my questions may seem irrelevant to you, and may even result in your feeling frustrated, but I need you to bear with me as I try to be helpful." The effect of this statement can often be enhanced by inserting a recognition of the feelings the client is presenting, saying, for instance, "I know you are hurting and probably feeling some resentment and frustration, but I need to do this to be helpful to you," and then continuing.

Some families or couples may be vague and have trouble identifying specific goals. In such a case, the therapist might suggest that all meet together for another one to three sessions to complete an assessment and to determine goals and the best way to proceed. Having several sessions allows clients time to better organize themselves as they respond to the new structure provided by the therapist and therapy. Also, the therapist is provided with an opportunity to proceed without having to accept the nebulous contract that might evolve by simply accepting the clients' ambiguity. Such a compromise by a therapist could hamper future effectiveness.

The purpose of this agreed-upon assessment phase is to identify goals of ongoing therapy to be negotiated. Clients' vagueness needs to be accepted at first to avoid amplifying their uneasiness and frustration prematurely. The therapist might explain, "The importance of these struggles and concerns to you is evidenced by your reluctance to identify specific concerns too quickly. That is encouraging, and for that reason I am willing to take a few sessions to attempt to determine what might be most helpful to you." The assessment phase can then continue, as the effort is completed to have clients specify what they want changed. This process also serves to metacommunicate to the couple/family that the therapist perceives that therapy exists to effect change and that the goal of change is paramount. New goals may surface as therapy proceeds, so negotiating time parameters as part of the therapeutic contract is valuable (see "Establishing a Therapeutic Contract" in Chapter 2).

## PRESENTING THE CONCEPT OF FAMILY SYSTEM

Through all phases of therapy, many new concepts may be presented to clients. In the initial phase of therapy, the concept of family system is often defined to help clients differentiate between family therapy and individual therapy. In the middle phase, the same concept can be used as the rationale for a reframing of presenting symptoms and other family problems. In the terminal phase of therapy, the concept is helpful in clarifying what changes in family organization may be necessary to accommodate upcoming developmental crises in family life. Teaching families about the concept of family system is a prudent investment of session time, if a therapist is able to define the concept clearly.

A number of methods have been described in the literature to aid in defining the family system concept. Analogies are helpful, and the most popular is the mobile. Many family therapists have made or purchased a mobile comprised of family figures so that when one figure is moved, all others move. When the family system is defined, the therapist can easily demonstrate not only that all family members affect one another, but also that change in one member does not necessarily mean an equal change in others. Family members may change more or less, depending on how directly they are connected to the figure that is moved. The mobile is also helpful should the concept of homeostasis need to be defined.

The principal task of defining any concept is to use language that the clients readily understand. Family therapy buzzwords such as circular causality, linear causality, morphogenesis, role, dyad, parental marriage, etc., are not appropriate, even if the client family is made up of family therapists. An appropriate definition of the family system concept might proceed like this:

> I think it is important here in the beginning of therapy to let you know how I think about families.

Families are like that mobile hanging above my desk. Every figure is connected to others. Notice that all the other figures move if I move this figure. Some move more than others, but they all move.

Your family is like the mobile, because everyone is connected, and when someone in the family changes, everyone else adjusts or also changes to some degree. For example, if one of you should win the Reader's Digest Sweepstakes, everyone in the family would feel the impact of all that money. Likewise, with the problems you are experiencing, everyone has had to change, some of you perhaps for the better, and others for the worse.

To work on the issues bringing you into therapy, no one will be blamed for causing the problems, because all of you have been changed by these issues, and changing is now everyone's responsibility and privilege. That is why the whole family is here in therapy. Everyone will need to help out if we are to get anywhere. Does everyone understand?

This statement serves a number of purposes. First, a new way of thinking about family life is introduced. Second, every member of the family is given responsibility for change, without having to feel responsible for the problems. Lastly, the need to have the entire family present in therapy is explained. The question at the end of the statement provides an opportunity for family members to comment on the thoughts presented and to reveal whether they will cooperate in the therapy.

The therapist may speak of triangles, alliances, coalitions, boundaries, and many other terms that label and describe family organization. As a result of using these new labels and concepts, the reframing and relabeling of symptoms and presenting problems become possible. Reframing and relabeling can be conducted without using family organization concepts, but both are much easier if clients are educated in foundation concepts such as the family system.

## MATCHING TREATMENT MODALITY WITH CLIENTS' PROBLEMS

Most of the original theories of family therapy evolved as a result of interaction between a founding theoretician and a population with whom they were involved. It is not at all unreasonable to assume that characteristics of the particular population worked with were as significant in shaping the subsequent theory as were the beliefs and characteristics of the particular theoretician. For instance, Minuchin and his colleagues (1981) were involved with juveniles and their families who appeared to be struggling for a semblance of productive structure. In Napier and Whitaker (1978), Whitaker worked with a responsible, well-educated population that could benefit from an injection of playfulness and more primary process interaction in contrast to being overly consumed with "correctness." As a result, Minuchin and his colleagues evolved structural family therapy, with its focus on hierarchy and productive structure, and Whitaker developed his symbolic-experiential approach, with the emphasis on injecting playfulness and greater appreciation for living with increased spontaneity and candor.

Bowen (1976) worked with schizophrenic patients and their families and developed a theory that worked with this population. Ackerman (1958) worked with families struggling with various neurotic conflicts and desiring greater closeness. Just as the thinking and therapeutic behavior of these early pioneers were likely influenced by the "type" of client population with whom they were primarily interacting, therapists today are primarily shaped by the therapeutic model with which they most closely align. Recognizing that most therapeutic models evolved as a result of influential interaction with particular populations, the wise practitioner needs to be attentive to and vigilant of whether or not a particular couple or family is a "good fit" or match with a particular therapeutic orientation. To assume one model is equally effective with all clients is as naive as assuming one size of clothing will fit all body types.

Recent research highlights this concern of fitting therapy to family. Hampson and Beavers (1996) have demonstrated that characteristics of each family have significant impact on what style of therapy they are likely to be most responsive to. For example, centripetal families (those characterized by desire for cohesion and mutuality) tend to respond more comfortably and favorably to nurturant therapists and therapeutic styles. On the other hand, centrifugal families (those characterized by disengagement and those who find it easier to express hostility rather than warmth and caring) distrust words and rely more on overt behavior. These family members are more likely to be distrustful of therapists who are "too warm too quickly." On this matter, Hampson and Beavers state:

> *Our experience has been that therapists accustomed to dealing with respectful centripetal families whose members usually internalize conflicts have a rude awakening as they attempt to form a warm and trusting working alliance with centrifugal families. Centrifugal families require leadership, structuring, and coherence initially, and may become distrustful or even drop out of therapy quickly if they have an apparently warm and friendly therapist. (1996, p. 348)*

Their very intriguing study revealed that centripetal families did better with higher degrees of therapist openness and partnership and a less overt power differential. Using the Beavers Assessment System to determine level of overall family competence, Hampson and Beavers determined that the most competent families, as determined by their assessment process and procedure, did best with a therapist style characterized by high levels of openness and partnership, and lower levels of power differential. The least competent families, identified by their assessment process, had better outcomes with a therapist style characterized by a high level of therapist power differential, less openness, and lower levels of partnership (a more authoritative, directive approach). As is suggested, the Beavers Assessment System equates greater family competence with families possessing more centripetal qualities and less competence with those families possessing more centrifugal qualities.

As we have done earlier in this section, Hampson and Beavers also applied their findings to some prominent family theorists. They suggest that Nagy's contextual family therapy and Bowen's family of origin therapy are low on power differential, high on disclosure of strategy, and high on inviting partnership. Therefore, in accord with Hampson and Beavers's findings, these approaches should work well with more competent families and those characterized as mid-range. They suggest that Whitaker's symbolic-experiential approach (Napier & Whitaker, 1978), replete with stories, tangential comments, and relative warmth and openness is a model appropriate for borderline centripetal families. Avoiding power struggles is very important in treating these families. Haley's approach (1976), with a high power differential, low disclosure of strategy, and modest effort at developing a partnership is best suited for more severely dysfunctional families.

Recognizing the suggestion evident in the work of Hampson and Beavers, as well as others such as Henggeler, Bourdin, and Mann (1993), we believe the wise clinician is one who quickly understands the nature of the client unit in the room with them and then selects a modality that is most likely to fit their style. We are now at that place in the evolution of family therapy that we can say with some certainty that "one size does not fit all." The most effective clinician is likely to be the one who is flexible enough to modulate his or her therapeutic style in relation to each client family seen. In this regard, the assessment procedures described in Chapter 3 become very important in determining which treatment procedures are likely to be most effective with a particular family unit.

## USING METAPHORICAL LANGUAGE

The utilization of metaphorical conversation, or speaking of one object or phenomenon as though it were another, can be a very important assessment procedure. Recognizing that most people are in therapy as a result of distress or duress, and that most people are not comfortable talking about their problems, it is important to make the experience as natural and comfortable as possible. The use of metaphors is one effective way of doing this.

By developing an understanding of the contexts people come from, and of how they formulate and describe their problems, the therapist can get valuable clues as to how to develop metaphorical ways of framing notions that will facilitate understanding. For example, a couple who owns a farm and are concerned about the absence of vitality in their marital relationship, despite their best attempts to "get the other to do what they want," may respond well to a metaphor. The therapist could compare marital relationships to the crops they rely upon for income:

> You know, a marriage is very similar to your work. You are unable to get crops to grow by going into the fields and pulling at them or demanding them to grow. Instead what you need to do is carefully plant them and ensure that appropriate fertilizer and other essentials such as water are available. A relationship does not prosper by someone pulling at it or being demanding, either. Like your crops, the relationship needs to be tended to and cared for by each of you. How about if we were to begin by each of you identifying what would serve to help you feel better and to promote your well-being and the relationship?

With the husband or father who is a mechanic by trade and appears to be relatively uninvolved in his family life, the following might be an effective metaphorical way of communicating:

> In working with cars, you know that the absence of routine maintenance will result in major problems. If routine tune-ups, lubrication, and oil changes are not performed, there will be major problems eventually. Relationships are very similar. Without routine attention and care, eventually there will be major problems. Let's brainstorm for a few minutes and determine what kind of things you might be able to do in this family that are like routine preventive maintenance in your business.

Metaphorical language can not only be very effective in drawing people into the therapeutic process; it also frequently encourages them to develop further metaphors from their own experience to describe problems. Whatever the clinician does to enhance people's capacity for understanding and communicating their experience is likely to be helpful, and the use of metaphors is one way of doing so. In this regard, the assessment process is facilitated while the clients' potential for learning about their perceptions is increased. Also, metaphors can provide a channel of communication that places clients at ease and helps them to understand their difficulties in ways that, many times, make more sense.

## REFRAMING SYMPTOMS

Reframing, as the procedure is called in the context of therapy, is designed to change the clients' views of their problems. Family therapists especially recognize that clients' definitions of their problems often perpetuate those problems by narrowing the range of possible solutions. Consequently, a first step in changing how clients act often consists of attempting to reframe symptoms and problems so new solutions can be tried out.

The reframing message itself can consist of a quick comment or a lengthy statement. When the therapist merely comments to reframe symptoms or problems, there is little attempt to persuade clients of the veracity of the reframe. For example, if the identified patient (IP) is a child who has run away from home, the therapist might comment to the parents, "You know, I think he's trying to help you two get your marriage together by giving you something to talk about." Such a comment may be influential in helping the child's parents begin to address their own marital relationship issues. If the spouses ignore or miss the point of the therapist's comment, which is likely, they will maintain their view of the family's problems and restrict solutions to those already proven ineffective.

Reframing is most successful when the therapist attempts to actively persuade family members that the reframe is not only a plausible reconceptualization of their problems, but also more accurate than their old conception. To take this persuasive tack, time must be invested in discussing the reframe, and evidence documenting the new conception must be cited. To continue with the example, the therapist might begin in the same manner:

> You know, I think he's trying to help you two get your marriage together by giving you something to talk about. I recall you saying that before John threatened to run away, the family, and especially your marriage, was dull and no one seemed to feel cared for. I know it may seem difficult to believe that John's behavior has the goal of bringing you two together, but consider what has happened. You two are spending more time together than either of you can remember having spent before, and the focus of your attention is inside the family. Also, consider the effects of his actions on the other kids. They are spending more time at home and they are quarreling less. I'm sure you can think of other ways that John has been helpful to

the family. Let's take some time to discuss this different way of viewing John's behavior.

The intent of both the comment and the more lengthy statement is to introduce an alternative view to the one currently used by family members to understand their situation. Instead of casting John as the bad child, he is praised, and a rationale is presented for some other aspect of family life—in this case, the marriage—to become the focus of treatment. As in all persuasive statements, the reframe message takes a specific form and has specific content. First, the IP's behavior is labeled. Then, the actions of all family members in response to IP behavior and the reactions of other family members to those responses are specified. The positive contribution of IP behavior to family functioning is described, and last, the cyclical nature of these responses is introduced. Such a complicated statement can be composed on the spur of the moment during a session, but more effective reframing statements are figured out between sessions when proper attention can be given to detail. The therapist's intent in delivering a reframe is to have the clients believe in the new conception, and a persuasive argument must be thought out to accomplish that end.

## RELABELING SYMPTOMS

Relabeling and reframing are components of the same procedure, because one often leads to the other; within the context of reframing, symptoms are frequently relabeled. By relabeling, however, a specific behavior or client characteristic is given a new name, the purpose being to aid the clients in reframing on their own.

Most often, therapists relabel behavior. Crying might be called expressing emotion, or controlling relabeled as structuring. On a system level, individual alcoholism is frequently relabeled as a family illness, or a family entering therapy is told that only a strong family can ask for help.

Whether relabeling at the individual or system levels, the new name can reflect either a change from positive to negative or vice versa. Examples of positive relabels that change a negative symbol to one less negative, or to neutral or positive include:

Temper tantrum: acting out, anger, expressing strong emotion

Beating child: spanking, swatting, disciplining

Withdrawal: silent, thoughtful

Drinking: medicating, anesthetizing

When clients minimize problems through labeling, a negative relabel might be called for. Negative relabeling consists of changing a positive label to one less socially desirable. Examples include the opposite of the positive relabels mentioned before and the following relabels:

Learning disabled: retarded

Extramarital fling: affair, intercourse

Close: strangling, smothering

As in reframing, the likelihood that a relabel will be adopted is primarily dependent on the esteem the client or the family holds for the therapist. If therapist esteem produced by reputation or client experience is high, clients are more likely to use the new label and attempt to change their actions. Where esteem for the therapist is low, relabeling will not be effective.

Instituting a change in labels can be conducted by merely using the new symbol when appropriate or by overtly discussing the label used by clients, asking them to use a different one, and explaining why. If the label that needs changing serves to control a wide range of family behavior, discussing the need for a different label is appropriate. For example, if a teenager is labeled a "bad" kid, the presenting problem includes violence, and the parents are considering foster care, a relabel of *strong-willed* or *immature* may change how the parents react and, accordingly, the child's behavior. Producing such major changes will be enhanced by openly discussing use of the label *bad* and the ramifications of creating more of a problem by continuing to use the label. Part of the discussion might include describing how the new label can be used in everyday family interaction and establishing clear guidelines for the new parenting behavior that will fit with the new label.

## DEFUSING A CRISIS

Just as there are times when therapy can benefit from the therapist's inducing a crisis, at other times, productive therapy dictates that a crisis be defused. To defuse a crisis, therapists have the option of using themselves to create an intentional triangle or referring the family to its past crises to activate resources that helped them in earlier circumstances. To illustrate the first option, assume, for example, that a family enters a session in crisis. As the family comes into the room, at least one family member is overtly and intensely irate with another member. The angry family member is shouting, blaming, and spouting accusatory indictments and appears intent on continuing these expressions. The other family member gets defensive, but that member's efforts do little more than further incite the angry person. A therapist can intervene at this juncture and begin to defuse the crisis by becoming triangled in the relationship.

One way of doing this is to say, "I can see and hear that you are really upset about this and I need to hear it, but I need you to slow down so I can fully understand, and I need you [said to the one who is the target of the anger] to just be quiet for a short while. All right, let's go ahead. Please tell me what this anger is about." The therapist then encourages the angry member to speak directly to the therapist and to quit attempting to get any further response from the person the anger is directed at. During this time, the angry member should receive the therapist's complete attention, along with periodic efforts by the therapist to clarify and ensure that this member feels understood.

Once the emotion has been stated, the therapist can turn to the family member who is the target of the anger and ask for a response to what the target has just heard. During this time, if the angry member attempts to interrupt, the therapist can say, "I know you're really angry, but I need to hear this completely. I assure you that I'll be coming back to you in just a minute. I want to make sure I understand all this, and I'm sure you want me to." By preventing them from directly addressing one another, the therapist allows the angry member an opportunity to ventilate and have the affirming experience of being heard and understood at the same time. Intercepting the direct interaction between these two members also prevents things from escalating to the point of destruction.

The interaction is continued in this fashion, with the therapist actively introduced as the third point in the communication triangle. Direct interaction between the partners at these times often activates old destructive patterns of defensive relating. As a more manageable level of affect is achieved, the family members can be encouraged to interact directly with one another.

Returning the family to their past is another means of defusing a crisis. Assume a family comes into a session in great distress over the fact that father has just been informed that he has been laid off from his job. After acknowledging the nature of the crisis and understanding the family's distress, the therapist might implement this procedure by saying, "I realize this may be the most upsetting thing to fall on you folks in some time, if not ever, but what was the last situation that was almost this distressing?"

This intervention does a couple of important things to defuse a crisis and enable the family to be more proactive. First, when confronted with a crisis, people tend to be so consumed with its immediacy that they lose sight of the fact that they have encountered and survived other crises. Asking this question reminds family members that they have encountered other tough times, and they are still here to experience this current crisis. It is important not to ask them about the last crisis that was "this bad," because the current crisis always seems to be the worst. Acknowledge this point by asking them about the last situation that was "almost this distressing." Second, once the last situation is identified, ask the following sort of questions: What did you find helpful that time? What did you do? Who was helpful to you then? These questions help the therapist to determine what resources the family has activated in the past that it may use once again.

In addition to confronting crises, therapists can take the preventive measure of predicting crises ahead of time. This encourages the family to do some preventive planning prior to being consumed by the crisis and increases the therapist's credibility in the family's eyes once the crisis does come. For instance, as a family resolves a problem, they might be asked to predict what the next crisis might be and to talk about ways to resolve it. The therapist may also simply predict that some crisis is about to occur, based on the family's level of readiness for difficulties. The prediction can help the family identify the next crisis in terms of the family's "readiness," rather than perceive it as a fault or weakness of the family.

## TAKING A BREAK DURING A SESSION

Where is it written that therapy sessions are to last a certain number of minutes and that no break is to be taken during the session? Even Freud was reported to interrupt analytic sessions for a visit to the bathroom (Meisel & Kendrick, 1985). The answer to the question is obvious; the routines we establish as service providers are learned, usually without question, from our mentors and they from theirs. The therapy session without a break is one such custom, not the product of research.

Family therapists have been willing to abandon traditional practice customs and establish service routines that better fit the needs of their clients. Families are often seen for longer than the typical one-hour individual session once each week. Many authors have recommended one-and-a-half–hour sessions for married couples and two- to three-hour sessions for large families (billing rates by the hour). Along with these longer sessions, however, comes increased client and therapist fatigue.

The initial session, when the therapist presents an overview of what therapy will be like, is a good time to state that short breaks will be taken. Then before the next session begins, the family can be reminded that a break will be taken at some time during the session. When the therapist notices fatigue creeping in, a simple statement such as "Let's take a five-minute break," delivered at a transition point in the session, will suffice.

As a result of changes in session time span, rest breaks are not the only kinds of breaks used by family therapists. Because longer sessions have meant that therapists have more information to process during a session, a few minutes spent away from the distraction of clients can be very helpful in collecting thoughts, reviewing, and reorienting session plans. There is absolutely nothing inappropriate in a therapist stating, "I need to collect my thoughts, so I'll step out for a few minutes. In the meantime, I would like you to . . . ." In this directive statement, the clients are given a task while the therapist takes a break, and the message is clear that they are to keep working.

Changes in treatment methods also have led to the need to take breaks during sessions. The therapy team approach in which the therapist(s) and a group of observers work together requires that a communication link between the two be established. Although technological aids such as the telephone and bug-in-the-ear serve this need quite well, there are times that the therapist and the observers need to get together face-to-face during a session, and a rest break or therapist break can provide that opportunity.

When the therapist steps out of the session with the sole purpose of consulting with the observing team, the clients should be given several messages. The statement "I'm going to consult with the team. I'll be back in a few minutes. I'd like you to continue talking about . . . ." will tell clients why the therapist is leaving and what they are to do in the meantime. Helping clients understand why the therapist is leaving prevents their misinterpretation of the break. It also forewarns clients that the therapist may come back to the session and deliver a message from the team or radically change the direction of the session. Without such an implied warning, the "doctrine of no surprises" may be violated and the therapist may feel awkward and hesitant either to deliver a message from the team or to change tactics in a session. Giving the clients a task helps keep the mood or theme of a session intact. The therapist can leave and come back without feeling disruptive and, as a result, consult with the team when necessary.

Taking breaks is a common feature of family therapy. With attention given to timing and the way breaks are initiated, fatigue can be relieved, a therapist can gain the opportunity to review and reorient the session process, and colleagues can be consulted.

A related way of taking a break comes from the work of Norwegian Tom Andersen and his colleagues and is referred to as the "Reflecting Team" (Andersen, 1990). This idea is clearly consistent with the post-modern, social constructionist/narrative traditions.

Andersen and his colleagues essentially stumbled upon the reflecting team format while observing a family session in March of 1985. He and his colleagues were observing a session with a family that related a long history of misery. On various occasions, they called the therapist out of the room to share ideas on how to interact differently with the family, but in spite of the new ideas offered the family quickly returned ". . . back and down to their misery" (Andersen, 1990, p. 26). After these abortive efforts to effect change had transpired, Andersen and his colleagues decided to attempt something different. One of the observers entered the consultation room and asked the family if they wanted to hear some ideas of the observers that might prove helpful to their talk. The family agreed and the lights in the consultation room were dimmed while the lights in the observation room were turned up and the speaking system reversed so the family could listen to what the observers were saying.

With the lighting and sound system reversed, the observers began to discuss their observations. They talked about the family's strength and endurance, wondered how the family's struggle with this unkind destiny distracted the family from awareness of their many unused possibilities and resources, and discussed what might happen if some of these possibilities and untapped resources would be used. When they finished and reversed the lighting and sound, they were prepared for anything from a very angry family to one that was simply bored. Instead, what they observed was a family that was very silent and thoughtful, who after a short pause started to talk among themselves with smiles and an optimism not previously observed. Andersen reports that at that time they realized this format captured the essence of Bateson's famous sentence, "The differences that makes a difference."

The Andersen group decided that there was no sense in hiding their deliberations from families. This new format was much more collaborative and served to level "the playing field" by identifying families as the ultimate experts on themselves. To enhance the process of collaboration and the recognition of families as the ultimate experts, there are basic guidelines the Andersen team found helpful. They observed that to be most helpful the reflections must truly be reflections, that is, offered with appropriate uncertainty or tendered tentatively, such as "I am not certain, but it seemed to me . . . ," or "When considering that, I couldn't help but wonder about . . . ." They believe this makes it easier for the family to pick and choose what they wish to respond to. They also found it to be valuable for the reflecting team to look at one another during this process rather than at the clients. Their belief being that this makes it easier for clients to really listen and attend to what is being said without the immediate social pressure that comes from experiencing a need to respond now.

Team members are also encouraged to avoid negative connotations; for instance, instead of saying, "I can't understand why they haven't tried this," say, "I wonder what would happen if they tried this." The absence of negative connotations and the related tentativeness serves to underscore a basic assumption, in fact, a key guiding principle, of the reflecting process: There are many ways to explain a situation rather than one right or correct way. This is reflective of the constructionist/narrative notion that we do not relate to life itself, but rather to our understanding of it.

Once the team has offered their reflections, the positions are reversed with the family encouraged to go back to talking and the reflecting team to go back to listening. The therapist in the room with the family starts the discussion with an open question such as "Is there anything you'd like to talk about from what you've just heard?" Every family member who has not spontaneously talked is asked this question directly and then the therapist may add their ideas or reflections to the discussion.

Andersen has stated that a mirror is not necessary, and often the team simply enters the consultation room and offers their reflections among themselves as if the mirror were present. Also, if there is no team present the therapist can promote "inner and outer conversations" as family members are asked to reflect on what they have heard another family member say, and then ask the initial family member to reflect on the reflections of these other family members. In this respect, the impact of the reflection process can be derived without the necessity of the mirror and sound system initially employed by Andersen and his colleagues.

## PRESESSION PLANNING

For every therapist who advocates extensive presession planning, another can be found who discounts value in this activity and may even consider it responsible for diminishing spontaneity. Practically speaking, there are legitimate arguments on both sides of this issue. There is value in considering patterns evident in a family's presentation and determining the most appropriate interventions at a particular point in time. On the other hand, spontaneity can be destroyed if the therapist enters the session with a plan that is quickly dashed by the family when they present a new crisis that does not fit with the plan.

Regardless of what position the therapist might have in relation to this issue, some basics do seem imperative. Minimally, the therapist should review past notes to keep current with the specifics of the case so that references can be made in therapy to what has occurred in the past. The therapist who never seems to remember what has occurred will quickly be perceived as not regarding clients as important as we all like to feel. When the therapist periodically refers to what has been presented in past sessions, clients develop a sense of being valued and special. Similarly, review of past notes increases the potential of a therapist's identifying recurring themes or patterns in a family's presentation and subsequently developing the most appropriate interventions.

Additionally, the presession planning period can serve to remind the therapist what homework might have been assigned and to ensure that the results of that assignment are checked out in the approaching session. The therapist who forgets to check out the results of assigned work runs the high risk of communicating to the family that homework assignments are "really not that important." As a result, it is likely that a family will be less responsive to future assigned tasks as they come to perceive them with the same degree of casualness as does their therapist.

5

# Middle Stage Treatment Procedures

Once the initial phase of therapy has been completed, it is time to undertake the middle phase in which most of the work takes place (Barnard & Corrales, 1979). Many of the procedures used in family therapy have been developed for use in this phase, and very few of them will be effective unless several conditions are met. First, procedures work best when a relationship has been established in which the client perceives the therapist as competent and authoritative. Second, unless the therapist has diagnosed the family in terms of its systemic functioning, implementing a procedure may be a waste of time or even lead to deterioration. Lastly, the therapist must have won, for the moment, the battle for structure, and act as the leader in the consulting room. As long as these conditions are met, the procedures described in this chapter may bring about the conditions in which change can occur.

## STEPS IN BEHAVIORAL TREATMENT FOR COUPLES AND FAMILIES

Treatment efficacy and effectiveness literature guides us in choosing interventions that are more likely to be successful than others. This literature has been accumulating for over thirty years in marriage and family therapy. For a host of reasons, most of the research has been done on behavioral treatments for a wide range of marital and family problems. Based on the conclusions of several meta-analyses of this research (Gurman & Kniskern, 1986;

Pinsof & Wynne, 1995), it is clear that the behavioral approach is effective. Some would say that it is the treatment of choice over the other modalities, most of which have not been tested using systematic methods.

Numerous concerns and qualms about the effectiveness of behavioral methods have been raised. Client dropout rates seem to be higher than for nonbehavioral treatments. The primary criticism though is that behavioral treatments focus on symptoms as described by the client rather than what adherents of other modalities would view as systemic causes for those symptoms.

Behavior therapists would agree. They would point out, however, that, from the client's point of view, the symptom(s) is (are) the problem and that the symptom(s) is (are) what need(s) attention. Reframes of the problem to other causes such as an enmeshed subsystem, as might be the case with structural and possibly psychoanalytic modalities, are constructions by therapists that must eventually be translated into behavior if change is to come about. Moreover, when clients succeed in changing the behavior comprising their symptoms—for instance, when parents learn to set and maintain limits for their children—they accomplish tangible goals that often generalize to other aspects of their lives. Despite the criticisms and concerns, the research tells us that every competent therapist should know how to implement behavioral treatment methods. Even if a clinician's orientation is not strictly behavioral, the steps making up behavioral treatment nicely augment the procedures of other modalities.

Below are the main steps making up behavioral treatment. These steps are greatly simplified, but the descriptions should provide enough to develop a treatment plan.

The first step in behavioral treatment is when the clinician focusses on actions (behaviors) that can be clearly and accurately understood. For the lack of a better definition, *actions* are what can be counted or seen. Included in this group would be:

> *Discrete thoughts,* which are self-statements, such as "I hate myself," "I hate him!", "She's smart," or "We are a good couple." Thoughts can be counted just as reliably as overt behaviors.
>
> *Overt acts,* such as crying, laughing, sighing, talking, running, hair pulling, hitting, etc.

Every client behavior should fit within one of these two categories.

Not in this group of actions are the fuzzier, nonbehaviors, such as kindness or independence or laziness. Clients often want more of what they cannot accurately identify. Their therapist's job is to help them state what they want to change in terms either of their own behavior or that of their partner. So, when Jane says, "I want to be more independent," her therapist should ask her what she means exactly. Often she will not know, and helping her decide what she wants in behavioral terms will be what is needed for her to change or for her partner to know what she needs. Sometimes clients hang on to these undefinable needs as a means of maintaining or gaining power in their relationship system. Considerable work in clarifying can be called for in such instances.

Another important and usually second step in behavioral treatments consists of asking the client to study the behavior that either is unwanted or desired for a week or even longer. For instance, to learn about his depressive episodes, John might count the number of times each day he experiences an empty, worthless feeling as well as the events that precede and come after those feelings. He would record these observations in writing and bring his records to therapy for discussion. Behaviors that occur several times each day might need study over one week for John and his therapist to learn the contingencies influencing his feelings of depression and to specify a change or a goal. Where the behavior occurs less frequently, a longer study time is required. If John only experienced feeling depressed every few weeks, for instance, the study period might be much longer so that several instances would be included in the analysis.

A complication in this study process is that as a result of watching and recording what they do, clients commonly make changes for the better. Without making changes in their lives, however, they usually drift back into their old routines. During the study phase of therapy, they should be instructed to avoid making changes. Interestingly, telling clients not to change is a paradoxical prescription, which would be issued by a therapist practicing one of the strategic or systemic modalities.

Actual change is designed in the third step. This is where the therapist and the client decide what will be the first goal in the change process. This is also the phase of behavior therapy or any modality of therapy that therapists, and clients as well, can easily become overconfident in the client's ability to change. Avoid lost time and your client's energy by rehearsing the behavior in session then choosing small changes both of you are sure will be completed successfully outside the session. A good first step might consist of the client merely recognizing when would be a good time to try new behavior. After this success, the client might try the wanted behavior once with no expectation of success. Successive steps would be more challenging until an overall goal was attained. As in the stock market, the trend is your friend, so you want to create a trend built of successes.

## Rewards for Good Behavior

When success occurs, the client needs recognition and reward. You can provide the recognition through your supportive comments. Smile and remark that you are happy about the client's success. There is no reason to underplay this expression of social support. Additionally, the client must give him or herself rewards, too. Choosing payoffs and when they are to be given can be tricky. For instance, when John begins to identify the times when he can say to himself, "I am confident," he could give himself some small reward. A stick of gum might be one example or if he stands most of the day, he might let himself sit down for a short time in a comfortable chair. Other possibilities for rewards include activities John enjoys. If he watches TV in the evening, watching a favorite show might be a good payoff for accomplishing the day's goal. Biking to work instead of driving or walking might be a good choice, if that is what he enjoys. Essentially whatever John does on a regular basis can be used as a reward if he withholds it until he accomplishes some goal.

In establishing the contract for rewards, clinicians can err easily by forgetting to structure in rewards for each performance of the wanted behavior. For instance, it would probably be a mistake for John to receive his reward on Friday only if he had successfully achieved his goal on the four previous days. A slip on Tuesday would let him off the hook for even trying to change his behavior on Wednesday or Thursday since he'd already lost the possibility of reward. A better plan would include a reward each day plus an additional reward on Friday. Contingency contracts for children often are drawn up incorrectly so that once the child makes a mistake, he or she cannot find success again until reward day has come and gone. Again, it is better for the child to receive a small reward with each successful try at the wanted behavior rather than a large reward after an extended series of efforts. Also, parents and their children tend to think too big when considering rewards. Even if the family can afford large purchases, head them away from costly items such as bicycles or trips out to dinner. Small is beautiful when it comes to rewards.

Behavioral treatments can include highly evolved teaching strategies. For instance, teaching your clients effective parenting and marital communication skills as fully mature interventions consistently produces good results. Every clinician should know these strategies as well as those making up traditional behavior therapy as described above.

## TEACHING PROCEDURES

Teaching is a most important therapist skill that is not talked about by authors of family therapy texts or by supervisors. The reasons for this omission are several, the primary one being that teaching is not perceived by mental health professionals, especially by those seeking to enhance the public image of their profession, as a therapeutic activity. In addition, most therapists are not trained to label, as teaching, those aspects of therapy that involve showing a client how to do something or instructing a family in the process of the family's interaction. Hopefully, however, family therapy clients do learn in the context of therapy; such learning is the result of a teaching process, no matter how dissimilar that process is to academic instruction.

Teaching, in the context of therapy, is an individualized process that consists of showing clients how to do something that will improve family functioning or relating information that will change client attitudes in order to motivate family members to take new actions. The important elements of successful teaching in the therapy are (1) a well-defined ability to know when to switch into a teaching mode (recognizing the teaching moment), (2) awareness of what it is that clients need to be taught and what they can learn in the context of a single therapy session or part of a session, (3) the ability to demonstrate what the clients are to learn and to clearly present new ideas when attitude change is in order, and (4) well-developed skills in providing actual instruction. The three steps in successful teaching are described next.

## The Three-Step Strategy

The key to success in teaching is to use a systematic training procedure, following three basic steps: First, discuss the skill and present a rationale for learning the skill to the clients. Second, the skill is demonstrated. Third, the clients practice and receive feedback while they perform the skill.

The first step, stating the rationale, is designed to explain what the skill is, why it is important to learn, and how the skill will benefit the client. People learn more easily and cooperate more when they understand the purpose of what they are to learn and what the payoffs will be. For example, eye contact is commonly taught as an attending skill to listening. The rationale for this subskill might be explained as follows:

> Good eye contact is designed to communicate that the listener is paying attention to what is being said so that the speaker feels attended to. When good eye contact is present, a speaker usually does not need to get angry or resort to some other attention-getting strategy to make sure that the listener pays attention. Good eye contact consists of looking in the pupil of another's eye and moving back and forth from eye to eye while the other speaks.

Typically, clients will want to discuss the rationale, especially for complex skills. Such discussions are important because misconceptions can be clarified when they occur rather than at some later time when they may result in client failure. In addition, during the discussions, the therapist can usually model using the skill while the discussion occurs and enhance the validity of the rationale in the process. Once clients understand why the skill is important and what the payoffs will be, the therapist can move on to the second step: demonstrating the skill.

Cotherapy teams have an advantage when modeling skills for clients. Unfortunately, most therapists work alone and often must ask a client to help with the demonstration, unless the skill does not require the participation of more than one person. A creative and efficient therapist will use a demonstration in which a client helps as an opportunity to do more than model a skill. For example, in demonstrating how family members can talk together without interrupting and how signals are to be used in asking for the floor, the therapist might ask the family member who interrupts the most frequently to play the role of someone who is speaking and who relinquishes that role when signaled by the therapist.

However, the most important factor to keep in mind when demonstrating is that the modeling must accurately depict what clients are to learn. A demonstration of good listening, for instance, should show good listening and not something else. That means you, the therapist, must know how to perform the skill you are asking clients to learn. In addition, the modeling should have a direct application to the problems confronting the family in therapy. For example, in demonstrating the time-out procedure for parents with young children, the behavior attended to during the demonstration should be one that the children in the family perform at home. The more clients can identify with the situation depicted in the demonstration, the more likely they are to value learning the new skill and to understand how they can use it at home in everyday life.

An excellent follow-up to a demonstration is to ask clients what they saw you doing. Spending a few minutes in discussion at this point helps clarify the specific behaviors clients are to copy and allows you to clear up misunderstandings about what is and is not to be done.

The last step in the teaching procedure is to have clients practice the skill and receive feedback on their performance. It is at this point in teaching that therapists most often make a mistake. Usually, the mistake is to demonstrate a skill and then ask the family or couple to continue the discussion that preceded the switch from therapy to teaching, while one family member attempts to practice. Not surprisingly, most clients have difficulty performing the skill well because the situation used for practice is emotionally charged. Always have clients first practice a skill in a low-threat situation. For example, when teaching listening to a married couple, assign them a nonrelationship issue to discuss in their first attempt to practice listening. As the spouses' skills improve, the topics can proceed from positive relationship issues to minor problems in their marriage, and then to the larger issues. As a result of controlling the content of their discussion, the spouses can concentrate on learning instead of defending or attacking.

Another important task in this phase is to let clients know that they are performing well, or at least in close approximation to what has been demonstrated. The easiest way to give clients this type of feedback is to say, "Good" or "That's it" or some other short phrase of reinforcement. When clients are first learning, they need this type of feedback fairly frequently (say, three times over a three-minute period). Once they know they are doing well, you can give the feedback every five minutes, and then reduce it to occur only after a practice segment has ended. When clients do not do well, stop them after a short time. Often, a second demonstration is in order, or perhaps one of the above factors that inhibit learning (i.e., topic too emotionally charged) is active and is affecting their ability to concentrate.

Once a therapist knows this three-step strategy of teaching, the steps can be applied to many different skills that clients need to help them interact better and to feel successful in therapy.

## RECOGNIZING THE TEACHING MOMENT

One of the most important teaching skills is recognizing when to leave the therapy mode and enter the teaching mode. Unfortunately no one guideline exists to help the therapist decide; several factors must be considered.

The presence of high emotionality indicates that the teaching mode is not appropriate. For example, when a wife finally explodes at her husband about his drinking, an appropriate response on the part of the therapist is to make sure her message gets through. An attempt to teach appropriate listening to the husband while he is in the midst of guilt or defensiveness will fail. Likewise, when a client is sobbing, therapist instruction in the skill of self-disclosure will be unsuccessful, and the client may even be offended at the therapist's inappropriate attempt to intellectualize and abstract. The emotional intensity of a situation, therefore, is one factor therapists must take into account when considering whether to teach or do therapy.

Another factor is the amount of time in a session that can be devoted to teaching. Skills training and attitude change do not occur without a substantial investment of time on the part of the therapist. A comprehensive skills training program, for example, that is designed to include both listening and self-disclosure skills for married couples requires approximately eighteen hours of instruction time when the instruction is carried out in a small group format. Less time is needed when both skills are taught to individual couples, although the amount of practice time needed is not significantly less. As a result, most therapists teach a component of the more generic skills. Rather than teaching empathic responding, most therapists teach eye contact or nonverbal attending. Teaching even these skills takes time, however, and it is important that enough time be devoted to their instruction that clients will be able to learn and practice the skills. Inadequately developed skills that are the product of too little time spent in explanation or practice are harmful, because clients will not successfully use them in everyday life and may also resist future instruction. Allocate enough time in a session to fully teach what is appropriate.

A third factor pertains to the need of the client to know or learn the new skill. Teaching is most beneficial when the client experiences a real need to know. For example, suppose a wife is disclosing her feelings about her troubles to her husband and comes to an abrupt halt, followed by a complaint that her husband is not paying attention, and his reaction is not defensiveness but puzzlement. In that moment, the therapist could, over a two- or three-minute span, teach him a nonverbal attending skill, and he would be able to practice the skill in a situation requiring it. Such moments abound over the course of a therapy session. Husbands and wives interrupt one another, children get noisy, and spouses distract and intellectualize; all of these incidents in therapy can be dealt with by teaching what clients need to know at the time they need to know it.

Another excellent time to teach is when a session gets dull. When you feel bored, it is likely that your clients are also feeling bored to some degree. Switching to teaching can be a change welcomed by all concerned. The difficulty is deciding what to teach. Naturally, what is taught is most helpful if it pertains to the interaction prior to the switch to teaching. If you cannot think of anything appropriate, a transition statement that specifies a change of topic is necessary to help the clients switch their attention from their previous interaction to learning something not associated with it.

## TEACHING LISTENING

Most often, listening is taught to married couples, family members, and individual clients who consistently break the basic rules of effective listening. To assess what to change, the therapist must know these basic rules:

### Nonverbal Rules

1. Maintain eye contact with speaker.
2. Use head nods visible to the speaker to communicate understanding.

### Verbal Rules

1. The intent of a listener's statements or questions should be to clarify the speaker's message, not to change the topic or gain control of the speaker role. The listener role should be that of a follower.
2. Therapists often attempt to teach reflective listening to clients. This attempt commonly fails because not enough time is allocated to the teaching process. When listening is taught in the context of therapy, it is far

better to change nonverbal behavior and to limit a listener's responses to those designed to clarify speaker messages than to attempt to teach reflective listening.

The steps in the teaching process are as follows:

1. Discuss

   Discuss why eye contact is important.

   Discuss why it is important for the listener to follow the speaker's lead instead of guiding the speaker's awareness.

2. Demonstrate

   Demonstrate eye contact (it may also be helpful to show clients what their current behavior looks like).

3. Practice

   Ask the client to copy you while listening to the spouse or other family member.

   Reward the client, if appropriate, and give feedback.

   If the client cannot do what is asked, change the topic of discussion, as it may be too threatening for skills training.

   Practice until the skill is understood and performed well.

   In future sessions, ask about the client's use of the skill and watch for its appropriate use in session.

## TEACHING SELF-DISCLOSURE

Of the two basic interpersonal communication skills, the speaking skill is not as well developed as the listening skill. The concepts of *I messages* and *ownership of feelings* are more like buzzwords than descriptions of concrete skills. Good self-disclosure consists of talking about yourself and your feelings and thoughts about yourself in relation to some event or situation. Opinions are not part of self-disclosure, nor are interpretations of others' actions.

### Rules of Effective Self-Disclosure

1. Speak about yourself, how you view yourself, how you contribute to relationship problems, how another's actions are a problem for you, how you react to another's actions.
2. Avoid statements or words that will interfere with getting a message through to the listener. Words such as *always* and *never* should be used with great care.

The primary difficulty in teaching self-disclosure is that many therapists emphasize the disclosure of feelings, and, unfortunately, clients (especially men) do not know the difference between thoughts and feelings. As a result, clients do not feel successful even when they try to be more feeling-centered and disclosing. A better tactic is to tell clients to talk about themselves, how they contribute to relationship problems, and how others' actions are a problem. Ordinarily, the client will talk about feelings in the process of answering these questions without becoming confused about whether they are talking about feelings. In addition, the therapist's use of phrases such as "disclose your feelings" and "own your feelings" may stimulate additional arguments in the family or marriage when one spouse accuses another person of not being feeling oriented. The steps in the teaching process are as follows:

1. Discuss

   Discuss why self-disclosure is important in a family or marriage. Through self-disclosure the important problems are identified, intimacy begins and grows, and personal burdens are shared.

2. Demonstrate

   Therapists who demonstrate self-disclosure should take care not to be too analytical about themselves or too intimate in their demonstration.

   The topic should pertain to the important issues being dealt with by a family.

   The demonstration should include the person most likely to be undisturbed by the therapist's intimacy.

3. Practice

   Ask the couple to continue their topic of discussion while using the new skill, but only if the skill is still applicable.

   If the clients cannot do what is asked, make sure they understand the rules of effective self-disclosure.

   If they do understand and still cannot stop themselves from accusing, interpreting, and intellectualizing, change the topic to one that is less emotionally laden.

## TEACHING FEELING AWARENESS

It is common today to encounter clinical problems that are partially based on deficient awareness of feelings and/or communication of feelings. Men and teenagers, it seems, are prone to not feeling or, at least, not disclosing their feelings at home.

Rather than first attempting to understand what role nonfeeling plays in maintaining homeostasis, a therapist might attempt instead to increase feeling awareness and expression by stating that feelings are OK and coaching clients to respond to questions such as "How do you feel?" Typically, the supposedly unfeeling client stumbles and mumbles until the therapist gives up and relationship homeostasis is retained.

Lack of feeling awareness/communication among relationship members is not always due to a simple lack of skill. The cold, withdrawn husband, for example, may be highly expressive about sports, elaborate technical schemes, or sophisticated business plans. In a similar manner, a withdrawn teenager may be highly disclosing in a nonverbal way with friends. In such cases, nonexpression may be an attempt to maintain interpersonal power in the family. Where nonexpression appears to be stable across contexts and relationships, however, a lack of skill may be the reason.

Whether inexpressiveness is a power play or the result of a real skill deficit, the therapeutic strategy consists of first encouraging talk, not the disclosure of feelings per se. Clients feel awkward and resist when asked to label their feelings in therapy with questions such as "How do you feel?" They will cooperate, however, if asked to simply describe some important part of their day or some discovery they have made about themselves. Some prompting and questioning may be required to keep the client talking. Most importantly, however, the client's spouse needs to pay attention to the talk, but differently than in the past. To learn how the client's partner has attended in the past, a role play will prove very informative, or the partner can be questioned.

When clients are able to talk about themselves, their reactions, and thoughts, a didactic discussion of feelings and their function in relationships becomes possible. Feelings in relationships serve two functions. First, disclosing feelings creates the opportunity to build trust, and then intimacy, between partners. Second, familiarity with emotional reactions adds zest, color, and meaning to personal life. Disclosing feelings in relationships also lets a partner know whether a request for change or a request for the familiar is important or unimportant. Feelings acquaint spouses with the vitality of their relationship, and feelings help them appreciate each other. When told of these purposes that the communication of feelings serves, spouses are usually motivated to express more feelings to each other.

## TEACHING PROBLEM SOLVING

Considerable research has been conducted on effective procedures for teaching problem solving in the context of marital and premarital intervention. Unfortunately, little of that body of knowledge is used by family therapists, because therapy is not viewed as an opportunity for clients to learn complex, new skills. Problem solving is one such skill that builds on clients' competence at listening and self-disclosing.

Problem solving is taught as a process of steps used to help couples find solutions that work. The process itself does not generate solutions, but it does provide a structure couples can use to identify, try out, and evaluate their own solutions. The steps of a typical problem-solving model include:

1. defining the problem or complaint,
2. expressing how each partner contributes to the problem,
3. brainstorming alternative solutions,
4. selecting and contracting a solution, and
5. evaluating the outcome.

The therapist's role in teaching problem solving is more like that of a guide than a model, because many of the steps do not require new behavior that must be carefully shaped. In the first step, defining the problem, spouses use effective self-disclosure and listening skills. Problem statements become less threatening and the usual attention-grabbers, such as yelling, become unnecessary. After a period of time spent discussing the problem or issue, and when the speaker can state the problem clearly, the couple should be told to move to the next step of the process in which they each discuss how they contribute to the problem. These statements tend to be surprisingly open, because the task's structure forces each partner to admit helping to cause the problem. Usually, very little therapist intervention is needed other than to make sure both spouses feel listened-to by their partner.

In step three, the process takes on a playful tone, with the partners listing alternative solutions without evaluating any proposed solution. Evaluating solutions as they are being listed tends to stifle creativity. The therapist's role is to encourage creative solutions and make sure the structure of the problem-solving model is adhered to. In the next step, the alternate solutions are evaluated, and one workable solution is discussed. In this step, the partners make an agreement or contract that details how the solution is to be implemented. The final step, evaluating the solution, is completed after a trial period of several days, weeks, or months, depending on the frequency of the problem and the nature of the solution.

Of the different types of training, problem solving is perhaps the easiest. It usually follows more basic training in communication skills after which couples possess a skill foundation that helps minimize bickering and passive-aggressive behavior. The role of the therapist is not so demanding, because although the skills are more complex, they involve behavior in which most people have engaged. The essential ingredient to effective problem-solving training is to limit the size of the issues that couples attempt to resolve until they have been successful in dealing with minor problems.

## TEACHING PARENTING

Many of the problems presented by families in therapy involve the skill of the parental subsystem in carrying out the parenting role. As a result, the family therapist is often called upon to show adults how to parent. Unfortunately, many therapists do not have a detailed knowledge of basic parenting skills; and all too often, therapists' recommendations are not understood, or they are forgotten, because time is not taken to teach clients how to carry them out. Following are descriptions of the procedures used to teach the most frequently needed parenting skills.

### *Rule Setting*

All parents need to set rules, and all children struggle to discover what they are. Most of the parents seen in therapy use the yell-and-hit method simply because they know of no other. Because so much emotional energy is required to carry out the yell-and-hit and because this sanction is so severe, it is not used consistently. It can result in withdrawn and acting-out children and abusive parents sentenced by the courts to family therapy. These parents need to learn a method of setting rules that is low cost in terms of emotional energy expended, allows for increasingly severe consequences for a child's noncompliance, and promotes consistent use.

One such method is the three-step procedure for disciplining young children that is taught in most of the currently popular parenting programs. The first step in this method is for the parent to explain what the child cannot do and then suggest an attractive alternative. For example, if a child is drawing on the wall with crayons for the first time, the parent should stop the child, look him or her directly in the eye, and calmly state, "You cannot use your crayons on the wall, but you may draw on paper." The second time the problem occurs, the parent should restate the rule and give a consequence for its violation. Following the same example, the parent should stop the child, look him or her in the eye, and state, "You may not draw on the wall with crayons, and if you do it again, I'll put you in time-out." The third time, the parent restates the rule and imposes the consequence without hesitation.

For very young children (between three and five years of age), the entire three-step sequence may need to be repeated if several days or so pass between episodes, because they may not be able to remember the rule. Older children (six through eighteen years of age) respond to time-out or to the loss of privileges ranging from watching favorite television shows, visits to and from friends, to receiving an allowance, using the family car, and favorite foods and beverages. Of utmost importance is consistency. Encourage parents to keep a few rules consistently and let the rest slide.

To teach this method, the therapist must know the rule-setting sequence and be able to cite examples, the best of which are based on incidents provided by the parent(s). The teaching procedure consists of first stating the rationale for changing the parents' current rule-setting method. The rationale for the three-step method is as follows:

1. The current method used by the parents does not work, and it costs too much in emotional terms.
2. The three-step method will encourage them to enforce rules more consistently.
3. Children will learn what they can and cannot do.

Second, the three-step procedure is described, using examples, and discussed in order to make sure the parents understand the rationale and how to implement the procedure. Finally, the parents are asked to role-play, using the procedure, in the therapy session. When they are able to go through it without prompting, they are asked to use the method once before the next session and to note other times they could have used it. The next session should begin with their report of how things went and when they could have used the method but did not, followed by role play using the three-step method in the situations they used the yell-and-hit method. Next, the parents should be asked to use the new procedure more often during the next week, but only in situations they think are appropriate for the three-step method. Over a few weeks, parents will stop using the yell-and-hit method, and a new skill can be attempted.

## Time-Out

Time-out is a child management procedure that all parents need to learn, even if they are not active child abusers. The procedure is very simple, and it is effective after a child learns that the parents will use it and use it fairly. The difficulty parents have in punishing children is that corporal punishment instills guilt in the parent and fear in the child; thus, physical punishment does not encourage parents to consistently enforce rules. Time-out helps parents establish consistency, and consistency provides children with the boundaries they need to feel secure.

Time-out should be used in the three-step procedure described previously. The idea of time-out is to move a child from a high-stimulation situation to one that is low in stimulation. The time-out place should remain the same; good examples include a chair in a corner, a dimly lit hallway, or a stairway. When step three of the rule-keeping procedure is required, the child is sent or led to the place and instructed to remain there for a short period of time. The length of time the child should remain in time-out is guided by the child's age. Two-year-olds should spend no longer than two minutes in time-out, three-year-olds three minutes, and so on, until the child is seven or eight, when ten minutes can be designated. While the child is in time-out, reading or any other activity should not be allowed; the experience is supposed to be boring. If the child does not voluntarily stay sitting or standing and remain in the time-out space, the parent must physically keep the child there.

In teaching this method of child control, the mistake most often made by therapists is in not requiring the parent to role-play placing the child in time-out during the therapy session. Instead, many therapists merely describe how to institute the procedure and then check up on its success the following week. For effective learning, the parent must be supervised while sending a child to time-out. If asked, children will gladly cooperate by misbehaving and allowing themselves to be sent to time-out.

## DESCRIBING THE PARENT ROLE

One reason that parents abuse or neglect their children lies in their misconception of the parent role. Helping children and their parents in such instances involves more than teaching child guidance and parent–child relationship skills. It is often instructive for the therapist to define effective parenting at an intellectual level, and in so doing change parents' expectations of themselves. The following is an example:

> I'd like to spend a few minutes defining the role of an effective parent. Raising children is a very difficult job. It takes a lot of time and a lot of hard work. By their nature, children need to be taught how to do nearly everything, and one part of being a parent is teaching them what they need to know. What that boils down to is being patient and understanding. When a child misbehaves, they may be seeking attention, or more frequently, they simply don't know how to do anything other than misbehave. Changing how your kids act is a long and frustrating job; no parent has a child who learns after being told how to behave just once. Part of parenting is telling children how to act over and over again.
>
> Another aspect of parenting includes punishing children. Research has pretty well shown that hitting children has side effects that in the long run produce more problems. Put a lot of effort into trying not to hit your kids. Use time-out, loss of TV or allowance as punishment.
>
> Children also need to spend time with you. It is not enough to park them in front of the TV for most of their waking hours. If taught, even the smallest child can do some part of the work needed

to keep a household running. Working together is equivalent to any other activity performed together except, perhaps, just listening to children talk about their day or their troubles. Reading to children is particularly important.

Like it or not, the parent role means more giving than receiving. Children do give back, but not in equal measure for the time and energy they take. Your parents may not have understood that, but it is up to you to change the style of parenting that has been present in your families perhaps for generations.

## ENHANCING THE PARENTAL ALLIANCE

As part of the assessment process, the state or condition of the parental subsystem can be indexed to analyze this aspect of family health. A breach in the parental alliance is easily detected from observations of family interaction or reports from family members. For instance, the children state that mom and dad have different rules; the parents complain that one is more lenient than the other; or one parent is responsible for all child care, leaving the other with no real parenting role. What can be done to strengthen the parental subsystem?

At the root of a broken or weak parental alliance is a lack of agreement on parenting standards and a lack of joint decision making on a day-to-day basis. The first step in changing these weaknesses involves requiring the parents to carry out their role during sessions. At all times, parents should be maintained in their role. When mild disagreements between parents occur in-session and out-of-session, discussions of parenting standards can be undertaken. The objective of these discussions is to arrive at agreement on standards.

More effective, however, is joint decision making that takes place as incidents occur that require parenting. For example, when children become noisy and distracting in session, the parents can be prompted to intervene. When they handle a situation poorly, the therapist can model what has been labeled the bathroom procedure (Smets, 1985). Several steps are involved. First, the parents and the therapist leave the consulting room and meet in a nearby bathroom to discuss how the parents are going to handle the children. The therapist helps them decide on a course of action that they are to carry out in the session. Upon returning to the session, the children are asked to act up again, and the parents act on their agreement. The homework assignment consists of bathroom meetings at home whenever the children require guidance. The bathroom procedure requires that both parents get involved, and it helps focus parental attention on bigger child management problems while decreasing attention to minor events.

## EXPLAINING CODEPENDENCE

Since the early 1980s and the seminal work on codependency and concern for adult children of alcoholics (Black, 1981; Ackerman, 1983; and Woititz, 1983), the amount of literature in this area has exploded. Today, it is not uncommon at all to have someone present the family's problem as residing in a member's codependency or the codependency of the entire family. Recognizing the widespread nature of knowledge on codependency, it seems to have become a buzz word for many, and like the "trendy" nature of drinking one of the sparkling waters, codependency for some appears to be a prestigious problem that can be worn as a badge. This should come as no surprise since barely a week passes that codependency is not a topic on one of the daily television talk shows. Further, this has been fueled in the last few years by a rapid expansion in the number of popular psychology and self-help books on codependency.

As the public develops a greater awareness of the problem known as codependency, helpers can expect to hear it more as a self-diagnosis. When working with families that diagnose themselves in this way, you must proceed with caution and not be too quick to assume that your understanding of codependency is the same as theirs. Instead, a wise approach is to use the presentation of this self-diagnosis as a signal to put on the "therapeutic brakes" and push for greater specificity. To continue working on the basis of assuming everyone in the room has a similar shared understanding of codependency is potentially disastrous to the effort to secure change.

At these times it can be helpful to proceed in a fashion such as follows:

> I'm glad you're aware of the issue known as codependency. People have come to recognize this is a widespread problem that can have very troublesome effects on individuals and their relationships. But we also know that the various behaviors that are part of what we call codependency are manifested differently from person to person. Some behaviors are more prominent among some people than others and may even appear in different ways, depending on who the participants are. For instance, in interacting with one person the codependent behavior of being overresponsible and quick to assume blame may be more evident than while relating to another person. Which codependent behaviors are you most concerned with attempting to change?

This clarification serves to validate the clients' self-diagnoses while simultaneously encouraging greater specificity. This avoids having them feel discounted and fosters them identifying concerns for change in a more behavioral fashion. Recognizing that the client group is a couple or family, the therapist can then proceed to help define the problem in relational terms; for instance:

> So when Jack says that in that fashion, your feelings of guilt increase, and you don't say what you would like different. You then become upset with yourself and bitter with him. Certainly these are ingredients for unhappiness, aren't they? Recognizing this, Jill, how might Jack respond differently to help you get better control of this piece of codependent behavior so you can relate to him with less bitterness?

The last question, along with defining the problem in relational terms, also serves to frame the solution in terms of a quid pro quo. Each gains something positive from the new interaction style that hopefully will evolve. Jack will receive less bitterness and more affirmation, while Jill will be assisted in securing greater control of the codependent behavior that consumes her. In this example, the problem was defined in much more manageable terms than the broad construct of "codependency." Also, by defining the problem in a more therapeutically manageable fashion, the potential for the clients to experience success was enhanced.

## ANTI-VIOLENCE TRAINING

When assessment uncovers family violence or a client is ordered by the court to go to therapy as a result of family violence, care must be taken in deciding whether family therapy, conjoint marital therapy, or individual treatment is best. Although it is not necessarily true, this decision may be influenced by community treatment standards. Some law enforcement and human abuse prevention groups, for instance, share a belief that those convicted of domestic violence crimes should undergo group therapy consisting of resocialization and skills training. These same groups may view family therapy as not only counterproductive but harmful to victims. They may assert this position regardless of the severity of the violence or whether both partners engage in violence. Their concerns stem from a mistaken belief that family therapists force victims to participate conjointly in therapy with perpetrators. Family therapists do not force any client to act against their perceived best interests, or at least they should not. Nonetheless, these critics are correct in focusing our attention on the safety of victims. A safety plan and a no-violence contract should be among the very first goals of therapy if the victim or victims are seen at all. Moreover, careful assessment is needed to determine a victim's safety concerns throughout therapy.

Whether therapy proceeds with the perpetrator alone or conjointly with the victim and the perpetrator, systematic antiviolence training is often part of treatment. Several models have been developed, all of which borrow from the social skills training methods described earlier. Presently, antiviolence training consists of the following components: no-violence contract, role of violence in relationships, anger management, situation recognition, time-out/cool down methods, and problem-solving training.

The content of the training changes as research reveals new understanding about domestic violence. For instance, the cycle of violence was once believed to be the dominant pattern among couples. More recently, another pattern has been defined in which conditions of intimidation and violence are stable characteristics of the system rather than cyclic in nature. Considerable research is being done on domestic violence, and therapists must continuously revise their training programs. The Internet is an excellent source for up-to-date information.

An important issue that must be dealt with at some point during the training is the perpetrator's attitude. Simply put, if the perpetrator is not genuine in claiming ownership for the violence, treatment can be an empty gesture, a waste of everyone's time and good will. Violence perpetrators often find this task particularly difficult. They may attempt to deny, minimize, obfuscate, and otherwise distract their therapist's efforts to address an attitude that supports violence. Where clients are court ordered for therapy, the therapist can state clearly and repeatedly to the client/perpetrator that treatment will not be considered complete until the client demonstrates a genuine change in attitude and behavior. It is the client who must persuade the therapist that he or she genuinely owns responsibility for the violence.

Because significant cognitive reorganization is needed to accomplish such an adjustment, several weeks or months of therapy may be required. Even good acting should not produce an attitude change after one session with even the most accomplished clinician. Where alcohol is involved, as it usually is, substance-abuse treatment can proceed conjointly with antiviolence training or as a prerequisite. Patience, clearly drawn boundaries, and clear expectations for performance are musts for working with violence issues.

## MANAGING COMMUNICATION WITHIN THE SESSION

Chitchat, or small talk, is an important part of all therapy, but especially of family therapy. Upon first meeting, individuals use chitchat as a way to get acquainted. After we come to know another person, we use chitchat as a preface to further interaction. Within a group of people, such as a client group, however, small talk is more likely to dominate verbal interaction unless the group is moved toward its tasks. Small talk can inhibit the progress of therapy unless it is controlled.

Controlling small talk means initiating it at the beginning of a session and then quickly communicating that the session is beginning through a transitional or directive statement. The question, "Well, how did things go this week?" often serves to indicate the end of small talk and the beginning of the session. Initial interviews often begin with the phrase "How can I help you?" or "What problems are you experiencing?" or the more provocative question "What do you want to change in your marriage [family]?" An alternative is to remain standing with the family during small talk and then sit down to indicate that small talk is at an end. Whatever signal is used, marking the transition from small talk to the task of therapy is the therapist's responsibility. Attention to this procedural detail will often result in a greater sense of movement by the therapist and greater confidence on the part of the clients that their therapist has the ability to be helpful.

## ENCOURAGING FAMILY GRIEF

Unsolved grief sometimes serves as an emotional brake to the development of a family and its individual members. The family that does not successfully mourn losses often stops growing from the time the losses occur. Losses may come in the form of physical death; loss of an ideal (for example, a bookish son instead of an idealized athlete); divorce or other loss of a significant relationship; not receiving an important promotion (in the case of a parent); not completing an academic goal such as graduation; or a child marrying someone other than the parents had desired. Therapists need to remember that losses comprise many human experiences besides the obvious one, death.

Significant losses can be determined in a number of ways. One way is to pay attention when a family identifies a loss as a significant time in the family's life. Another way is to inquire during intake about significant losses/disappointments the family encountered in the last twelve months. Research by Holmes and Rahe (1967) has documented the importance of this period, although losses earlier than this may also be very significant. When a family identifies a particular problem as having begun at a certain time, the wise therapist will inquire whether significant losses occurred at about that time, because unresolved grief may have provoked the family's presenting problem. For instance, problematic drug use by a family member often closely relates to a significant death in the family. Remember that a family member's death will result in the loss of several important roles that the dead member had filled and the disruption of rules that the dead family member had helped to maintain. Also, death accentuates issues for survivors that relate to belongingness and separateness, or closeness and distance in relationships. These all constitute important accommodations the family must make that can provoke faulty adaptations culminating in a multitude of family problems. For example, death may result in the family's pulling together more strongly just at the time an adolescent member is in the process of leaving the family (as part of the differentiation process resulting in rebellious behavior by the teenager).

In general, the more open the family, the more effective the family members are at coping with losses and the accompanying grief. Lewis, Beavers, Gosset, and Phillips (1976) have examined the family's potential for dealing with death, finding that the families most open to discussing death are also the ones most functional in other ways. Consequently, the therapist's task consists of identifying important losses that have not been successfully resolved by the family, or by particular members, and then facilitating resolution. Norman Paul (1967) refers to the process of facilitating belated resolution as *operational mourning.* According to Paul, this process consists of the therapist's inviting exposure and expression of feelings attached to the loss by repeated and direct inquiries. It is important to recognize that the family may have developed fairly rigid and dysfunctional rules governing the expression of this affect that will need to be penetrated and changed.

Similarly, Bowen (1976) has identified the importance of using direct words to communicate a new comfort level to the family in discussing death (such as *death, die,* and *bury,* instead of *passed on, deceased,* and *expired).* Using empathic relating demonstrates to the family how to talk about sensitive issues attached to losses. It also desensitizes death issues and shows that they can be confronted directly without the family's falling apart. Having all family members present during the process of operational mourning helps them learn how to relate more empathically, and reap the immediate benefit of sharing the experience. The immediate experience can also be used to promote family discussions about how family members might help each other deal with the present loss and with future losses. Last, the belated resolution of losses can help the family establish permission, rules, and procedures for adapting to the inevitable.

## MANAGING ANXIETY WITHIN THE SESSION

Typically, the therapist's and family members' experience of anxiety fluctuates during the course of a session. A certain look on a wife's face provokes anxiety for her husband; older sister's hand on little sister's knee lowers anxiety; the adolescent stands and rushes out the door, which raises anxiety for the therapist; dad's talk of hopelessness and suicide intensifies anxiety for all family members. Each person's experience of anxiety can be affected by the various behaviors and interactional sequences present in the session. Because anxiety occurs on an ongoing basis, most often out of the control of the clinician, situations will arise requiring the clinician to appropriately manage anxiety-inducing cues.

When a family seems to have become complacent about the change process, without sufficient anxiety to provoke further change, the clinician has a variety of options for stimulating anxiety. The number of options is limited only by the clinician's perceptions of the family's organization and creativity. For example, the clinician might refer to "the family that was seen a few months ago" that resembles this family:

> They were saying things exactly as you folks are now, and seemed to be feeling the same things. It seemed that just when they thought they had things fairly well under control, all hell broke loose. You know, the similarities between you now and that family just before the intensification of problems are spooky. I've seen it before, too. It seems too bad, when folks have made the kinds of advances you have up to this point.

This type of comparison often piques the family's curiosity and anxiety enough to induce the family to explore possible ways to secure further change and maintain change effected already.

Sometimes, however, a particular subsystem of a family is so firmly entrenched in its attributions to, and perceptions of, a family member that change seems highly unlikely. In the absence of anxiety that might stimulate change, the subsystem's perceptions have created a self-righteous sense of indignation and anger. For example, recently a family was seen by one of the authors that contained two parents and two daughters, ages six and ten. The parents presented the problem as that of the ten-year-old's being obstinate and unmanageable. It was quickly determined that as obstinate as the ten-year-old was, the parents were at least as obstinately critical. These two crucial components of this apparently endless cycle acted as both cause and effect, and at least one needed to be altered if there was to be hope for change.

At one point in the conversation, the parents mentioned how similar the ten-year-old was to the husband's brother, who had been extremely depressed at various times in his life. The parents made it evident that they had been very helpful and responsive to this brother and prided themselves on their contribution to his "recovery." This similarity was explored and became the focal point for increasing productive anxiety to stimulate change. The similarities between the brother and daughter were amplified by the therapist until the daughter was viewed as being as much depressed as "obstinate." The obstinance that was present was related to depression, and a plan was devised so the parents were as helpful to their daughter as they had been to the husband's brother. The concern, or anxiety, for the daughter becoming as depressed as the brother was sufficient to motivate the parents to change their obstinately critical way of relating to their daughter. As suspected, the parents' more moderate and compassionate way of relating to the daughter was quickly met by her becoming much more cooperative and caring. A benevolent cycle had been developed between the parents and daughter, replacing the old destructive one.

Just as there are times when it is valuable to intensify the experience of anxiety, there are also times when it needs to be mediated in order to open a pathway for change. One of the authors recalls working in a clinic at a time when a local newspaper carried an article by a psychoanalyst that declared that playing with matches by five- and six-year-olds suggested a multitude of future problems for these youngsters. During the next several weeks, the clinic was flooded with intakes of five- and six-year-olds who had been caught playing with matches. Predictably, the parents of these children were experiencing intense anxiety secondary to a concern that their child was doomed to an adulthood ravaged by a variety of unknown mental disorders. A crucial task in working with these parents was to attempt to ameliorate their anxiety and normalize the curiosity of their children. With few exceptions, there was considerable evidence that the children were simply responding in a curious fashion to fire as an interesting phenomenon in their world. If the parental anxiety had not been mediated, it is reasonable to assume that their overresponsiveness and concern could have increased the likelihood of problems being observed in these children as they grew and developed.

As was true in the previous example, providing information to replace the destructive notions that current behavior is based upon frequently reduces anxiety. In another case, the couple who presented concern for the wife's being unable to experience an orgasm in spite of penetration for at least three minutes responded very quickly to the correction of their notion that three minutes should be enough. Clinicians often waste valuable time searching the depths for the etiology of a problem, only to stumble across the discovery that all that was needed was a simple piece of information to replace current erroneous information. Frequently, information that normalizes and reframes, or places behavior or an experience in a different perspective, is what the family is most in need of in order to moderate anxiety. While this sort of intervention is not what makes for dramatic case presentations, it is often what can be most helpful to concerned families.

## INDUCING A CRISIS TO STIMULATE CHANGE

There may be times in working with a family when the clients' anxiety levels have fallen too low, and the uneasiness or tension that can be so important to stimulating change is lost. At these times, the therapist might consider inducing a crisis by amplifying a particular deviation already present or manipulating the family affect so that dynamic tension is rekindled (Minuchin, 1974).

Amplifying a deviation can take a variety of forms. Assume that a couple has been seen for some time and appears to have settled into a complacent pattern. The therapist may choose to identify a particular piece of behavior in their relationship and then amplify it. If the husband, for example, makes a comment to his wife that could be interpreted as demeaning or discounting in nature, either in its content or the style used in delivering it, the therapist could amplify this deviation by saying to the wife: "How do you feel about his saying that or the way in which he said it? I can really appreciate that if I was in your shoes, I would probably feel hurt, but also angry too." This form of amplification involves the therapist's assuming what Zuk (1981) refers to as the side-taking function, by aligning with the wife to support her in addressing the husband's discounting style. The husband's behavior may otherwise go unnoticed by the wife, and the therapist's effort to amplify the deviation serves to promote interaction that can result in change. As Zuk indicates, though, the therapist must be sensitive to the dynamics of the clients' relationship. For instance, in the example offered, it would be wise for the therapist to create some sense of alliance with the husband to serve as a buffer or shock absorber against his possible perception of being ganged up on by the therapist and wife. If the appropriate alliance is present, the husband will not become unduly defensive and will be able to productively address the concern identified.

Manipulating the family affect is another means of promoting a productive crisis within a family. This refers to changing the affect a family member attaches to a particular experience and assumes that a change in affect will also promote a change in behavior. Take, for example, a family with a mother, father, and some children, including one adolescent who has been disruptive and problematic. Assume the adolescent's disruptiveness is correlated with the parents' apparent inability to activate some authority and set limits with contingencies identified for transgression of these limits. The adolescent makes a comment that is disrespectful of the parents, perhaps even a blatant put-down. The therapist asks for the parents' feelings about the comment, and the parents report: "Well, I don't know for sure, but I imagine it's his right. You know, I'm just not certain what to say."

This would be a time when the therapist may move to manipulate the client's emotions by making a comment such as:

> I'll tell you, I'd be mad as hell if he said that to me. I don't believe you deserve that, as I think about how concerned and helpful you've attempted to be. Perhaps the problem is that you've been too concerned and understanding. I definitely believe that you are deserving of more respect than that comment suggests.

The effort is then continued to promote the parents' having some righteous indignation to the point that they begin to assert themselves as parents and executives in the family. The effort is made to initiate new behavior by creating a crisis or, as in this example, manipulating the affect that the parents are attaching to their son's behavior.

Therapists who are not comfortable enough to periodically promote a crisis could be destined to many episodes of apparent lethargy and no change by the families they are involved with. In using this procedure, though, it is important for therapists to be candid regarding their motivation and ensure that it is not to satisfy their own feelings of frustration with the family. If there is any reason for doubt, the therapist should probably discuss this possibility with a supervisor or colleague.

## ASSESSING WHEN TO CONFRONT

Confrontation is a valuable though potentially explosive technique when used appropriately. Just as nuclear power has tremendous positive value to humankind, yet equally destructive power, confrontation has the same potential in relation to family therapy. In general, confrontation has its greatest therapeutic value after the development of a relationship that provides for adequate shock-absorbing quality. If confrontation is engaged in without evident caring and commitment, it can be perceived as caustic or designed solely to injure. Certainly, confrontation is a procedure that could provoke termination by the family but, perhaps more importantly, create an impression for the family that all therapy is more injurious than it is helpful so that they never seek help.

Gerald Zuk (1981) has written the most explicitly about confrontation with his description of the process of side taking by the therapist. Zuk goes so far as to say that families will not allow the therapist not to take sides, and even if the therapist attempts to remain neutral, the family will perceive the therapist to be taking sides, anyway. Consequently, Zuk encourages the therapist to accept side taking as a natural part of the therapeutic process and to use the process of confrontation to produce the greatest therapeutic value. Cautions about this process have to do with becoming too predictable and the need to monitor the structure of the family to avoid injuring clients. For instance, always confronting the adolescent member of a family could encourage the adolescent to develop a rigidly organized set of defenses to the therapist that prove impenetrable later on. Or confronting a mother who feels her husband and children have ganged up on her could lead her to terminate therapy.

The therapist can apply confrontation to a variety of issues, such as family members' definitions or labels attached to a person or behavior; communication styles that are counterproductive; patterns of responding to others in a fashion that curtails productive relating; unwillingness to compromise;

and reluctance to acknowledge another's point of view. The confrontation can take the form of a direct confrontation between therapist and another person, or between therapist and subsystem of the family, such as the parents. The confrontation can also be packaged in a variety of ways, depending on the therapist's perception of the situation. For instance, the confrontation may be presented in a teasing and playful fashion in the case of a client who seems to be tenuously engaged in therapy, or it may be offered as speculation that really does not demand a response—for example, "You know, I think you probably do that just to get the type of reaction I saw you get. Makes sense to me." Naturally, the confrontation can also be very direct and truly confrontational. Confrontations that are more direct may be necessary to underscore the seriousness of whatever is at issue. They might also be the most appropriate way to get a message across simply to a client.

The use of confrontation is probably one procedure in the therapeutic arsenal that is most reflective of the art, rather than science, of therapy. The therapist must assess a family's circumstances at the time of the confrontation, as well as its appropriateness and likely consequences, before implementing it. The therapist who does not do this is likely to find that many families terminate without explanation.

## CONFRONTING CLIENTS

As defined by the lay person, confrontation is a hostile, unpleasant, demeaning, and anxiety-provoking experience that is best avoided. These feelings result from confrontations in relationships and encounters that produce frustration, irritation, and anger.

These same feelings are often experienced by therapists toward clients. In family therapy, such feelings are good indications that the therapist is becoming enmeshed in a family system. If a therapist acts out these feelings, the result is often client hostility, appointment no-shows, or at the least a "stuck" case. Talking with a colleague helps to disengage from the family and reestablish a therapist role. There are times, however, when therapists need to confront clients with their feelings. When fees are not paid or when therapy is not taken seriously by court-referred clients, for example, feelings are created that need to be communicated.

The essence of good therapy is confrontation, but of a different sort. Therapeutic confrontation involves close examination of client's patterns, or feedback about client behavior, followed by a statement of what is not obvious or is not easily revealed. For example, in listening to a daughter describe her relationship with her mother and her lack of sorrow when the mother died, a confronting statement might be, "It doesn't sound to me like you two were very close to begin with," or "In talking about her, you seem to be stifling a lot of strong feelings." These two statements are confrontational but can be stated in a manner that is not offensive or demeaning. The crucial difference between offensive versus therapeutic confrontation lies in the therapist's tone of voice and intent to be helpful.

## DESCRIBING A BEHAVIORAL PATTERN

In attempting to promote behavioral specificity with clients, modeling the process of describing a behavioral pattern for them can be valuable. For instance, assume that whenever a wife says to the husband, "There you go again, will you grow up!" he becomes withdrawn and appears to retreat. Then she escalates her attack, and he responds with greater withdrawal, and so on. To describe this pattern, based upon observing it more than once, a therapist might say:

> Did you two notice that when Joan said, "there you go again, will you grow up," Larry, you became quiet and began to drop your eye contact and appeared to become inattentive. Joan, his actions seem to promote more anger and frustration from you, along with an increase in verbal statements that seemed to get more of the same withdrawal and inattention from you, Larry. I have observed this on more than one occasion, and I'm wondering about its usefulness to your relationship.

They are then invited to comment on this observation. The question at the end of the statement supposes that the patterns exist. It also serves to imply that the pattern ought to change.

The value of describing behavioral patterns lies not only in helping clients become aware of behaviors that would otherwise remain automatic, but also in introducing the possibility that the identified patterns may evolve into new treatment goals (see "Establishing Therapeutic Goals" in Chapter 4). Although the therapy may already have more general goals, an identified pattern can facilitate the achievement of a larger goal (such as improving communication effectiveness to diminish a sense of not being valued by one another) or it may become a specific minigoal by itself.

Patterns are often more easily detected early in treatment, before the therapist has become so familiar with a couple or family that everyone is oblivious to reoccurring behaviors. In this regard, reviewing audio- or videotapes of sessions can be particularly valuable, as can inviting a colleague in for a consultation session with the specific identified purpose of observing, and then guessing at what might constitute patterns.

Clients' responses to reports of behavioral patterns by a therapist will frequently cause them to use those very patterns. For instance, with the example used before, it would not be surprising to observe Joan beginning to attack Larry as he becomes withdrawn, and so on. The astute therapist will be sensitive to this behavior pattern and be prepared to use it to confirm the presence and strength of the pattern. Once the behavior pattern has been identified, it is valuable to have each client identify how the other might help that client stop contributing to the pattern in order to prevent its occurrence, and then rehearsing these proposed behaviors in session. For example, Joan might ask Larry to tell her when he is feeling accused/attacked by her by simply saying so or combining his report with some clearly absurd behavior, such as pointing his finger at her and crossing his eyes. By incorporating the absurd component into this reporting process, the sharpness of the exchange can be minimized while still conveying the necessary information. Continuing with the example, Joan might report to Larry when she perceives him withdrawing and appearing to become inattentive and accompany this statement by holding her hand to her mouth like a megaphone and saying, "Am I being received over there?"

## REWARDING CLIENTS

Therapists correctly assume that they are psychologically important to their clients, and that their approval can help clients change. The ways of showing that approval range from making a long statement that might follow successful completion of homework to simply stating, "Good." The longer statement has the most effect if it is stated in terms of the therapist's feelings. For example, if a father and son have successfully negotiated a rule on their own, their therapist might say, "I'm glad you two were able to sit down and calmly agree about the time you are to be in on school nights. Getting that issue settled has made me confident you can tackle your larger issues just as effectively."

Shorter rewarding remarks typically are used in situations when skills are being taught in session. When, a spouse responds appropriately during a session in which a couple is being taught problem solving, for instance, a quick, unobtrusively stated "good" or "that's it" immediately after an effective response will communicate approval. In teaching situations, such remarks need to occur frequently (approximately one per minute) until the client knows what is expected. Then the rate can be gradually lessened but not eliminated. Appropriate behavior, if it is to continue and generalize, requires attention supplied through social reinforcement.

## SETTING UP A ROLE PLAY OR ENACTMENT

Whether for educational or therapeutic reasons, role play is used quite extensively by family therapists. In the initial phase of therapy, therapists often use the role play to communicate family system concepts and to reframe symptoms. In the middle phase, role play can help clients experience contrasts between old and new behavior and the outcomes of each. Together with family sculpting and many psychodramatic techniques that are forms of role play, asking family members to take on roles and act them out in accordance with specific guidelines is a powerful procedure.

There are three rules to follow in setting up a role play. First, the doctrine of no surprises dictates that clients be forewarned that they may be expected to role-play. If a therapist plans to conduct role play on some issue in a session, the clients should be told at the beginning of the session that they may be asked to role-play later on. Second, when it comes time to set up the role play, clients are not asked whether they would like to participate. Instead, the therapist moves participants into their roles without asking for cooperation. Third, and most important, the role-players need specific instructions regarding the setting and what they are to do.

In specifying the roles that players are to assume, detail is crucial. For example, if a husband and wife are to play out their last fight in order to discover how to avoid such flare-ups in the future, several pieces of information are required. The therapist should find out where the fight happened, how the spouses were feeling and what they were doing before the fight occurred, who said and did what during the fight, and how they ended it. Once these details are known, the couple will be able to act out the fight, because they will have refreshed their memories as to what happened.

Similarly, if clients are asked to engage in new behavior, detailed role descriptions will allow them to pay more attention to the role and less to figuring out what to do in that role. The easiest way to quickly provide the required amount of detail is for the therapist to model. When teaching time-out, for example, the role of the child and the role of the parent should be modeled first by the therapist, then tried on by the clients. As with all therapeutic procedures, many outcomes are possible when clients role-play. The likelihood that the outcome of a role play will be the one desired is enhanced by taking the time to set it up carefully.

Examples of what families can role-play are numerous. Couples can act out their latest scrap or how they compliment one another, providing greater understanding of what the spouses actually do to and with one another. In a family context, children and their parents can role-play stressful interactions to achieve the same end of providing added insight into interactional patterns and the possibilities for change. Finally, role play can be an extremely powerful educational tool. For example, instead of merely describing how parents are to use time-out with their children, a role-played situation in the therapy session in which a child pretends to misbehave and a parent implements time-out is an excellent opportunity for the therapist to observe and supervise parenting behavior.

## INTERRUPTING TO CHANGE INTERACTION PATTERNS

Frequently, in the midst of a session, a therapist will observe an interaction between clients that plays a role in maintaining either the symptom or a dysfunctional family structure. The dilemma is whether to interrupt the session and change the interaction or let it go, hoping it will occur again at a more opportune time. Experience will be the best guide on whether to intervene. Generally, however, it is best to intervene rather than wait until later; a better opportunity may not present itself.

Therapist willingness to interrupt a session primarily depends on the ability to smoothly stop interaction, transit to the intervention, make the intervention, then return to the original topic. For example, suppose a husband and wife are discussing their feelings of being trapped in their marriage:

*Wife:* "When I go out, you always quiz me about what I've been doing, who I was with, and where we went. Well, I—"

*Therapist:* "I'd like to interrupt here for a second. I need to comment on how you are talking together. Jane, I noticed that one of the words you used may stop your message from getting across. As much as possible, I would like both of you to try not using the words *always* or *never.* They tend to create an argument about how often something happens, then the real issue gets sidetracked. Now, say the same thing but leave out the argument word."

*Wife:* "When I go out, I don't like it when you ask me a lot of questions about who I was with, what we did, or where we went."

*Therapist:* "Good, go on."

Interrupting clients to make a change in their behavior is less threatening for the therapist who knows that it is possible to do so gracefully. Such interruptions end with the therapist's directing the clients to continue with what was interrupted.

## REDUCING FAMILY LOYALTY

The book *Invisible Loyalties* (Boszormenyi-Nagy & Spark, 1973) loudly proclaimed the important role that family loyalties play in family processes.

The authors skillfully portrayed the role of relationship ledgers and the importance that the balancing of these ledgers has in relationships. As a result, many family therapists initiated efforts to understand families in relation to loyalties. The two family life-cycle stages in which loyalties are most influential are as follows: the family with an adolescent and the newly married couple.

The family with an adolescent is typically confronted most dramatically with a member beginning to shift attention and allegiances outside of the family. Although this is not a problem for some families, others experience this shifting of loyalty as a form of rejection and heresy by the adolescent. This perception typically results in the family's becoming more constrictive and attempting to further prevent the adolescent from engaging in the age-appropriate process of beginning to leave home. Predictably, the adolescent responds by behaving in ways that are perceived as being even more dramatic evidence of wanting to leave, and the "runaway equation" effect develops in which the more the parents do something to squelch behavior, the more the adolescent feels that the only option is to escalate the behavior. This problem is particularly evident in families best described as enmeshed (Minuchin, 1974). Interestingly, these families are frequently those in which the parents themselves are still struggling with attempting to resolve loyalty issues with their families of origin.

This type of family is often helped by having the problem with the adolescent framed in the context of loyalty issues for the adolescent and that client's apprehensiveness about beginning to leave home. Helping the parents recall their own leaving-home process and then encouraging them to coach their youngster about leaving home can be very helpful. While the adolescent is getting what is wanted (leaving home and individuating), the parents gain some sense of control and involvement that eases their distress over feeling abandoned or rejected by the adolescent. During this time, it is important for the therapist to frame this process or place it in the context of a developmental process that is normal for our society. To describe the parents' facilitation of this process as a gift to the child can be helpful, as can identifying how the parents as a couple can be helpful to each other during this time. This suggestion serves to stabilize and strengthen the marital relationship that may otherwise seem jeopardized by the potential loss of an important family member. This crisis situation may be the first time the parents have ever openly discussed the issue of loyalty or commitment to the family. The act of openly discussing it may dislodge them from the unspoken fear and apprehension that has been blocking their engagement in the natural process of evolution from one stage of the family life cycle to the next.

The newly married couple is at the other stage of family development during which the problem of family loyalties is most often observed. As the new spouses develop and organize their own relationship, attempting to incorporate rules and patterns from their respective families of origin, loyalty problems may surface. These issues can arise because one of the spouses feels disloyal to his or her own family and must fight to have old family patterns incorporated into this new family, or the spouse may be stimulated by one or more parents who feel abandoned. This apparent crisis can often be used to motivate the young couple to make a commitment to focus on the type of family the couple wants to develop; specifically, what the couple most wants to bring into this new family from the families of origin, and what the couple most wants to leave behind.

The process of having the spouses talk concretely and specifically about these issues takes the loyalty struggle out of the shadows of their current relationship, and places it clearly in perspective. This intervention places the process of the couple's developing a new relationship in a new context; it becomes purposeful and future-oriented rather than one contaminated by the past and by the pull of being loyal to the spouses' respective families. Therapy consists of developing a loyalty to the couple's own relationship, and a negotiation process to aide the transition.

## CHANGING THE SEATING PATTERN

As has been noted by many therapists, the seating pattern chosen by clients often indicates family structure. After the initial phase of therapy, seating patterns may change from one session to the next to reflect new coalitions or alliance breakups. As part of treatment, a therapist may choose to change a seating pattern to symbolize new family structure or to make an intervention easier.

Changing a seating pattern is an easy task that can be made difficult, if not impossible. If a therapist pleads for the clients' permission, the likelihood of noncompliance increases. The change is easy if the therapist says, "George, I'd like you to change seats with Marjorie. That will make it easier for you two to talk directly to one another." Typically, clients will cooperate. If George balks, the therapist can stand up, grasp him gently by the arm, gesture him to stand, and steer him over to Marjorie's seat. If she does not move, the therapist can use the same physical management to get her to stand and move to George's seat. The easiest way to get clients to cooperate in changing seats is to direct them to do so.

## INTERACTING WITH YOUNG CHILDREN

The family therapy process usually includes young children. A prominent danger in working with their families is to ignore the young children, only addressing the adults and older children who are capable of speaking the same logical language that the therapist does. In doing so, therapists deny themselves the rich advantage of joining the family through young children and the benefit of the understanding so often afforded by the young, who can utter truths without defensiveness characteristic of adults and teenagers.

Few parents can avoid developing feelings of fondness for those who positively attend to their young children. Consequently, therapists who are kind, attentive, and interactive with a family's young children are bound to engender fondness in the parents toward them. To avoid this simple, but powerful, means of initially joining the family is a gross oversight. Attending to children also conveys to the family that children are valued in the therapy context, and they are perceived as being as much a part of the family as any other member. Further, such attention can serve to model, for one or both parents, how to effectively interact with young children. Typically, it will be a more valuable lesson for the father than the mother.

Interacting with the children can also quickly provide valuable information about the structure and operation of the family. For instance, interacting in the following fashion with the four-year-old who clutches his teddy bear closely to his chest upon entering the room can produce valuable insights:

> That teddy bear looks as though he gives you lots of good feelings. I had one like that when I was your age and I loved him as much as it looks like you love that one. It's nice to feel close, isn't it? Who else in this family can you cuddle with like you can cuddle with your teddy? How about your brother over there; who can he cuddle with? How about Dad, Mom, etc.?

Using the child's world, and whatever toy might be important to the child, can provide a valuable path to a quick understanding of important dimensions of the family's structure and operating schema. A child's responses can disclose where the alliances and coalitions are, who the child looks to for permission to speak, what silencing mechanisms are employed by the family to keep children quiet, which family member is overresponsible for the children and tries to get them to say the right thing, and other equally important bits of information relevant to the development of a therapeutic plan.

As suggested by Haley (1976), it is always valuable to have toys and puppets available in the therapy room, to give children the opportunity to communicate in play form. Toys not only provide a conduit for the children to convey their messages, but also provide a means of assessing how the parents play with the children and what skills parents have for interacting with their children in the child's world. Having toys available provides the opportunity to tap into children's intuitive world, which tends to be more sensitive to emotion than adult cognitive powers. Drawing paper, crayons, chalkboard, chalk, finger paints, blocks, dolls, and a dollhouse all provide a communication channel for children. Toys also provide children with the opportunity to escape into fantasy when the therapy process proves too much for them.

Having children present in the sessions also provides the therapist the opportunity to directly observe the parent–child interaction style prevalent in the family. Once the style has been observed, specific interventions to assist in the development of more positive parenting techniques can be offered. In addition, having children present and interacting with them promotes the preventive component of family therapy. Children have the opportunity to participate firsthand in the process of effecting family change, acquiring this learning which they can use to prevent similar problems in their future relationship spheres.

## INDICATORS OF RESISTANCE

Resistance is the act of being in opposition to or avoiding something. More recent analytically oriented writers such as Anderson and Stewart (1983) regard resistance differently than writers such as Erickson (see Haley, 1973), Watzlawick, Weakland, and Fisch (1974), and de Shazer (1982). The latter authors' views on resistance most adequately represents our own view, which is that the construct of resistance is much ado about nothing.

We must remember that what we call resistance is a two-person phenomenon; a relationship between persons must exist before any behaviors can be identified as resistance. We must keep in mind the utilitarian value of this construct: As long as this concept is available, we can avoid responsibility and project the blame for lack of progress onto our clients by saying, "They are just too resistant!"

Resistance as a two-person phenomenon means that we have some responsibility for its existence or nonexistence. To avoid resistance, the therapist must maintain a sense of balance within the client relationship and, in addition, the potential for retreating and regrouping with the client group. This is particularly important in the early stages of therapy when the relationship with the client has not developed sufficiently to serve as a shock absorber for direct confrontation. Once this shock-absorbing quality is present in the form of a relationship commitment, behaviors reflecting resistance are far less likely.

Retreating and regrouping with the client group refers to the capacity to sense client irritation likely to be counterproductive, and then to make necessary shifts such that a more productive interaction can occur. Rather than engaging in battle, employ the philosophy and technique of judo: The opponent's force is not opposed by an action of equal force but is accepted and then amplified by first yielding to it and then going with it. For example, assume that during the initial session someone appears to be very antagonistic and irritated. Perhaps the clinician has provoked it or maybe something totally unrelated to the therapy has. Whatever the case, the wise therapist will initiate moves that will effectively neutralize this potentially problematic behavior. One way is to identify with the client by agreeing with a statement said or a point made, perhaps even by placing yourself in a symmetrical relationship with the client, saying: "I can see that you and I are going to get along well because we are so much alike. I often feel and think just as you do, and I don't have the opportunity to meet many like us." The goal is to change the interaction that is apparently becoming oppositional or resistive to interaction that is more cooperative and potentially productive.

Not infrequently, entire client groups that do not follow through with assigned tasks or activities are identified as being resistant. Again, it is much easier for us as professionals to define them as resistant than it is to realize that we have blundered in not providing them with sufficient understanding, skills, or motivation to be cooperative and successful. Or, the family that seemingly refuses to talk as freely as the clinician might like is referred to as resistant, without the clinician even considering that this family is not accustomed to talking with strangers about their problems. Perhaps the family has been cautioned about going too quickly with therapists "because they tell everything to the courts" by neighbors whose therapist had to report them to the local social service unit for physically abusing a child. What is more important is to observe the clients' behaviors, then define them as cooperative and reaffirm them. For instance, with family members that refuse to talk, we might thank them for being courteous and demonstrate our appreciation for having clients who "think before they talk, because so many don't." Further, they can be acknowledged for caring about themselves and their family so much that they exercise "good, cautious judgment." These efforts at retreating and regrouping will effectively eliminate the occurrence of behaviors conveniently referred to as resistance.

Whenever therapists find themselves wanting to refer to a family or couple as resistant, they should stop and ask, "What could I be doing differently with these people to foster cooperation and further enhance our relationship?" As the relationship improves, behaviors typically characterized as resistance will not likely occur.

# ▶ 6

# Termination Procedures

Even though all cases end eventually, not all terminate. The word *terminate* means to end actively, and that is what should happen but sometimes does not. For many reasons, some clients abruptly stop coming to therapy while others seem to fade away. Many, however, do choose to end their therapy formally because their goals have been met. The potential for this development can be strengthened by contracting for a termination session during the initial phase of therapy. This serves to elicit a commitment from clients to recognize termination as an important element of the therapeutic process. Also, addressing termination at the initiation point of therapy underscores that this is a process with a distinct endpoint and, contrary to what some clients believe, does not exist indefinitely over time.

This chapter describes when to terminate and details related to how to facilitate the termination process. Dependency is a primary confounding variable to effective terminations. As a result, the section to follow is designed to address how to best assess for and rectify problematic dependency.

## ASSESSING WHEN A FAMILY IS TOO DEPENDENT

While the therapist is concerned with developing a therapeutic alliance sufficient to effect change, there is also a need to ensure that the family does not become too dependent. Signs of problematic dependency might become evident in the form of phone calls between sessions to receive confirmation of particular ideas or perceptions, requests for sessions more frequently than what the therapist deems appropriate, or comments made in session, such as "We agreed that we would wait to discuss this until we were here and you could tell us if we were right."

With couples or families who make frequent phone calls between sessions, a simple prescription is often effective. They are instructed that the next time they feel disposed to call and report an incident or ask a question, they are to wait twenty-four hours from the moment of the initial impulse before calling. If the desire is still present at the end of that period of time, they are to call; otherwise, they are to make note of the incident and report it in the next session. Most frequently, they already have the answer to their question or ideas about possible solutions to an incident and are simply looking for affirmation or approval rather than relying upon their internal resources. In the vast majority of situations, their ideas and solutions are appropriate. The situations they might otherwise call about will typically require some action within twenty-four hours, and asking them to be responsive to a twenty-four-hour phone moratorium increases the likelihood that they will implement their own ideas.

When these incidents are reported in the next session, it is important for the therapist to recognize the nature of the clients' actions and to emphasize the positives that are inherent in what they did. On those occasions when they do call after the twenty-four-hour moratorium, it is wise to ask what they have been thinking about doing and encourage them to select from among the options they have identified: "It seems you are definitely on the right track and have thought of good options." In the next scheduled session, it will be important to reinforce the clients for the insight they have manifested in regard to the situation presented over the phone and underscore it as evidence of the progress they have made.

Dependence might also be evidenced when the therapist states the belief that it is appropriate to consider less frequent sessions and/or termination, and the couple/family responds by requesting maintenance of the same schedule or even more frequent sessions. In these circumstances, there is value in asking clients what they are uneasy about. As they describe their fears and apprehensions, the therapist listens and determines how these uneasy situations develop and what can be done to prevent them from occurring.

There is also value in having them identify what is the worst that could happen if their fears materialize. Once their worst fears are identified, the therapist is wise to explore with them options for action in response to these developments. Oftentimes this discussion will serve to ease their apprehensions; if not, they should be encouraged to "give it a try" and then implement the options they just discussed.

There may even be times when there is value in encouraging clients to attempt to develop one of these uncomfortable or fearful situations to practice implementing the various options identified. This suggestion serves to take the edge off of their apprehension and allows the therapist to metacommunicate a sense of conviction and belief in the clients that they may not otherwise have in themselves.

Those who appear to be manifesting problematic dependence by frequently reporting the decision to wait until they are in session to discuss an issue or to get feedback should be encouraged to talk about the issue at that time while the therapist observes. This serves to desensitize discussing issues to resolution, and it also provides the therapist with an opportunity to observe communication styles on issues that clients perceive as sensitive. By intervening at the process level of their communication, the therapist can facilitate the development of skills and resources that result in clients feeling more competent and less restricted, and subsequently less dependent upon the therapist as a mediator or insurance policy against the total destruction which they fear.

## WHEN TO TERMINATE

The issue of termination in family therapy is not nearly so crucial an issue as it is portrayed to be when working from an individual perspective. Family therapy is oriented to facilitating family members' coming to use one another, rather than the therapist, as primary resources. The notion of cure is not nearly as prominent in family therapy as it is with individuals, because families are continually evolving through a life cycle with predictably difficult times and because of family therapy's tendency to be more problem-specific than is most individual therapy.

One way of reducing, if not eliminating, the issue of termination is to work on the basis of specific temporal boundaries. From the outset of therapy, there is agreement among all involved that therapy will last for a certain number of sessions. If the agreement is to meet for five sessions, it is understood that everyone, including the therapist, will decide if they have accomplished the goals by the fifth session and then enter into a decision-making process about the value/need of negotiating for more sessions to reach a particular goal. If an agreement to continue is reached, the purpose and time frame is once again agreed upon. As a result, everyone gains a temporal orientation similar to those to which we have grown accustomed in daily life: watches on almost everyone's arm, clocks on many walls, calendars distributed liberally at the start of each year, and pocket calendars in purses and vest pockets. There is a feeling of comfort, if not security, in having some sense of time—and the same holds true for therapy.

At the end of each negotiated time period, the therapist can facilitate the discussion about continuing with another "treatment block of time" and/or encourage clients to go home and discuss continuing and then contact the therapist with a decision. Should they call and desire to continue, there is value for the therapist in asking them to explain not only what area of change or goal they wish to achieve, but also how they decided. Frequently, the description of how they decided to continue suggests termination because they have demonstrated the capability of operating in very independent and functional ways. If the therapist agrees to continue, it is understood to be for a time-limited period once again.

Working on the basis of these temporally specified treatment blocks significantly minimizes the issue of termination and provides everyone with recognizable times when it is easy to terminate. It is not unreasonable to assume some families may develop a loyalty and liking for the therapist that makes termination uncomfortable enough for them to postpone. While some might suggest that this is an indication of the family's need for more "work," it is incumbent upon the therapist to make it easy for the family to exercise free choice in ending *their* therapy, for most assuredly it should be theirs.

Families may give other clues of their desire to terminate by not showing up for scheduled appointments or asking questions such as "Do you think we're accomplishing anything here?" or "We've been talking among ourselves about coming only once a month rather than every other week. What do you think about that?" When these and other such behaviors that may suggest the family's readiness to terminate are present, there is generally value in offering to terminate rather than going to greater spacing between sessions. This way it can become the family's free decision in response to the therapist's invitation, and they can also sense the therapist's autonomy from them and the fact that there is no dependency or urgency in continuing on the therapist's part. It is still possible for the family to suggest greater spacing of sessions rather than outright termination, but at least the invitation/permission for them to terminate will have been given. Regardless of whether they decide to terminate or opt for greater spacing of sessions, it is advisable to explore with them likely struggles or tensions in the future so that when normal crises or tensions arise, they do not attribute this directly to the decision to terminate.

At the point of termination, there can be value in suggesting another session in two to four months. While a follow-up session can facilitate the termination process for the family, it can also be a rich source of data for the therapist. By seeing families after two to four months, the therapist can assess the effectiveness of various interventions over a period of time and enrich his or her experiential base regarding what is helpful to families with various presenting problems. This practice is one way of preventing therapeutic burnout resulting from an absence of feedback on the effectiveness of various practices.

## COMPONENTS OF THE TERMINATION SESSION

Successful termination is a useful procedure that can yield firm and positive closure for the clients and their therapist. This is in contrast to the dribble-out style of termination in which the client misses one session then two then never returns. A more active, planned style of termination will feature a specific session designated several weeks before therapy is to end.

A good way to begin the termination session is for the therapist to quickly summarize the presenting problem and the main events that occurred over the course of therapy. Looking over the case notes before the session is a considerable aid in recalling the course of the therapy. This brief statement helps remind clients of their accomplishments. Then the clients should be asked for their recollection of those events so additional details about the therapy can be identified. When the family omits or forgets to mention significant events, the therapist can offer prompts or otherwise fill in the gaps. From this point, a pattern is followed in which the family speaks first and the therapist fills in.

Predicting relapses and/or coming difficulties can be extremely helpful. Of course, such procedures are time honored paradoxical procedures, but, in this instance, the therapist should encourage conversation rather than minimize it. First, ask clients to identify the conditions that will result in reappearance of the symptoms or other problems. Fill in where they are not clear enough to establish a profile that will be easy for them to recognize. Then ask the family to speculate on some difficulties they see coming, either because of changes in the environment or among themselves. Mentioning developmental difficulties that they may encounter based on the stages of the family life cycle can produce a helpful discussion.

Very helpful toward the end of the session is inquiry about what aspects of the therapy the clients found helpful and what they thought was unproductive. Some therapists use prepared feedback forms to collect this information throughout therapy as well as during the termination session.

Lastly, the therapist should explain what he or she gained as a result of working with the family Every couple or family is unique and teaches us something, perhaps even a great deal. Part of our job as therapists is to find out what that is and to nurture it. Revealing what we receive from therapy—besides the financial reward—establishes our personhood and may help clients avoid feeling guilty about ending therapy and possibly about ending a significant emotional relationship.

The end of the session presents the opportunity to remind clients that therapy is not the same as a graduation. They can return at any time. A follow-up session at some point in the future, say in three or four months can be beneficial. Increasingly common is the yearly family checkup as a preventive service for past clients. Mentioning these options along with the open door invitation is a positive way to punctuate the end of the session so clients can leave without awkwardness. Handshakes all around are usual. Hugs may be in order where the client signals and the therapist feels the client will benefit. Care should be taken to avoid even the mere suggestion that as a result of termination the therapist is open to a social relationship. The discipline is very clear that such relationships are not to be pursued with clients until at least two years after termination.

# ▶ 7

# Specialized Treatment Procedures

This chapter is more than a mere collection of procedures that do not fit neatly into the categories discussed in preceding chapters. All professionals confront unusual problems and issues in practice. Family therapists are no different and likewise need to know what to do in such circumstances. For example, what does a therapist do if a member of a client family is handicapped? Under what conditions is bibliotherapy appropriate, or when can letters be most helpful to clients? How can a family member who is important to the therapy or a particular session but lives far away become constructively involved? In these situations, a single procedure is not sufficient, and a style of therapy somewhat different from the usual is needed.

## VIOLENT RELATIONSHIPS AND NO-VIOLENCE CONTRACTS

In her highly acclaimed book *The Battered Woman*, Walker (1979) identified three distinct phases in violent relationships. She describes phase one as consisting of minor incidents of violence, which gradually escalate in seriousness and finally culminate in a phase two, or acute battering, incident. Phase two is generally no longer in duration than twenty-four hours and is followed by phase three, called the "honeymoon phase." This phase consists of a cessation of the violence and an expression of remorse on the part of the violent partner, who becomes gentle and attentive and promises not to be violent again. Walker's research suggests that as the cycle repeats, both phase one and phase three become shorter in duration; in other words, a violent relationship is likely to become more violent rather than less violent unless the cycle is interrupted.

Consequently, when violence or even the fear of violent reprisal is reported, it is important for the therapist to address it directly. It is generally valuable to develop a no-violence contract, to take effect immediately and to last until the next scheduled session. Although some therapists advocate getting an agreement in writing because doing so extracts another level of commitment, a verbal agreement is often sufficient.

To negotiate a no-violence contract, it is important to secure information that describes the evolution of the violence and its maintenance in the relationship. Walker's cycle of violence can be particularly helpful in guiding the information-gathering process. Determine what seems to provoke or establish conditions that can trigger the violent episodes. It can be very helpful to use the most recent incident as an example, since it will in all likelihood be representative of all the others. Have each partner describe, as specifically as possible, his or her behavior during each of the three phases. Once the specifics are identified, new options can be introduced to replace behaviors previously linked to violence. For instance, the husband who recognizes that each violent incident is preceded by a clenching of his jaws might be encouraged to use a time-out. The wife who comes to understand violence is preceded by changes in her own behavior (increased crying, for example) might use this perception to call a time-out.

Time-outs will not be very helpful, however, unless agreed-upon rules are attached to their use. For example, such a vaguely defined time-out as leaving the house may serve to escalate the incident if the partner left behind is jealous and wonders where the other is going and for how long. Useful time-out rules that can be negotiated during a session include no drug or alcohol use, agreed-upon people to be used as resources during the time-outs so as not to escalate a partner's jealousy, and means for communicating the amount of time needed on a specific occasion.

It is also valuable to have each spouse describe how the other can help curb behaviors identified as contributing to the violence. Developing this form of cooperation can help decrease the violent behavior, but the therapist must be sure to prohibit the violent spouse from holding the other responsible for his or her behavior. Individual responsibility and potential for self-control must be kept clearly in focus.

Finally, a no-violence contract needs to ensure physical safety of the spouse in danger of being physically hurt, who is usually, of course, the wife. Most communities have homes designated as safe houses, or shelters, for battered women. The use of this resource must be identified as a way the woman can not only care for herself but aid the relationship as well. If this resource is not used, the violence can escalate to a point where the wife is seriously injured and the husband faces criminal charges. While the husband may not experience the wife as caring for the relationship at the time she uses this resource, establishing the shelter's importance beforehand and again when the crisis has passed can help prevent disaster.

Beyond negotiating the initial contract, it is also important that the therapist spend time in future sessions discussing the role of violence in relationships. Weitzman and Dreen (1982) have identified issues around which most battering couples become locked into rigidly complementary relationships with little room for negotiation. These issues include the regulation of distance and intimacy, jealousy and loyalty, dependence and independence, rejection and unconditional acceptance, adequacy and inadequacy, and power and powerlessness. It seems that most problems of battering couples are anchored in attempts to resolve one or more of these issues, which will eventually have to be addressed in therapy. For instance, Hoffman (1976) has discussed how violence can become a perverse way of developing periodic closeness in a relationship, followed by predictable distancing. In this sense, distance in the relationship comes to be regulated by the violence. The goal of therapy in such a case becomes regulation of distance in the relationship without reliance on violence. If this goal is not met, a separation or other form of treatment, such as the many groups for batterers and the battered, may also be needed. Regardless, it is important to keep communicating to all involved that no one deserves the ill will and shame that emanate from interpersonal violence—not to mention its potential for lasting physical harm. Violence is an issue that needs ongoing therapeutic attention.

## STRUCTURING A THERAPEUTIC SEPARATION

The objective of separation is change—change in the direction of greater closeness or distance. Hopefully, old interactional patterns can be interrupted through creation of an environment that is more favorable to positive and productive change.

Granvold and Tarrant (1983) offer the following factors which may provide the rationale for a couple to implement a therapeutic separation:

1. The conflict has become so intense in the relationship that the aversiveness present limits the potential for any positive change. The therapist may have much more leverage for introducing change if the spouses have only brief contacts through the benefits of the structure provided by the negotiated elements of the separation.
2. The couple's relationship has a history of low reward-exchange (exchange of pleasures, satisfactions, and gratifications). A separation may increase the potential for raising the level of mutual positive exchange

between spouses and for experiencing greater freedom from a marriage that has become unrewarding.

3. One or both partners have a sense of being restricted or bound by the other or by the relationship, and may benefit from a respite.

4. The problems of sexual unhappiness or involvement of a third party may benefit from a separation that promotes experimentation without complete dissolution of the marriage. As with the other factors listed above, experimentation would need to be negotiated and agreed upon by both partners if it were to be a part of the separation.

5. A situational or midlife crisis may enhance the value of a structured separation. Separation may be better than divorce, with its long-range consequences. During a transition point in a person's life, deciding to separate can introduce a greater potential for objective decision making.

6. The separation can help stop one or both spouses from taking the other for granted and introduce greater objectivity into their perception of the marriage.

7. The separation can approximate life after an actual divorce. In this respect, a couple can try the separation as a test of what divorce might be like for them and of their individual potential for developing greater independent living skills and emotional independence.

In creating the structure through which spouses might more genuinely make an autonomous move toward or away from their relationship, and in assessing their individual and relationship needs more objectively, all can benefit from addressing certain issues (Barnard & Corrales, 1979). The spouses should incorporate these issues into their separation agreement, although the therapist should feel free to suggest them for their consideration.

1. Address the length of the separation to be negotiated, recognizing that six to twelve weeks is most often identified as reasonable. In fact, there is some evidence that separation longer than one month is counterproductive.

2. Divorce is not to be used as a threat during the separation, and it is usually best to agree not to consult attorneys during this time.

3. Frequency of contact and arrangements for dating each other should be addressed, if the spouses agree.

4. The issues of the children's residence and visitation should also be negotiated.

5. What to tell friends, children, and others about the separation can be discussed and agreed upon.

6. Involvement of the spouses with others, sexually or otherwise, during the separation should be addressed. Hopefully, the spouses will under-

stand the potential destructive effect of becoming involved with others during the separation.

7. The nature of sexual contact between the two spouses during the separation is another important point to address.
8. The role and goal of therapy during the separation should be agreed upon. How often? Individual or conjoint? Goals to be addressed?

These are examples of the kinds of questions that will need to be negotiated for the separation.

It is true that a structured separation can be used for devious purposes by one or both of the spouses, but the family therapist needs to acknowledge that it is *their* separation. The therapist is merely a consultant to their negotiations and, hopefully, one who can share some insights derived from past experience with the process.

## THERAPY WITH AN ADHD CHILD IN THE FAMILY

Attention deficit hyperactivity disorder (ADHD) is the most common behavioral disorder diagnosed in American children, believed to afflict as many as 3.5 million youngsters or 5 percent of those under the age of eighteen. Ritalin, the prescription drug of choice for ADHD, has increased in the rate of being prescribed by 390 percent in four years (Henkes, 1994). Among the various criteria used to identify this problem, three of the main hallmarks are extreme distractibility, an almost reckless impulsiveness, and in many cases, a knee-jiggling hyperactivity that makes sitting nearly impossible. It has been noted that this is a difficult diagnosis to make prior to age five because the distinguishing symptoms are difficult to distinguish from age-appropriate behaviors in normal active children (American Psychiatric Association, 1994). For this reason, clinicians are well advised to caution parents about too quickly diagnosing their preschool child as being ADHD. There are many checklists and other resources available to assist in diagnosing this problem, but all clinicians should be familiar with the diagnostic criteria for ADHD identified in the *Diagnostic & Statistical Manual of Mental Disorders* (American Psychiatric Association, 1994).

A child with ADHD can be taxing on the available resources of the marital/parental dyad, which can in turn impact the child. Both Bogus (1993) and Nathan (1992) have discussed the interactive effects of a child's disability and family functioning. These authors describe how the cycle of frustration, guilt, and blame observed among parents of these children can serve to exacerbate the child's problems/behaviors, which in turn exacerbate the parents experience, and so on. A study by Taylor-Jones (1997) suggests that the disorder can promote a constraining function on the marriage and creates divisions in even the healthiest relationships. Among other things, Taylor-Jones recommended that therapy with these families focus on increasing family cohesion, structure, and connectedness. She cautioned clinicians against being too quick to limit their therapeutic efforts to either the ADHD child or the parental unit exclusively. Instead, she encourages a multi-modal approach that encompasses the needs of the entire family. Some of Taylor-Jones's specific recommendations that clinicians are well advised to attend to are to separate inherent marital difficulties from those imposed by ADHD; to offer support for and to be sensitive of differences in couples' orientations to their child's problems; to recognize and accept spousal differences in personality, temperament, and parenting acumen; to promote education and awareness of the potential for triangulation; to advance awareness of parental expectations for the child and how this impacts the couple's sense of loss; to promote awareness of the potential for the grieving process being ongoing; to maintain awareness of the disorder's waxing and waning quality of its interaction with the couple's hopes and fears; to assist in encouraging the parents' involvement with available support networks for parents of ADHD children; to focus on the couple's and the child's strengths rather than being consumed with weaknesses; and to educate and assist the parents in creating and maintaining a structured environment and utilizing behavior management techniques.

Most of the experts on ADHD suggest that these children need the benefit of structure and consistency. Some parents will find it more natural and easy to provide these elements, while others may need the benefit of more therapeutic attention to these dimensions. Also, those parents who find it more consistent with their natural styles to provide structure and consistency may benefit from encouragement to also be supportive and affirming, while those parents who are more naturally supportive and affirming may need attention to the structure element of parenting. Clinicians are well advised to be attentive to the potential parental need for assistance in enhancing their knowledge of child-management techniques, such as token economy systems and other similar tools to enhance structure and consistency in the family.

As with any chronic problem, families can become consumed with and by ADHD. Recognizing this fact, the family therapist is encouraged to attend to all individuals in the family and their respective needs, desires, and perceptions of relationships. There is always the risk of other children in these families feeling "lost" and unimportant as a result of the parents' preoccupation with the child with ADHD or of the parents having their emotional resources diminished to the point of being unable to adequately attend to either their marital relationship or the needs of the other children. Promoting each family member to take the opportunity to express his or her perceptions cannot be emphasized enough. This process can be enhanced by employing the procedure of circular questioning described in Chapter 3. Instead of simply asking each person to share his or her perceptions, circular questioning broadens the potential for identifying who may be feeling neglected. For instance, circular questioning may be employed in one of the following ways to facilitate this process:

*Addressing the father:* "Can you tell me which of your kids feels most in need of receiving more attention from you and their mom? Please tell me which you believe may be feeling the biggest void, followed by which other one, and so on."

*Addressing the mother:* "How about you? How do your perceptions compare to those of your husband's in this regard?"

Circular questioning can quantitatively and qualitatively expand the family members' understanding of one another. With the potential for preoccupation that is observed in families with a child with ADHD, this effort to expand perceptions, understandings, and appreciations can be a key element in the therapeutic process.

## THERAPY WITH A HANDICAPPED FAMILY MEMBER

Families will often be seen wherein one member has a particular disease or anomaly that may not be the primary presenting problem but does constitute a chronic stressor that depletes the family's resources. Examples include Alzheimer's disease, cerebral palsy, mental retardation, diabetes, learning disabilities, cancer, heart disease, and brain disorders. Although therapy may help the family to organize and realign itself in ways that lessen the impact of these problems on their functioning, the wise therapist will also be alert to the many community resources that are developing to assist with these types of matters. For instance, many departments of social services have developed programs that make available respite care opportunities to those families with a disabled member. These services can provide families with assistance that allows them to take long-postponed vacations or periodic breaks. Also, many communities today have support groups available to members of families with someone who has a learning disability, cancer, retardation, heart disease, or other such condition. These groups, populated by others in similar circumstances, can provide valuable education and support that cannot be offered in the same way by family therapists. Perhaps Al-Anon and Alateen—the services provided to spouses and children of alcoholics, respectively—have best demonstrated over the years the value of community-based support groups to family members. This type of referral and subsequent involvement can often prove therapeutic by involving family members in the community outside of their obsession with themselves and their family. Certainly, most who have lived in a family with a member with a chronic disorder can understand how this sort of problem can exacerbate other problems of family living.

The availability of these types of services can usually be determined by contacting the local chamber of commerce or the director of the area social services department. Learning the name of a contact person in each of these groups to facilitate the referral process can prove to be the most therapeutic activity a family therapist can perform.

## THERAPY WITH A MENTALLY ILL FAMILY MEMBER

Occasionally, a family will be seen with a member who has been diagnosed as having one of the major affective disorders or schizophrenias and is being treated by a psychiatrist. In these situations, it becomes imperative to develop an understanding and, one hopes, a therapeutic alliance with the attending psychiatrist. To do otherwise, and particularly to do battle with the psychiatrist, can prove counterproductive to the family and the diagnosed family member, not to mention the energy and reputation of the family therapist. For example, psychiatrists have frequently used psychotropic medications to treat various mental conditions, and these have proven highly successful in resolving troublesome symptoms. The family therapist who is too quick to encourage a family member to stop taking prescribed medications "because your mental illness is only a reflection or metaphor for what's happening in this family" could run the risk of a territorial battle with the medical profession and possible lawsuits for malpractice or negligence. Just as a diagnosed mental illness can serve to mask major family problems as the family becomes consumed with the illness, a battle between therapist and psychiatrist could serve to distract the family and provide them with other "hiding places" that postpone or prevent the most effective treatment from being delivered.

While family therapy is partly rooted in work with schizophrenia and attempts to describe the mental illness as being reactive to, and a metaphor for, the family process, psychotropic medications are now widely accepted and successful in addressing many of the major distressing symptoms observed. For these reasons, the therapist is well advised to develop a cooperative relationship with the attending psychiatrist that will enhance the potential value of family therapy. Naturally, trying to convince psychiatrists of the potential negative ramifications of their medications is unlikely to foster this type of cooperative relationship. It is more important and valuable to enlist the psychiatrist as the valuable member of the treatment team that he or she can be. Without understanding the treatment plan and receiving input regarding progress and interactions observed in the family sessions, psychiatrists will not be nearly so able to respond to their patients in the most effective manner. With the benefit of a cooperative relationship, attending psychiatrists are typically very responsive to suggestions that are offered. As might be expected, while some are very aware of principles of family therapy, most psychiatrists are more keenly aware of medications as their special treatment modality; thus, cooperation of the family therapist and psychiatrist can promote a definite synergistic effect for the patient and family.

David Keith, a psychiatrist also well known for his family therapy skills, has noted the following regarding the use of lithium in the treatment of manic-depressive illness: "Lithium is helpful and should be used, but it does not define the parameters of the family struggle" (1980, p. 53). While Keith's article focuses on how medication, particularly lithium, may be viewed as the panacea to all of the tensions present in the family, there is also present the recognition of the value medications can have in facilitating family therapy and what is in the best interest of the diagnosed person.

An interesting and effective approach to working with families having a member experiencing schizophrenia has been developed by Anderson, Reiss, and Hogarty (1986). Along with medical supervision and drug therapy provided to the victim to moderate the symptoms of schizophrenia, the family is educated about the disease. This is an educational model intervention designed to change the family's interaction with the member. This is a second-order change that minimizes the influence of the disease and also has curative value. It is a good example of the benefits accruing to clients when marriage and family therapists work cooperatively with physicians.

## PARENTS PRESENT WITH SEXUALLY ABUSED CHILDREN

Clinicians are currently encountering this situation far more frequently than what has been the case in even the recent past. As society appears to have broken the taboo that inhibited people from disclosing this experience and enhanced methods of identification have developed, the incidence of reporting has increased. This should come as no surprise when we consider the contention of Peters, Wyatt, and Finkelhor (1986) that incidence of abuse for females is from 6 to 62 percent and 3 to 31 percent for males.

Although "survivor's groups" for sexually abused children are definitely becoming available on a more widespread basis, parents often find it difficult to find organized assistance, and they turn to therapists. In cases where the abuser was someone outside of the family context or someone in the extended family, both parents will frequently appear for the appointment. When the abuser was a parent, typically the other parent will appear in the clinician's office. It is not uncommon for these parents to be experiencing anxiety regarding how best to assist their abused child and resolve possible guilt over not being more vigilant and protective of the child. Naturally, this anxiety and/or guilt must be addressed immediately for their benefit as well as their child's. The child has likely been traumatized sufficiently already and now needs the benefit of a parental subsystem that is feeling confident and competent. To facilitate this effort, and assist the parents in helping their child, a psychoeducational approach is often most helpful. In this regard, the work of Finkelhor (1979) can provide a helpful model to share with the parents. Finkelhor describes four potential factors that influence the impact of sexual abuse on children: traumatic sexualization, betrayal, powerlessness, and stigmatization. This can be presented in the following fashion, recognizing some adaptations would be made depending on the particular needs of the parents and their child:

> I can certainly appreciate your distress over this situation and I'm encouraged by the fact that you are so concerned and motivated to help your child through this. Even though we know countless other children have gone on to live productively after having been similarly abused without it being detected and treated, you are right in being concerned for wanting the best for your child.
>
> Simply making your child aware of your concern, love, and desire to be available and supportive will be a major component of what will be helpful to your child. Beyond that, you can be helpful to your child by being sensitive to four elements that can influence the impact of the abuse on a child.
>
> One element relates to how the experience may shape your child's notions of sexuality in an inappropriate fashion. For instance, as a result of the experience, does your child believe this is what all adults want from him or her, or is this what one does to please adults? Or may your child now give distorted importance to a part of his or her anatomy or regard a body part as dirty? Or might your child, because of experiencing some pleasurable sensation during the abuse, attempt to provide a peer with this same experience?
>
> We do know that the younger the child, and the less understanding, the less sexualizing the abuse is likely to have been. To help your child in this area you can attend to him or her and discuss openly, at his or her level of understanding, any questions they might raise. If you observe any behaviors related to the sexual anatomy of your child, his or her peers, or yourselves, certainly pro-

vide information and corrective feedback, if it seems appropriate. For instance, if you observe your child touching his or her organs or those of his or her peers, provide the child information about a "right time and place" for this activity and, as it relates to peers, the need to respect others' privacy. It would be important for this information and/or corrective feedback to be offered in a calm and loving fashion, in spite of the fact that I'm sure you would be alarmed.

Another key element potentially influencing your child is the amount of betrayal he or she perceives in the experience. For instance, we know that the degree of betrayal experienced is proportional to the level of regard and trust the child had in the abuser. As an example, there is a greater sense of betrayal for that child abused by a grandpa than if an adult in the neighborhood was the abuser. We know that a child's resolution of feeling betrayed is best facilitated by experiencing support from parents and an absence of feeling condemned or held responsible. Related to this, it may not be surprising if you observe your child being somewhat more 'clinging' and maybe even more dependent and regress somewhat in his or her ability to care for himself or herself. Older children, rather than becoming more clinging, may have more tantrums and episodes of being angry. You can be helpful in this regard by being available, supportive, and loving of your child even before he or she manifests increased clinging or tantrum behavior. Reassure him or her of your availability and unchanged love and connection.

The third element has to do with the degree of powerlessness with which the child may have left the experience. Because your son or daughter's body space was invaded, to the extent he or she recognized this the child may feel disempowered. The fact that you, and others, have believed the child's report and responded supportively to him or her will be very helpful in counteracting the potency of this possible impact. If he or she feels disempowered, he or she may be somewhat more tentative than before and may seem to feel less competent and ascendant than previously. Some children may behave in a much less competent fashion and need your reassurance and encouragement to regain their previous level of confidence. Other children may react through extreme efforts to control and dominate others in order to regain a sense of competence. If this does happen, children can be helped by reassuring them of their ability to influence their environment without these necessary extremes and, in conjunction with this guidance, remind them of their parents' love for them.

The last element is that of stigmatization, or the extent the child connotes badness, shame, or guilt to himself or herself. Children who are younger and less able to understand may not experience this. Also, children whose parents do not respond in exaggerated ways and don't impute blame to the child are less likely to experience these feelings. Children who weren't encouraged or coerced to keep the abuse a secret also experience less stigmatization. Once again, as a parent, your ongoing support and reassurance of your son or daughter not being responsible and your continuing to show your child that he or she is every bit as lovable as ever will prove helpful in this regard.

For the purpose here, the foregoing was offered in an uninterrupted fashion. But that would be unusual; typically, the clinician would want to ensure the parents' understanding of each of the four elements. They would apply their understanding of each to their child as well as guess the impact of each on their child. How might their child react? How might they best provide reassurance, guidance, and support?

Just as abused children are frequently observed to be confused and bewildered, so too are their parents. Using a psychoeducational model and information such as that just described can reassure parents and provide them with an orientation to restore a sense of understanding and mastery in their roles as parents.

## THERAPY WITH COURT-REFERRED CLIENTS

Many therapists have mixed feelings about working with court-referred clients. Whether the court refers for chemical abuse evaluation, incest, or family violence treatment, such clients typically have many problems (for example, low income and minimal education) that are not amenable to therapy treatment alone. The problems that are amenable to treatment tend to be those in the category of more severe pathology. In addition, chronic offenders who are sentenced to treatment typically have had a good deal of experience with social workers, psychiatrists, psychologists, and other mental health professionals who are perceived as allies of the courts and not to be trusted. Family therapists may be seen as more threatening than individually oriented helping agents because the therapy will invade the offender's intimate interpersonal life and involve persons who may have a great deal of power. All of these issues compound the usual difficulties encountered in therapy.

The training that therapists receive is also a hindrance. Most clients seen by therapists in training are those who have sought out therapy. Consequently, the therapist has no need to exercise power other than that naturally produced through displays of competence and interpersonal skill. The therapist of a court-referred client, however, can exercise real coercive power. Since most therapists are not trained to use this power and are socialized not to coerce clients, the tools provided by the courts often are ignored.

In working with court-referred clients, clinicians have been most successful when they have clarified their role at the outset. Role clarification consists of first conferring with the county attorney or other legal officer to determine the therapist's responsibilities. Most often the referral of a perpetrator to therapy means that instead of jail, the perpetrator will attend sessions and cooperate. Referral to a family therapist implies that the perpetrator's family must do likewise. The only way to find out who must attend sessions and for how long is to ask the supervising officer.

The therapist's role must also be clarified with the clients in the initial session. With clients who are in trouble for the first time, it is helpful to state that the therapist is not a police officer or their parole officer. Commonly, reports of the client's progress will be asked for by the court, and the client should be made aware of that fact. Even so, the therapist can differentiate himself or herself from the authorities by stating that family therapy is designed to help the family function better, not to analyze the family for faults or to serve as an alternate punishment. When the client can differentiate between therapy and punishment, therapy can proceed as with a typical client family.

For the vast majority of court-referred clients, however, the therapist needs the power granted by the courts, and the client needs to know that he or she will remain in therapy and perhaps out of jail only as long as therapy progresses satisfactorily. The therapist does not attempt to establish difference from the authorities, but instead joins with them to work on improving family functioning. The client is told that regular attendance at sessions and cooperation by family members is expected. If sessions are missed or if the client refuses to cooperate, therapy will terminate and a report detailing the client's behavior will be sent to the supervising officer. After this discussion, therapy can begin with a discussion of what family therapy is about and a statement of the goals of family therapy before the actual treatment process commences.

## LETTERS TO CLIENTS AS THERAPY

There are times when use of letters can constitute a significant part of therapy. Letters are appropriate when used (1) to express appreciation and caring beyond the usual in-session means, (2) to send a message that the therapist wants to assure is "received," (3) to ensure a time of family togetherness with a focus on a particular topic, or (4) to share a forgotten assignment or the therapist's afterthoughts to a session.

In the busy schedule of most therapists there are times when apprecia-tion or caring for particular clients is not voiced. For instance, while doing an intake with a family, the therapist is reminded of another family that had a similar initial presentation and has now progressed considerably. That reminiscence also reminds the therapist that he or she has not provided them with the affirmation they are due. At this time an unexpected letter of affirmation to that family can prove very therapeutic as they collectively share the affirmation and acknowledgment of their accomplishments. Therapists can take their clients for granted as easily as family members can do with one another.

Putting a message in writing can also serve to accent its importance and improve the chances of its being received. For instance, there may be a time when the therapist desires to prescribe the symptom presented by the fam-ily, or the therapist may think that a prescription for a piece of particularly troublesome family interaction could benefit from being placed in writing and sent to the family with the directive that they all read it at least once and then discuss its implications before the next session.

Letters can also be used as a means of directly intervening with the fam-ily. For instance, the family may be told to expect a letter from the therapist and to be prepared to engage in what the letter requests. This creates an air of anticipation and excitement that better ensures completion of the assign-ment than does having the same message uttered at the end of a session. For example, a letter may be sent asking the family to identify a thirty-minute period within three days of its receipt to be used by each family member to identify two things they believe they could do to help the family situation. The outcome of this assignment can then be dealt with in the next session.

When the therapist simply forgets to make an assignment or issue a re-quest of the family, a letter can prove helpful. Rather than waiting for the next session, and possibly losing time, a short handwritten note can serve to cover for the oversight and better capitalize on the time available in session. This type of letter also seems to have the effect of providing the family with another means of feeling affirmed by the therapist, as they realize they are in the therapist's thoughts beyond the time they are together.

## BIBLIOTHERAPY

The use of reading material as part of the therapeutic process, or biblio-therapy, can be a valuable therapeutic adjunct that expands the impact of a single session. Using assigned reading material to prepare clients for a ses-sion or as a follow-up to what transpired in-session can significantly in-crease the efficacy and impact of therapy.

Areas of focus for which bibliotherapy is applicable include parent-child interactions, interpersonal communications, and family activities; it can also enhance cognitive understanding of phenomena such as depression. More recently, an impressive and helpful body of literature appropriate for use with the lay public has evolved around the issue of being the adult child of an alcoholic. These resources can help individuals and couples in the process of developing a new understanding of the behavior that has proven troublesome to them, and this understanding could provide a valuable springboard to effecting change. Books such as the following are particularly helpful in this regard: *It Will Never Happen to Me* (Black, 1981), *Children of Alcoholics* (Ackerman, 1983), *Guide to Recovery: A Book for Adult Children of Alcoholics* (Gravitz & Bowden, 1985), *Adult Children of Alcoholics* (Woititz, 1983), and *Another Chance* (Cruse, 1983, 1989).

An important issue in utilizing bibliotherapy is the makeup of the client for whom the reading is intended. Those clients who have had unpleasant school experiences and who do not read extensively should not be encouraged to read a large, hardcover book with small print. Such a book will probably not be read, and the client will feel embarrassed about returning for the next session and/or angry at the therapist's apparent lack of sensitivity to the client as an individual. The books identified above are all paperbacks, and they are very concrete and practical in style. Typically, a paperback book is less intimidating to the reader and is more likely to be read.

A frequently used bibliotherapeutic aid is *Single Parenting: A Practical Resource Guide* (Atlas, 1981). It is a paperback and—true to its title—practical in its orientation and the ideas provided. Although it is not a how-to book, Thurber's story *The Secret Life of Walter Mitty* (1967) is a good resource to illustrate how one can indulge in fantasies to the extent that life passes by without being recognized for what it is, or could be.

A derivative of this approach is that discussed by Hamburg (1983). He discusses how he frequently has couples read aloud, alternating reading time, *The Intimate Enemy: How to Fight Fair in Love and Marriage* (Bach & Wyden, 1970). He has found the experience to have immediate "face validity" to distressed couples, helping them to understand their damaging conflict styles. The book universalizes and normalizes their difficulties and introduces them to new options for conflict resolution. He maintains that reading aloud encourages them to engage in a cooperative endeavor that is not patronizing, but that directly addresses the concern they present while stimulating cooperative behavior.

As with other assignments, it is crucial for the therapist to check with the clients to determine their reaction to suggested reading. If the reading is suggested and then never followed up, the client may conclude that the therapist throws out ideas with little regard. Also, the greatest benefit from bibliotherapy stems from its integration into the therapy and the clients' lives, which will involve some discussion to promote application.

# ▶ 8

## Alternate Service Delivery Procedures

The decade of the 1980s brought to social service delivery systems a new way of working with families. Prior to that time, delivery systems conformed to societal notions of how things should be. Most practices were characterized by investigative, monitoring, and enforcement activities. In performing the duties associated with these activities, a negative image was attached to some professional groups that persists yet today.

The Adoption Assistance and Child Welfare Act (PL 96-272) of 1980 changed the goals and makeup of social service intervention. While primarily designed to avoid increasing numbers of out-of-home placements, this legislation also promoted better use of resources. The legislation was predicated on the concern that social service systems had become as reactive to family crises as the families themselves. Troubled families were perceived as underorganized and without proactive capabilities. So too were the social service systems.

When this legislation was introduced, there was concern that social service systems were too quick in removing children from their natural homes and placing them in alternative care. This approach sent a message to children and families. Did the greater society want families and children to believe they were not capable of resolving difficulties themselves and instead needed to be dependent on some outside force to resolve conflict? Under these circumstances, no wonder families seemed to develop a dependency on social service systems that in some instances lasted for generations.

The shift in orientation of delivering services to conflicted families was also based on the realization that the traditional delivery system expected families to organize and appear in a therapist's office at some designated future date. The system was "crazy-making" in nature. Combrinck-Graham stated:

> When it [family service] is available, and often it is not, it is fine for chil-dren, as long as the family is healthy enough to make it to regular appoint-ments at the therapists' offices. This has usually excluded the poor, the under-organized, and the beleaguered from treatment. (1988, p. 11)

Troubled families, particularly the poor, were believed to be in need of a service that acknowledged and responded to their intense needs con-founded by deficient organization and/or numbers of resources. Out of these concerns evolved a delivery system that attempted to bring supportive services to these families in contrast to a service that was intrusive and adversarial in nature. This new delivery system attempted to be more re-spectful of the family and focus on strengths and pockets of health that could be supported. The deficit detective game ended, and energy allocated to determining all the reasons a family could not make it on their own was directed to preserving and supporting families.

This shift came at about the same time a similar change occurred in the practice of medicine, particularly regarding surgery. The medical profession recognized that the frequency of surgery employed as a treatment was not justified. The concern focused on acknowledging surgery as a solution pos-sibly more traumatic than the problem being treated. Instead, medical prac-titioners emphasized strengthening the diseased system in more natural ways. Similarly, social service delivery systems came to recognize that the surgical removal of a child from the family was oftentimes more detrimental than it was helpful. In this respect, removal was iatrogenic; the treatment was more of a problem than the issue being addressed, and research docu-ments that removing a child can lessen the likelihood that problems will be solved. Even in cases where the parents request removal of their child, ac-commodating that request only convinces them of their incompetence and increases the likelihood of future dependency upon the system.

Rather than fragmenting the family even further than may already be the case, the family-based services orientation promotes accepting the fam-ily as the target of intervention to:

1. mobilize the system and bring the service to the family's environment where the difficulty is occurring;
2. approach the family members as allies to address their struggles, rather than perceiving them as pathological and consequently approaching from an adversarial posture;
3. stabilize the initial crisis that brought the family to the attention of help providers;

4. assess and identify pockets of strength and other resources to be activated and/or augmented to prevent future incidents; and

5. offer services to help family members evolve beyond their current level of capabilities or terminate services and leave the family to independently use its own newly discovered or rediscovered resources.

In response to the increasing acceptance of the family-based services orientation among marriage and family therapists who work in social service settings, this chapter identifies the stages typically observed in the delivery of in-home services as well as descriptions of specific interventions and procedural considerations that have proven helpful. Many of the ideas described elsewhere in this book can also be applied in the course of providing family-based services.

## STAGES IN THE DELIVERY OF FAMILY-BASED SERVICES

In delivering a therapeutic service, it is valuable to recognize recurring behaviors, or patterns, that seem to characterize the process. The following section discusses the stages frequently observed in the process of providing family-based services. While stages in any process may occur with some degree of regularity, there are always exceptions. Some families will not stay involved in any service delivery system long enough for the usual stages of treatment to unfold. Many families probably do not need to stay involved as long as we might think they should. Zuk (1981) suggests that some families only want their therapist to serve in the role he refers to as the celebrant. Zuk describes the celebrant as similar to the role society attributes to the priest or judge; someone who is socially sanctioned to acknowledge that something significant has happened and who serves to accentuate this for the participants prior to their going on about their business. Obviously, those families that are after someone to fulfill this role only will not stay engaged in a process long enough to observe all the stages about to be described. Also, some families may stay involved in one stage much longer than any of the others, and then move on to termination very quickly. With these variations acknowledged, the stages we have observed are (1) initiation; (2) crisis stabilization; (3) family therapy/reorganization and enhancement of the family's positive support network; and (4) termination.

### Initiation

As the Chinese characters for danger and opportunity are combined to portray the concept of crisis, in the initiation stage the therapist attempts to respond as quickly as possible to dissipate potential danger and capitalize on the opportunity to bring about change. We know that families are often the most malleable and available at times of crises. The rapidity of delivering family-based services attempts to act on this. Further, bringing the service to client families' homes is a way of acknowledging the frequency with which these families' current crises immobilize them and make it even less reasonable to expect them to come to us for help. For too long we have offered services to families and then branded members as being resistant when they do not appear in our offices for scheduled sessions. For many families in crises, it is simply not reasonable to expect them to organize themselves sufficiently to attend a session scheduled into the future. In fact, it is crazy for us to assume as much, with so many families bogged down and overwhelmed by other major issues such as ill health and poverty. The chaos and underorganization that may characterize members ordinarily becomes even more pronounced by their current crisis. Further, by bringing the service to the families' homes, many perceive an interest and commitment not previously observed in contacts with professionals.

During this initial stage, marriage and family therapists are advised to extend every effort to recruit as many family members as possible—hopefully, all of them for the initial sessions. The presence of each family member obviously increases the accuracy of the therapist's assessment. The National Resource Center on Family Based Services (1988) has determined a direct positive correlation exists between the number of family members attending the first session and both the success of treatment and rapidity of effecting positive change.

## Crisis Stabilization

Ordinarily, the therapist sees the crisis family as a result of a child being placed out of the home. The attendant sense of upheaval created by this change causes people to behave in reactive, impulsive ways that tend to foster escalation of destructive patterns. This initial stage is designed to counter these proclivities.

In the face of intense emotionality, there is value in the therapist's demonstrating competence and an ability to be active and directive. The escalating behaviors need to be short-circuited if family members are to experience an increase in their sense of hope for change. While the communication of caring is a valuable therapeutic aide, in these situations, demonstration of competence is essential. Family members need the assurance provided by someone who seems to know what he or she is doing. Their current difficulties point out that their own resources are not adequate. In this regard, the therapist is advised to define the family's situation as capable of being resolved and to communicate to the family that this is familiar territory. One way to do that is for the therapist to state that other families in similar situations have been helped, and the crisis is not as overwhelming as it probably seems. To create this perception the therapist might say:

> Obviously, you are hurt, frustrated, and angry about this. I know from past contacts with many families who have had similar struggles that until they get to the other side of the struggle and resolve things, there is a sense that nothing can be changed.

This type of statement demonstrates to the family that the therapist has worked on the problem before and that other families have been able to change. This message is powerful. It is designed to introduce the therapist's competence and to increase the family's level of hope. It provides a powerful antidote to the negativity and frustration that usually prevails. Also, it introduces the necessary conditions for increased optimism and hope.

While assessment occurs from the moment of first contact with the family, at this stage the therapist is exposed to information on how the family is organized and how it operates to create the problem and escalate a crisis. Some therapists may focus on alliances and coalitions and how various roles and rules are more predominant, while other therapists may be sensitive to determining what happens in this family that is different when such destructive behaviors are not in evidence. Each therapist's background and training will influence what and how he or she assesses, but the one dimension that is probably constant among all therapists focuses on the communication form and style displayed among family members.

Distressed families typically externalize their problems by blaming other family members, who respond in kind, and an escalating cycle of anger grows explosively. This cycle needs to be interrupted, and that can be accomplished when the therapist becomes triangled in the destructive communication. While the therapist wants to eventually produce a capacity for the family to engage in direct person-to-person communication, the current breakdown can benefit from the therapist's becoming triangled to the problematic relationships. For instance, let us assume mother and daughter are engaging in reciprocal blaming of one another that escalates to hitting and throwing objects at one another. The therapist may become a third point in their communication by stating, "Ruth, it is obvious that you're hurt and upset about this. Tell me, as clearly and directly as you can, what you would like to have different about this situation." After Ruth responds, the other is consulted to ensure the message was heard accurately, and then the therapist acts to secure a response: "Sue, before responding, what is it you just heard Ruth say? Please let me know this, and then I'd like to hear what you would like different about this situation, too." By becoming triangled in this fashion, the therapist reduces the participants' level of frustration by making sure they each are understood. Much of their frustration probably is fueled by not feeling heard and then responding out of that frustration.

Their communication has also probably been laden with references to the past and by broad generalizations such as "You never . . ." or "You always . . . ." The therapist can be helpful in providing initial stabilization by organizing their communication so that they begin to focus on solutions and resolution rather than continuing their struggles with reciprocal blaming. For instance, the therapist may say something such as "Sue, as you think about what you just heard from Ruth, what is one small thing you can do during the next twenty-four hours to make things improve somewhat?" In this statement, the therapist attempts to introduce solution talk in contrast to the problem talk that has predominated. Efforts are expended to have each person make a commitment to a small behavior change that may improve their circumstances. The change is to be made in the context of the next twenty-four hours, not some indefinite time in the future. Others in the family can prove helpful at this time as each, in turn, is requested to contribute his or her ideas on one small thing that each of the primary participants can do to immediately begin restoring stability. This effort increases the potential pool of solutions from which the participants can select, and further increases potential for change. These efforts are all geared toward increasing hope and replacing the problem talk with solution talk.

During this stage, the therapist can also use redefinition and positive connotation whenever possible. Use of these interventions can decrease family members' attempts to attribute only negative intentions to the others. For instance, a therapist might say:

> It is certainly evident that each of you is angry and frustrated, but I also sense the hurt in each of you. The hurt that is present tells me there is some caring and concern present here. We are most hurt only by those we care about and are concerned for. Let's work towards making that caring and concern more evident.

In stating, "Let's work toward . . . ," the therapist communicates a working with, or willingness to establish an alliance with the family, in contrast to doing something for them. Families who have frequent contact with social service staff commonly view themselves as victims of the system and wait for professionals to act upon them.

Another intervention consists of a therapist's helping to promote stabilization by reminding the family that its members have dealt with a particular crisis before. A therapist might say something such as "The last time things were almost this uncomfortable, what happened or what did you do that changed things?" By prefacing this question with, "The last time things were almost this bad . . . ," the therapist short-circuits the family's thoughts that things have "never been this bad before." In directing them to the past, for purposes of exploring past solutions, the therapist reminds them that they have coped before and somehow made it. This intervention is another way to increase their sense of hope, because they recall previous accomplishments at resolving tensions. Stimulating recollection of past resolutions can reactivate solutions otherwise forgotten in the midst of a crisis.

During this stage of working with families in crisis, the therapist can further help the family by not "overpathologizing." A family in crisis usually shows dysfunctional behaviors in a magnified fashion that is not at all a reflection of how things are. Recognizing that our perceptions influence our subsequent behaviors, the therapist should defend against viewing the family as sick. Pathologizing may prevent the therapist from attempting more creative interventions and could also prove destructive to the members as they sense the despair and hopelessness of the therapist. Accordingly, there is real value in using the team approach when working with families needing extensive support. If two or more therapists intervene, each can monitor the other and prevent pathologizing or losing sight of the family's strengths and other resources. One therapist alone may focus on solutions that reinforce the notion that the family is flawed and won't change.

## Family Therapy/Reorganization

The goals of this stage are to enhance and augment the accomplishments evolving from the first two stages. As the family is stabilized, it can be encouraged to establish new goals that help reorganize itself in a way to decrease the potential for future crises. For example, family rules that may have been overly constraining or otherwise unrealistic can be changed.

Those in crisis frequently function in the absence of a positive structure. Families appear to have given up and let life happen to them instead of engaging in positive and proactive behaviors. In this stage, the family develops new skills to introduce a semblance of positive order and activates old skills and resources.

Overlap among stages can be easily discerned at this point. For instance, recruiting or engaging family members in the first stage will be influenced by the therapist's orientation to families, as well as the efforts of members in the second stage.

A most important resource to mobilize in this stage is the family's positive support network. While the therapist conducts an assessment of the family, one would expect a determination of resources available in the family's extended network to occur. Knowing the family's available resources and the current difficulties the family is struggling with advances the therapist's ability to support the family by linking members with previously unrecognized community and/or extended network resources. Experiences in both rural and urban settings suggest the following typically available and frequently activated resources:

Friends and neighbors as respite care providers

Social service resources, such as county homemakers, emergency financial assistance, mental health services, respite care, parental aides, or parent education groups

AA/Al-Anon groups

Vocational rehabilitation services

School-related services

Churches

Kinship/Big Brother/Big Sister organizations

A frequent observation made of families in distress is that the members tend to seal themselves off from the outside, if for no other reason than to conceal their internal difficulties. As family members become more consumed with their strife, their internal obsession serves to blind them to resources available in their extended network. The activities of this stage are designed to remind them that they have resources accessible that can promote their own more independent and positive functioning without the assistance of outside help such as that provided by the therapist. In this regard, members are helped by the therapist to use resources that are a natural extension of their world.

## *Termination*

One goal of family-based services is to terminate as quickly as possible. Most delivery systems offering this service consider three to six months as the outer limits for intervention. Families in a position to accept or request further services can be referred on, or continued with, as the organization of the delivery system dictates.

Terminating as quickly as possible increases the likelihood of the family using its own resources in the future rather than feeling dependent upon an outside source when confronted with struggles. If the members do need help, the belief is that time-limited therapy will help the family feel more disposed to use the family-based service in a consultant role without fear of having to engage in a long course of therapy. For instance, if the service provided seems to continue on and on, the family may be hesitant in the future to merely consult with the therapist, out of concern that contact is tantamount to another long-term course of treatment, when all they want is a brief consultation.

Therapists should shift their role to that of consultant as soon as possible. The goal is to terminate services to the family before they feel compelled to do so themselves. If the family believes they have accomplished what they were interested in but perceive the therapist as continuing to push them to do more, they may terminate and thereby diminish the likelihood of ever seeking out the therapist for future consultation. In this regard, therapists will occasionally struggle with the temptation of responding to their own grandiose notions of what they believe the family wants or needs, rather than what the family is prepared for and interested in. A seductive trap to be avoided is wanting to keep the family engaged until they have successfully addressed the therapist's agenda. As a result, the family can end therapy only by becoming resistant. There is a temptation to believe that families want all that we have to offer. By listening to the family and respecting their beliefs and requests, the therapist can transit from the role of therapist to that of consultant and better ensure that the family will feel comfortable about future consultations.

Just as families in crisis can become so consumed by the immediacy of the current situation that they lose sight of past situations they have resolved, at the point of termination families can feel so relieved that they lose sight of what they have done to promote this resolution. For this reason, there is value in the therapist's using the termination stage to rub their noses in their success. The therapist should encourage each member to acknowledge what he or she has done and/or changed to promote resolution of his or her circumstance and to encourage each family member to communicate what he or she believes each other family member has done to advance change. This action serves to underscore what they have accomplished and, subsequently, what they can continue to do.

Highlighting the notion of the family being the source of change in contrast to the therapist or other agents outside of the family is very important to successful termination. During this stage, there is also value in encouraging the family to project themselves into the future and anticipate future struggles. As they identify possible future tension points, they are also encouraged to identify ways of addressing them. This is another way of encouraging them to engage in proactive behaviors, in contrast to their past reactive pattern of waiting until the crisis is upon them. Projecting into the future serves to burst whatever utopian notions they may be deluding themselves with and helps them accept that, while they will have struggles in the future, they are now prepared to accommodate and adapt in more productive ways.

## PROCEDURAL CONSIDERATIONS AND INTERVENTIONS

This section is designed to identify procedures and interventions that are helpful in the delivery of family-based services. The criterion used to select items for this section is the demonstration of the greatest impact upon the effectiveness of delivering home-based family services. While each delivery system has its own idiosyncratic ways of organizing and delivering this service, the following have been demonstrated to be valuable considerations in the implementation process. As suggested at the onset of this chapter, most other interventions described in this book can also be employed.

## The Seductiveness of the Utopian Syndrome

Therapists are well advised to defend against being seduced by the Utopian Syndrome—the belief they can and will bring about change in every family encountered so it becomes an optimally functioning family unit. Addressing the family's immediate crisis, stabilizing, and introducing some small changes that will help members become organized to operate in somewhat more productive ways need to be the immediate goals. Remembering that a primary driving force in the evolution of family-based services was to avoid the increasing numbers of adolescents being placed out of home, the immediate sense of crisis that may otherwise provoke the placement must be the initial target for intervention. Beyond this initial stabilization lies the concern for prompting change that addresses issues that provoked the crisis.

The immediate crisis is what the families are most concerned about resolving. They have no immediate interest in becoming a model family. Imagine how you would feel if you contracted with a carpenter to repair your broken door and he then went on to reshingle your house even though you were not dissatisfied with the old siding. Most family-based delivery systems, recognizing they are working on a time-limited basis of three to six months maximum involvement, intervene to stabilize and promote some small and hopefully significant changes that can have a snowball effect within the family. For those families who seem motivated to effect more radical change, referral to the traditional outpatient delivery system is suggested. In fact, research suggests that of those families who are responsive to family-based service, two-thirds seek further involvement with the human services delivery system (National Resource Center on Family Based Services, 1988).

## The Seductiveness of Pathologizing the Family

Therapists are wise to avoid pathologizing the family and instead to emphasize strengths and resources that can be activated to assist the family in achieving change. Unfortunately, much professional training focuses on pathology to the detriment of what constitutes health.

Figuring out what is wrong with a family is inviting and enticing, but it can paralyze the change process. This negative attributional set, often observed by family members at the point of first contact, can prove destructive to the therapist. The more pathological elements identified, the more over-whelmed and immobilized the therapist can become. Also, as the therapist views the family as pathological, to a greater degree the family members can become angry and distance themselves from treatment. Pathologizing is an activity pursued for the enjoyment of the therapist; it does not benefit the family for either the short or long term. To counter it, there is real value in having a cotherapist available to monitor the amount of pathologizing either explicit or implicit in the initial stage of therapy. Hopefully, cotherapists can keep each other aware of the strengths and pockets of health to be intensi-fied and activated in addressing the family's problems.

## Avoiding Isomorphic Reactivity and Fragmentation

Recognizing that most families encountered by family-based delivery sys-tems will be in the midst of a crisis, and typically with high risk that a child will be placed out of the home, therapists need to monitor the tendency to become equally reactive and fragmented. The principle of isomorphism sug-gests that neighboring and interacting systems can take on characteristics of the other.

Rather than being proactive and intentional, a family in crisis will often be reactive and fragmented in efforts to resolve the problem, thereby mak-ing a bad situation even worse. For instance, each contact with the family seems to suggest a new problem and introduces the realization of another helper being involved with this family, such as a school counselor, a minis-ter, or the like. The therapist can quickly come to feel as confused and over-whelmed as the family does.

An effective way to prevent reactivity is to introduce order and organi-zation. For instance, to respond to the new-problem-every-session phenom-enon, the therapist can establish a menu of treatment issues with the family. This menu is then used to determine the treatment focus by cataloging the struggles. Simultaneously, the therapist can help family members look for common trends that run through the problems identified. This organiza-tional shift provides an order that creates an increased sense of ability to manage and resolve difficulties, and efforts can begin to orchestrate the vari-ous helpers involved with the family in a synergy that gives their efforts greater effect than a simple addition of separate efforts. Not to provide this sort of order and organization can make the family's difficulties appear even more dramatic than they are, and all participants become reactive and frag-mented and work at odds.

## Keeping Initiative for Change with the Family

When a therapist is too quick to assume responsibility for resolution of the family's difficulties, an adversarial relationship with the family can result, and this is particularly true if the family presents with a child at immediate risk for out-of-home placement. If a therapist is quick to assume responsibility for resolving the conflict, the family may then work to sabotage those efforts because its members have an interest in the therapist's failing to be more successful than they have been. By the therapist's accepting responsibility, and even usurping family members, the message conveyed to the family is "We know better than you—you're incompetent!" Therapists should extend every effort to ally with the family to promote a symmetrical relationship characterized by equals working together on resolving difficulties. This concern can be expressed immediately by having a therapist use phrases at the outset of his or her involvement such as "Let's see what we can figure out together to try to improve things here. Obviously, you know a whole lot more about his circumstance than I do, and hopefully we can work on this together." The frequency of employing the plural *we* suggests to the family that this is what this work is all about—it is a joint, cooperative effort, and they are experts, too.

This value stance is reflected in the following statement from an article written to promote human service providers' efforts to keep children and families together:

> *Unfortunately much family involvement in treatment is towards teaching families how to function rather than supporting them so that they can function. Most therapists act as if they know more about other people's children than those who have lived with them all of their lives. (Combrinck-Graham, 1988, p. 11)*

## Timing Is Crucial

Years ago Virginia Satir referred to those times when families gather together at the end of the day or week as the arsenic effect. She used this phrase in reference to how pungent and aversive relationships can become as families reunite after their busy and harried times outside of the family. In this regard, evenings, weekends, and vacation periods are those times when there is increased risk for toxic and explosive episodes. Successful family-based delivery systems accept the fact that crises may occur outside of normal business hours. Frequently, therapists will need to go to the family home rather than expect the family to organize itself and come to the office.

Timing is also a key variable regarding accessibility to the family. We now know that families will make themselves most accessible and visible at times of crises. Just as we tend to bring guests for a visit into those parts of our homes that are neater and more tastefully appointed, we will encourage these same guests to enter our closets, junk drawers, basements, and attics should a crisis such as a fire develop. Remembering that all families strive to return to a level of equilibrium as quickly as possible, putting them on waiting lists or otherwise being unavailable at times of crisis increases the likelihood that we will miss the opportunity to assess and intervene when they are most willing to make changes resulting from assessment and intervention. A window of increased opportunity is available, and every effort should be expended to capitalize on it. Not surprisingly, a National Resource Center on Family Based Services (1988) study of eleven family-based agencies found that a delay in responding to family crises increased the risk that adolescents in these families would be placed out of the home.

## *Monitoring Grandiosity*

Not all families want everything available in a therapist's therapeutic arsenal. We can easily delude ourselves into believing that every family desires all we have to offer and that its members wish to move from their current level of functioning to one we might regard as optimal. Wise therapists accept that most families do not want all they have to provide and that a family's current resources and level of differentiation may require two or more generations of change in a progression toward more optimal levels of functioning. For instance, imagine a family where the mother, an incest victim, is from an alcoholic family and has married an alcoholic man. Reasonably, we may hypothesize that neither of these parents had a happy and successful adolescence. Consequently, we can assume that they are functioning with what is referred to as adolescent hangover. As these parents deal with their adolescent daughter, they create something akin to an adolescent gang war. All participants tend to be reactive and impulsive and to function with bad judgment. The teenage daughter acts out, which stimulates family-based services to intervene. Let us assume that involvement results in the mother's going to an incest survivor's group, and that an improved mother–daughter relationship occurs, but that the father continues with his drinking and distancing from the family.

While some changes have been introduced that are immediately helpful, longer-term changes may be observed in the next generation as the daughter is prompted to make a better selection of a mate than might have been the case otherwise. She may provide her children with better parenting. Overall, minimal changes were effected immediately that may not have equaled what the therapists hoped for, but these minimal changes reverberated through the future generations and promoted potential for even greater change.

In contrast, had the therapists kept pushing or insisting that the father go into treatment for his alcoholism, he might have resisted so dramatically that mother and daughter left the treatment and no changes occurred. In-home therapists have moderate goals for their families.

### Remembering the Past without Obsessing

While avoiding becoming preoccupied with the past, the therapist should not forget it! When confronted with a crisis, it seems to be reflective of human nature that we become so obsessed with the immediate situation that we lose sight of the fact that we have experienced similar, if not worse, encounters in the past. For this reason, in-home therapists can benefit from routinely asking family members about the last time they experienced a situation almost this bad. Qualifying the question with the word *almost* avoids the likelihood of a family member reporting that things have never been this bad before. The therapist communicates his or her sense of appreciating their circumstances because the question conveys their perception of the severity of the family's problems.

Having families recall the last time things were almost as bad can accomplish several important goals. Without saying so directly, the question reminds the family that its members dealt with the crisis before and survived. This, in itself can serve to modulate the current reactivity. Next, the therapist can determine what they did at that time—what resources, internal or external to the family, were activated, and which of these helped? Was an aunt or uncle's house used as a respite? Did dad intervene and assert himself as he usually will not? Was a spiritual leader or neighbor brought in to mediate? Did the mother and an adolescent child negotiate some type of temporary relationship agreement? By determining what was helpful in the past, the therapist can develop quickly a good understanding of the resources the family used previously and can perhaps activate once again.

Therapists must recognize that, left to its own devices in the midst of a crisis, the family's capacity to recall what was helpful in the past has been diminished. With most families in crisis, talk of the past is more problem talk and likely only to worsen situations through blame and increased acrimony. As suggested here, reference to the past is designed to promote solution talk by identifying helpful recollections.

### Avoiding Working Merely with Those Easily Available

It is tempting for the therapist to see only those family members who make themselves readily available. But this is usually not in the best interests of a positive therapeutic outcome. Seeing only those who are eager or willing provides them the experience of being heard as they ventilate. Such exercises do not necessarily ensure that things will improve, and the crisis may worsen because the family members doing the ventilating don't get their message to the right person.

Imagine meeting with a son and mother who express concern about dad's inattentiveness and rigid, unyielding ways. The therapist provides them a positive experience of being heard that serves to make the mother and son even more hurt and angry about dad's behavior in contrast. When they confront dad, he becomes suspicious and angry with his wife and son, as well as with the therapist. As things deteriorate in the family, the therapist's potential for having a positive impact on family members falters.

Research with family-based delivery systems (National Resource Center, 1988) documents that the sooner more family members are enlisted into the helping arena, the more likely they will stay involved in significant ways. Further, the greater the number of family members recruited and maintained in the treatment process, the greater the likelihood of successful outcome. While it may take more time and effort on the part of the therapist to recruit as many family members as possible, practice and research show the time is well invested.

Once the family is gathered to give the therapist as comprehensive an understanding of the family's operation as possible, other decisions can be made more easily. For instance, which subsystems would be best seen alone? Which subsystem may provide the greatest therapeutic leverage for effecting quick change?

## Assessing for Losses

In responding to families in crisis, it is important to acknowledge family members' perceptions and descriptions of the problem. Disavowing their views in the initial stage of involvement is likely to result in their believing that the therapist just doesn't understand and will probably discount almost everything they say. These feelings and conclusions compound what they are already feeling—misunderstood and discounted by some other family members.

After the therapist hears their initial description of the problem and begins to promote stabilization and change, there is value in routinely assessing for the presence of significant losses within the family. While not all problematic behavior is directly attributable to a death in a family, that event has been found to be overly represented among families where problems such as alcoholism or mental illness are found.

The death of a significant person can skew the family into a sense of being out of balance, and the result is problematic behavior. For instance, in the family in which mother has relied on her mother for emotional closeness, members may experience problems in the aftermath of grandma's death. When the mother turns to her husband seeking emotional closeness, he may feel inadequate and unprepared for this new demand. The mother then may turn to her eldest daughter, who is involved in the process of emotionally leaving the home and engaging in age-appropriate activities such as investing in relationships outside the family. When the daughter, like her father, does not respond, the mother begins to feel panicky and increases her efforts to derive this satisfaction from the daughter. This struggle between mother and daughter escalates until the daughter runs away, creating the presenting problem. Although initial efforts with this family must address the running-away behavior, the therapist must address the death that triggered the crisis.

If a significant loss has occurred, there is value in determining how the need for that role and function in the family can be eliminated or be addressed by someone else. For instance, in the foregoing example, the therapist may help the husband feel more comfortable with providing his wife the emotional closeness previously provided by the grandmother or help the mother link up with outside resources, such as a women's support group. As a result, the daughter may be able to engage in the age-appropriate task of leaving home without running away. In this case, identifying the family's loss guided the treatment plan. Failure to identify loss and to fulfill a human need assures continuance of uncontrollable behavior, regardless of the therapist's best efforts.

## *Monitoring Premature Side Taking with an Adolescent*

More often than not, among families seen in settings employing an in-home family-based delivery system, an adolescent is the identified patient. In these situations, some therapists find it easy to fall into the trap of quickly identifying with the adolescent and viewing the parents as intolerant, rigid, and unrealistic.

This posture by the therapist is likely to make things worse for the adolescent and decrease the potential therapeutic alliance with the parents. The parents may feel embarrassed and resentful toward the adolescent, with a predictable increase in their demands. They may end up thinking the therapist doesn't understand, whereas the adolescent perceives the therapist's support and further acts out against the parents. The irony of this situation is that the therapist—motivated by a concern for the adolescent—has probably made the family circumstances even worse. Therapists must remember that it is the parents who are most in command of whether or not the family will continue in therapy. Losing the parents can abruptly terminate any hope of helping the adolescent or family. As Zuk (1981) suggests, if side taking is going to occur in the initial stages of therapy, it is almost always advisable to side with the parents. While initially side taking with the parents, there is also value in balancing this with support for the adolescent in order not to promote escalation of the adolescent's acting out as a result of his or her feeling further misunderstood and even more powerless.

An important shift in most families is moving from the fault finding and blaming that is so prevalent to acceptance of everyone's being capable and responsible for changing the current circumstances. The therapist might say:

> It is apparent that each of you is currently feeling hurt and misun-
> derstood. For this reason, I am confident we can only secure change
> by having each of you make an effort to change things so that there
> is more cooperation and you can feel more respected and under-
> stood.

This type of statement begins to shift the family from obsessing on current feelings of hurt and blame to focusing on each member's responsibility for moving the family to a place where there is less hurt and more respect and cooperation. In doing so, the therapist takes sides, or joins, with all family members and establishes their collective involvement in the business of change.

## *Monitoring Your Own System*

Therapists engaged in family-based treatment, particularly those who work with families in acute distress, are well advised to continually attend to their own needs to prevent acute distress. Given the intensity of family-based treatment, it is all too easy to become as fragmented and reactive as the families served and to mirror their feelings of being overwhelmed. Obviously, as is the case with families, fragmentation, reactivity, and feelings of being overwhelmed are fertile ingredients for the fueling of pathological or dysfunctional behaviors. The dysfunctional behaviors can take a variety of forms.

Therapists who are not sensitive to their own needs are at increased risk of scapegoating the families served. Rather than recognizing that resistance is always a two-party phenomenon and examining what he or she is or is not doing that may make it difficult for the family to trust and invest in therapy with the therapist, the distressed therapist scapegoats the family by pointing a finger of blame and categorizing the family as resistant and not amenable to change. In so doing, the therapist denies his or her own dysfunction and distress by externalizing blame onto the family, further reducing the likelihood of that family being helped by anyone else in the future.

Another possible manifestation of the therapist's response to internal dysfunction is the situation in which a therapist competes for the affections of the family and/or supervisory staff. Obviously, this is not likely to prove helpful to the families served and may even make things worse by providing a poor model in integrity in relationships. Family-based treatment is a powerful mode of treatment, and therapists must take care of themselves. Therapists using an in-home treatment model should strive to maintain proactive and intentional behaviors that are characterized by clear and direct internal communication and reciprocal respect. If this is not monitored, the family's dysfunction is likely to be acted out within, or projected onto, other families.

## PRAGMATIC CONSIDERATIONS
## OF IN-HOME THERAPY

Minuchin has said the following about serving as a supervisor in a particular setting:

> *As a supervisor, I must enter into the world of organizational politics. I am supervising a director of a psychiatric hospital. To help the therapist change to work with families I must first help the hospital change the way they do intakes. We then realized that we had to change the way the hospital was constructed to arrange for space to interview families. We must create new social structures that are family therapy friendly. (Storm & Minuchin, 1993, p. 2)*

Minuchin is describing the pragmatic considerations necessary to successfully deliver family therapy services in a setting other than the traditional outpatient clinic setting. Obviously, delivering a service in the home of the clients can be dramatically different than either an outpatient or inpatient setting. As one experienced clinician recently said, "It's difficult to act professional in a nonprofessional place" (S. McGee-Wirth, personal communication, Sept. 11, 1997). There are numerous pragmatic considerations for the in-home therapist to successfully navigate. For instance, the neighbors dropping in during a session, the distracting TV in the living room, allergenic agents such as cats, and a therapist being alone in a remote setting in the midst of heightened affect. These and other circumstances and situations are ever present, and the in-home therapist must be prepared to adopt or accommodate to them.

To address these pragmatic situations, the clinician may need to be more structural in his or her behavior than is otherwise characteristic of them. For instance, in relation to the distracting television, the clinician may need to say something such as:

> What each of you has to say is important to me and I want to make sure I hear it all without distractions. I'd really like to ask you to turn the TV off. I'm interested in being as helpful as quickly as I possibly can and being without distractions will help that to happen.

The issue related to friends or neighbors dropping in is best handled ahead of time. For instance, during the first session the clinician is encouraged to say something such as the following:

On other occasions, while seeing people in their homes, the situation has arisen where a friend or neighbor has dropped in to visit during the session. I'm sure you can appreciate that this could prove very distracting. What can you do to insure this won't happen while we're together and how would you like to handle this situation should it occur?

Addressing this issue ahead of time can spare everyone involved a possible embarrassing moment, while also encouraging the family to engage in proactive behavior. Recognizing that anticipatory planning is a frequently observed problem among families in the clinical population, this may constitute the beginning of an intervention for the important issue of enhancing proactivity.

Just as discussing ahead of time the issue of someone dropping in unexpectedly can be valuable, there are other situations that can appropriately be addressed during this initial "ground rule" phase of the first session: the importance and value of not receiving phone calls during sessions and how this can be insured; if smoke is problematic to the clinician, asking them if smokers make the sacrifice of not smoking during the clinician's visits; discussion about whether or not they have concerns about the clinician and/or clinician's car being seen at their house and, if so, how they would like to address this issue; encouraging them to identify the location in their house where it would be best to meet in order to minimize distractions; and asking them what they would like or expect of you as far as being respectful to their living environment, such as removing your shoes at the door.

While considerations such as the above are unique to doing in-home therapy, there are certainly advantages as suggested earlier in this chapter. In-home therapy typically makes it far easier to involve members that otherwise may not come to a clinic. Also, particularly with families that are more underorganized, the chances are far better that they will be present for in-home sessions than is the case when they need to organize and mobilize to make a clinic appointment. The in-home therapist is also afforded the opportunity to observe the family in their more naturalistic environment. How does their home seem to be managed physically? What is present that is important to them and may be very revealing, such as collections? What members of the family have what space allocated to them and how do they manage their individual space?

Recognizing these inherent advantages, there is still need for the in-home therapist to probably possess more flexibility than is necessary for the clinic-bound clinician, and to be secure enough that they do not need all of the professional trappings of a clinic to provide a professional service.

# ▶ 9

## Procedures
## for Challenging
## Situations

The focus of this chapter is on procedures designed to address events and situations that complicate therapy. Thank goodness for complications. Without such events, psychotherapy would be a much less rich experience and clients could do just as well with a book or a tape recording as their therapist. To a large extent, managing these situations is what makes up the competence of the experienced clinician and the training of the beginning practitioner.

## PARENTS WILL NOT
## CONTROL CHILDREN IN SESSION

The opportunity to observe how parents interact with their children can prove invaluable to the therapist. As with most interactional behavior, though, eventually patterns already observed repeat themselves, and little, if any, new behavior is observed. This is one reason there is no sense in allowing disruptive and disturbing children to continue to act out during sessions. Another reason may be concern for the safety of the therapist's office and belongings and the personal safety of all. Further, assuming the parents are unable to productively control their children, not to do anything about the kids may simply add to the parents' sense of embarrassment and futility, and lead them to prematurely terminate therapy. For these reasons, it is important for the therapist to promote some new behaviors among parents with disruptive children.

One procedure to implement with disruptive children is to encourage the parents to intervene with them. This gives the therapist the chance to observe parenting styles and offer feedback on how the parents might improve or add to their management style and repertoire. Many times, parents are quite unaware of the variety of management strategies available, and they continue to relate to their children with an impoverished parental arsenal. In these cases, providing information can be tremendously helpful. For instance, teaching parents techniques such as time-out or the Premack principle, which consists of exchanging high-probability behavior for low-probability behavior, can be energizing. Perhaps the parents threaten the children with consequences they are highly unlikely to enforce. Such parents can benefit from learning how they create ongoing struggles for themselves. Regardless, it is important for the therapist to begin to intervene and model a sense of competency for the parents. Along with information, the therapist can also help the parents by encouraging them and providing them with support and reinforcement for their accomplishments.

At other times, the therapist may choose to model implementing child management techniques with the children. For instance, the therapist may use time-out with a child during the course of a session or utilize the Premack principle by informing the child that if she sits in a particular fashion for a designated length of time, she can then play with a particular toy for a few minutes. The therapist may also simply model the direct and clear communication of expectations to a child, unlike the equivocal and apologetic style typically employed by the parents. This modeling can be followed up by coaching the parents on how they might do the same, fully expecting children to test whether or not this new behavior of the parents is for real.

There are also times when children are disturbing to the therapist but not to parents. In these instances, a therapist should act anyway and not allow the children to violate the therapist's standards. This is particularly true when a therapist feels that his or her ability to attend to the family is impaired by child disruptiveness or is concerned about the safety of personal belongings in his or her office. Although the therapist may want to consider child-proofing the office, it is unreasonable to do this and then end up with unspoken resentments toward a family. In these cases, therapists should clearly identify their needs and expectations, avoiding, as much as possible, demeaning or condemning behavior. For instance, a possible request might be worded as follows: "Would you please have the children stop that? Perhaps I'm overly sensitive, but I find it very difficult to listen to you the way I want to with that happening," or "Would you keep the kids from doing that, please? Those [some personal belongings in the office] are very valuable to me and I don't want anything to happen to them." In all likelihood, if therapists model this type of self-affirmation and directness, it will prove helpful to most families, regardless of the presenting problem.

## CLIENT ABRUPTLY LEAVES SESSION

On occasions, a member of the client unit will abruptly leave a session amid an intense display of emotion. In view of the intensity of affect often observed among family members, the therapist should not be surprised by this occurrence. It often provides important new observational data about family organization and operation. Who appears to be most affected by the display of behavior? What do the remaining members say and do in response? Who are the ones activated to comfort, distract, or behave in some other way at this time? Answers to such questions can provide information to the therapist that may otherwise be unobtainable. This is also a time to determine what family members want to do to make their response differ from their predictable one and what prevents them from doing so.

The therapist may also want to use this situation to effect change by moderating a family's usual pattern of not allowing a member to be angry, for example, or by securing some individual space, or even by encouraging a family to react in a way that provides too much space and evidences an absence of responsiveness to the member's affect. The therapist can also negotiate with the remaining family members the decision of who will go to retrieve the departed family member or to comfort them, whatever is therapeutically dictated. Whether the member returns to that session or does not return until the next one, it is usually valuable to process with the entire family what provoked the display and the way the members responded.

During such a crisis, beginning therapists will often have to control their impulse to assume responsibility and do something that a family member could benefit from doing, such as going out to retrieve the departed member. To become overly responsible for the family in such an instance could deprive the family of a valuable learning experience.

## CLIENT SHOWS UP WITHOUT PARTNER

When one partner comes to a session without the other, a choice is presented to the therapist: whether to go ahead with the session with one partner or wait until the next time both can attend. Generally speaking, if a therapeutic alliance is established with the couple, an individual session can occur without damage, assuming certain precautions are taken. On the other hand, if it is doubtful that the alliance has been established with the couple, an individual session could prove difficult to the development of future couple-oriented work.

Assuming the couple appears to be engaged sufficiently, an individual session could be productive in addressing items such as family-of-origin issues for the partner present. This is particularly true when a client's history includes issues such as an alcoholic parent or physical or sexual abuse. The couple alliance can be protected by suggesting that the session with the spouse be tape-recorded, so that the absent spouse can listen to it prior to the next conjoint session, or by having the understanding that this session will be reviewed with the absent spouse at the next session. It is also valuable to relate to the spouse seen individually that the therapist preserves the prerogative of determining what needs to be shared with the absent spouse. Establishing this rule prior to beginning the session can serve to prevent the attending spouse from being tempted to develop an unfair alliance with the therapist by sharing a secret. If this rule is not clearly stated, a secret can put the therapist in a compromised position, with the spouse present thinking they have a different and special relationship. This can prove counterproductive to the future conjoint therapy. Surprisingly, stating this rule to the spouse present can also be reassuring, because of the realization that this is a therapist who will neither allow nor promote the debilitating effect of secrets.

If therapy has just been initiated, the therapist may tell the spouse present that an individual session at this stage of therapy may prove destructive, and reschedule another conjoint session. Typically, a statement by the therapist such as the following proves sufficient:

> It is my experience that to conduct an individual session at this stage of therapy proves counterproductive, and out of fairness to the two of you, I believe it is important for us to reschedule another appointment when both can be present. I realize this may not make sense to you at this time, but hopefully, you can trust me that I want to be of the most help possible, and this is the best way.

Naturally, this is a situation that can usually be avoided by clearly stating during the initial session that both partners, or all the family members, need to be present for any session to be conducted, unless the therapist indicates otherwise in advance.

The process of rescheduling another session may be irritating to the spouse present, but simultaneously, it will likely convey that the therapist is a professional who is consistent and strong. If a client has come from a chaotic and underorganized family of origin, the therapist's decision to reschedule can develop the client's sense of confidence, and it also allows the therapist to model how to say what he or she means and then follow through. In this respect, the struggle for determining the structure of the therapy, which the therapist should determine, is maintained, and it better ensures that the initiative or work to be done will be up to the clients.

The precautions that apply to a one-partner session also apply to therapy work with entire families. If the therapist has requested the entire family show up for a session, but one or more members are absent, the therapist is confronted by the same dilemma. To proceed without these members present may communicate that although the therapist values the entire family, the therapist's behavior communicates otherwise. Obviously, this message can be a dangerous one for the family to believe, as they begin to wonder about what else the therapist said but did not really mean.

## CLIENT ASKS FOR INDIVIDUAL SESSION

When one family member requests an individual session, the therapist needs to address that person's intentions, as well as the perceptions of the others. Even if it does not seem that there is anything that needs to be said in an individual session that could not be said in the couple/family context, it is important to adequately process these requests. If the request comes in the context of a couple/family session, the therapist can clarify the intent of the person making it and the perceptions and concerns of the others present. If the request seems appropriate and the others do not react adversely, the session can be conducted, but with the therapist's conditions identified ahead of time. Some valuable conditions that might be communicated include the following: the therapist has the prerogative of choosing what to bring into the couple/family work from the individual session; the session will be audiotaped so that others not present can review it before the next conjoint session; the person attending the individual session must assume responsibility for sharing the outcome with the others; and the therapist will clarify the focus and intent of the individual session with all members present, with no digression from this focus allowed.

In the case of a family member who disagrees with another member's desire for an individual session, the disagreement should be resolved between the clients, not by the therapist. The processing of this disagreement, and the apparent suspicion it reveals, can prove valuable to understanding the organization and operation of the clients' relationship. Frequently, this disagreement reflects other tensions and differences present in the relationship.

There may be times when the therapist believes individual sessions are indicated. For instance, assume a couple has been seen for several sessions and a sound therapeutic alliance is present. The couple informs the therapist that one of them will be out of town, or otherwise occupied, at the time of the next scheduled session, and the therapist determines it would be an appropriate time to address such issues as family-of-origin concerns with the one client available. Discussing the intent of the individual session and determining the reactions of each spouse prior to scheduling will usually avoid provoking suspiciousness or distance and can be used to continue to provoke positive change instead.

Choosing to amplify an alliance with a particular family member is another example of a time calling for an individual session. One instance might be when spouses present themselves for conjoint work out of primary concern for the husband's drinking. Assume the wife presents herself as angry, at wit's end, and obviously committed to therapy, while her husband is just as obviously exercising caution, concerned that the therapist will just be an extension of his wife who, according to his perception, has a combative nature. Considering that the wife appears invested in therapy, she will likely accept an individual session between the therapist and husband without feeling unduly threatened. After all, the husband is in therapy and this is what she has wanted for some time. The individual session can be used to relate to the husband in a nonaccusatory fashion, and to develop his sense of trust and belief in the therapist's competency and desire to provoke positive change, rather than a belief that the therapist is someone who needs to be defended against. In this regard, the individual session facilitates the conjoint work and, perhaps in this case, increases the ease of confronting the issue of the alcohol problem without activating too much resistance.

## CLIENTS DO NOT SHOW FOR SESSION

Most clinics and practitioners today have a rule specifying a cost for any session that the clients miss without giving prior notification. This rule is important to enforce, because it communicates to clients that the therapist's time is valuable, and models self-valuation to them. At times, at least a portion of the family problem is poor organization and low capacity for following through on decisions. Allowing families to be irresponsible about the time committed to them by the therapist cannot be condoned. Although all of us experience the unexpected, and even emergencies, at times, promoting irresponsibility on the part of clients is not productive. Perhaps the first missed appointment can be excused because of an emergency that arose, but to do so consistently is to invite more such incidents.

A call after the first missed appointment can serve to convey the therapist's concern about the clients' behavior. On very rare occasions, a second missed appointment might call for another direct statement of the therapist's concern about the family's interest and commitment to the therapeutic process. This phone call might sound something like this:

I'm calling about the appointment that was missed today. I realize there could be many reasons, but hopefully you can appreciate that my time is valuable and that I cannot afford these missed times. As explained to you in our first meeting, I will charge for missed appointments. I'm wondering what might be done to avoid this happening again in the future; would another scheduled time within my regular hours perhaps be helpful, or what ideas might you have?

At other times it may be more convenient for the therapist to send a letter instead, and in fact, many therapists have a form letter to send at these times. The letter would have essentially the same content as the sample phone conversation and, depending upon circumstances, convey to the family that the therapist will assume therapy is terminated unless informed differently by a specified deadline (within two weeks, for example).

Keeping in mind the fact that many families seen in clinical settings are underorganized, it is important that the therapist seize the missed appointment as an opportunity to communicate to the family the importance of structure/organization, that the therapist values self enough to adhere to established rules, and that behavior has consequences. As mentioned, although there are always exceptions to rules, the behavior of missing appointments must generally have certain consequences attached to it, or else the therapist may fall into the trap of unwittingly encouraging more irresponsible and underorganized behavior by the family.

## ENGAGING AN UNWILLING FAMILY MEMBER

Throughout the family therapy literature, the firm sense is that therapy with entire families is the treatment of choice. Consequently, therapists should not be afraid to refuse services to a part of a family or to postpone an interview appointment to a time all family members can be present. An alternative to refusing service, however, is to actively attempt to influence uncooperative family members.

In most cases, the client's spouse or other family members will come in for at least one session. Positive reframing and extensive joining might seduce the visitor into becoming a full-time participant. Typically, unavailable partners or unwilling family members will attend sessions if personally requested to by the therapist. Reframing their presence with the idea "Help me help your family" can be a useful tactic. Stanton, Todd, and Associates (1982) suggest that several home visits by the therapist may increase family member cooperation.

Another approach is to start therapy with one spouse or a partial group, but concentrate discussions on how to get the missing client(s) into therapy. The therapist should keep in mind that there may be powerful resistance on the part of all involved members to the participation of other family members. Many times, however, cooperating clients do not know how to phrase a request for their partner's participation or fear their ability to explain therapy to a child. In-session practice of how to explain therapy and the need to have the partner's cooperation in attending sessions are appropriate in these instances.

When these more straightforward approaches do not elicit participation, other strategies can be used. The therapist might call an unwilling spouse during a session with the other spouse and state, "I'm Dr. So-and-So and your wife [husband] is here in therapy. I'm hearing her [his] side of the story and I would like to hear yours. Can you join us next week?" If the answer is "No," the response might be: "You mean you'll leave changing the relationship up to her [him]? Well, I'll try to protect your interests, but I can't promise you all that much," or "As your wife [husband] changes, you may find yourself being depressed without knowing why." Along these same lines, the cooperating spouse can be coached to tease an unwilling partner by making comments at home that catch the interest of the unwilling partner such as "The therapist thought you'd feel that way," or "The therapist thinks I have too much of the power in our marriage," or "The therapist said that adolescents need to have more of a chance to make decisions on their own than we have been allowing you."

The most common result of the clinician's use of these procedures is whole-family participation in therapy. The pragmatics of professional practice dictate, however, that family therapists broaden their theory and skill base to include methods of working with individuals that produce whole-family changes.

## GEOGRAPHICALLY UNAVAILABLE CLIENTS

As society has become more mobile, the problem of absent family members has been encountered more frequently. From a family systems perspective, helping parts of families may end up being problematic, may take place at the expense of those not present, and may lead to long-range problems. For instance, imagine a family that is in treatment as a result of the father's alcoholism, and the therapist leaves out an adult child because of geographic unavailability. The absent member may become the family scapegoat and be assigned a troublesome role in the family that serves only to reproduce the family's basic structure with a different person occupying a certain role. Whereas the family used to be occupied with father's dysfunction, now they have changed to being consumed with the problem of the member absent from therapy.

Because of these concerns, it is important to ensure the involvement of all in the therapeutic process. Although great distances and responsibilities may exist that interfere with all being present for therapy (such as the family in therapy in Nebraska with one member going to college on the East Coast); they may be accommodated. For instance, each session can have an empty chair present to represent the absent member, with a tape recorder placed on it. At the end of each session, the family mails that audiotape to the absent member, with the understanding that the absent member will respond to the tape with a tape recording, phone call, or letter. The easy availability of video cameras, or camcorders, presents an option that is even richer than the audiotape. Another option is to use a speaker phone that allows a group to converse with a person on the other end of the line. This innovation presents an opportunity for immediate interaction not provided by making tapes but is more expensive. Many families have resolved this problem by sharing the expense among themselves, recognizing that all may reap the benefits. In the absence of these options, or in conjunction with them, letter writing can keep the absent member informed, with the added value that the writing responsibility is shared among the members present.

Regardless of the method employed to involve unavailable members, the availability of resources today and the value of using them seem to leave no excuse for not following through with one. Even disregarding the efficacy of this approach, it would still seem that family therapists are professionally responsible for making these options and the importance of taking advantage of them known to families.

## NEW INFORMATION REVEALED
## AT THE END OF A SESSION

Occasionally, a member of a family will regularly express a desire to communicate "something very important" when there are only a few minutes left in the session. Although from time to time, as a natural evolution of a particular session, someone may disclose something that requires a few extra minutes beyond the scheduled time, some clients attempt to do so with regularity. With these clients, it is amazing how unusual it is for the "important" information to be important. Most typically, end-of-session disclosure is an effort to postpone the termination of the session, to test the therapist's capacity for maintaining some control of the session, a means of attracting extra attention, or some combination of these factors.

When this practice seems to be a pattern, rather than a chance occasion, it is important that the therapist not inadvertently reinforce this behavior. A valuable way to address this problem is to say the following:

> From the urgency on your face [or "the way you are presenting this" or "from hearing what you've said so far"] it is apparent to me that this is too important to address in the few short minutes remaining. Out of fairness to you, I would far rather wait until our next session and address this at the outset, so we can give it proper attention.

After having said this, it is important to bring the issue back to attention at the start of the next session. Interestingly, however, the issue frequently turns out to have been discussed or resolved and no longer possesses the same degree of urgency suggested at the last meeting.

If the behavior continues, despite the therapist's efforts (and this is, indeed, a rare occurrence), the therapy can probably benefit from the therapist's confronting the issue more directly, stating something like:

> If I recall correctly, this is about the fifth or sixth time you've brought up an issue that seems to have some degree of urgency attached to it at the end of a session. Because of the time crunch we are confronted with in the last few minutes of a session, it proves distressing to me, and I'm assuming it must be equally uncomfortable for you. What do you believe accounts for this, and what can be done to avoid either one of us having to be uncomfortable like this in the future?

In all likelihood, ignoring such behavior will only promote more of it in the future. This continuation will likely culminate in mutual dislike between therapist and client and, in any case, it is unlikely to be a positive influence on therapy.

## ALCOHOLIC RELAPSE/SLIPS

Vaillant, in his book *The Natural History of Alcoholism* (1983), asserts that the recovering alcoholic's regression to drinking should come as no surprise to those working with this population. Recognizing this fact, clinicians are wise to be prepared for episodic regression and to know how to help clients move beyond it.

Recognizing the low self-esteem and prominence of shame (Fossum & Mason, 1986) experienced by the recovering population, particular efforts need to be expended to support its members at times of relapse. Without therapeutic assistance, recovering clients are at marked risk of resuming alcoholic drinking in an effort to mask the rekindled unpleasant emotions provoked by the relapse. Also, the hopes of family members may be dashed at these times and replaced by the old feelings of hopelessness, betrayal, and increased feelings of frustration and anger. This can result in their withdrawing from the recovering alcoholic and/or increasing their angry attacks. Either response can serve to intensify the alcoholic's sense of hopelessness and experience of shame and worthlessness.

Recognizing the foregoing a clinician needs to respond quickly to the slip by doing the following:

1. Gather the family and recovering alcoholic together as quickly as possible.
2. Acknowledge their shared feelings of frustration, shattered hopes, anger, and worthlessness.
3. Remind them of the magnitude and nature of the problem they are confronting (see "Externalizing Alcohol Problems" later in this chapter), and encourage them to maintain their collective resolve to "win this battle" by learning what they can from this relapse to prevent reoccurrences.
4. Ask them to collectively identify cues that were present and that they could have used to predict and avoid this incident.
5. Encourage each member to use his or her powers of recollection and collaborate with other family members to generate a list of cues (recognizing each person's individual efforts at recalling can serve to remind others of further examples).
6. Rather than allowing the relapse to become a problem that overwhelms them, encourage each member to embrace this occurrence as an opportunity to learn and advance their efforts to better ensure lasting change—the current situation is defined as an opportunity to identify more potential and lasting solutions rather than viewed as simply another problem, or possibly the "last straw."

At these times, it is also important to "rub their noses in their success." In contrast to becoming so immersed in their frustration and hopelessness that they are blinded to the successes they have secured, the clinician must raise their most recent accomplishments to a point of high visibility by reminding them of the days, weeks, or, perhaps, months of nondrinking behavior that have been achieved and what they have been able to accomplish during that period. All the members should be asked collectively to identify the progress each has made and how their relationships have been different as a result. Clinicians want to reactivate their sense of hope and renewed commitment to advancing the recovery of the alcoholic member and advancing their relationships and themselves as individuals.

Clinicians who are not prepared for these regressions are at risk to perceive a slip as a personal affront to their professional competence. If perceived in this fashion, the clinician may be quick to become judgmental and make a bad situation worse. At this time, and in this way, the clinician is no longer a catalyst for change but rather another problem for the recovering family to accommodate. Very few recovering individuals secure sobriety without at least one slip, and all involved need to be prepared for this possibility.

## CONNECTING CLIENTS WITH AA AND AL-ANON

Berenson (1976) has suggested that as many as 50 percent of the outpatient population have either a personal struggle with alcohol problems or with the alcohol-related problems of someone closely related to them. Alcoholics Anonymous for alcoholics and Al-Anon for those involved with an alcoholic have demonstrated themselves to be highly successful agents of change. In spite of this demonstrated effectiveness, it can still be difficult to encourage clients to connect with these groups.

A primary reason for the difficulty in securing a commitment and appropriate follow-up with this referral may stem from a characteristic frequently observed among those struggling with one or both of these issues. This characteristic is low self-esteem and the subsequent increase in uneasiness experienced in new social situations. Most of us can probably acknowledge some uneasiness when entering a group of strangers and understand how this uneasiness is even further intensified by feeling so powerless in being able to control or influence our own drug use or that of someone we love.

To counteract this uneasiness and enhance the likelihood of clients availing themselves of the benefit of AA and Al-Anon, clinicians can benefit from having available to them a male and female member of both AA and Al-Anon. These people can then be activated to attend initial AA or Al-Anon meetings with clients who may benefit. By having a male or female member of both groups available as resources, the clinician can allow the client to select the person he or she would feel most comfortable with. Typically, AA and Al-Anon members are readily available and willing to assist in this fashion because both programs are based on the Twelve Steps; the Twelfth Step encourages them to assist others in reaping the benefits of recovery. In this respect, the AA and Al-Anon members not only are helping those referred to them but are also enhancing their own recovery.

Once the clinician has identified the two members from AA and Al-Anon, he or she can say to clients the following in an effort to enhance their resolution of alcohol-related difficulties:

In therapy with several others in circumstances similar to yours, I have found that AA and Al-Anon have oftentimes proven very helpful. AA and Al-Anon offer support, understanding, and sound ideas on how to resolve the struggles you're identifying. I know some people who have been involved with AA and Al-Anon, and they are willing to meet with people such as yourself to explain how they have been helped and go with you to a few meetings so you can find out for yourself. I can assure you that meeting with them will not make your situation worse and, as I suggested, it has been helpful to many others I have worked with. If you're interested in pursuing this, I personally know both a male and female from AA/Al-Anon who would be interested in meeting with you. Assuming you're interested, what would your preference be?

Assuming clients are willing to pursue this option, and most are, the connection is then made between the client and AA/Al-Anon member. Involvement with AA and Al-Anon, helpful agents in and of themselves, can provide a tremendous synergistic boost to ongoing therapy. If the therapy involves an individual or marital/family group, the collective impact of therapy and AA/Al-Anon often supersedes what either could give the client if offered independently. Barnard (1990) states that AA or Al-Anon alone may miss treating the "invisible patient," the relationship of which the AA or Al-Anon member is a part. Similarly, relationship work in the absence of AA or Al-Anon involvement can often miss addressing issues specifically connected to the addiction. Unfortunately, for too long, those in the mental health and chemical dependency/AA treatment fields have failed to recognize the potential value to their clients of one another's expertise, and the clients have been the subsequent losers.

## NEGOTIATING A NO-DRINKING CONTRACT

The use of alcohol and other drugs by family members can prove to be a major problem that needs to be addressed before other changes can be effected. When a spouse presents a significant concern for the other spouse's drinking, the negotiation of a contract can prove helpful. The contract can be developed into a quid pro quo, or behavioral exchange, in which the one spouse relinquishes drinking behavior in exchange for a particular behavior desired from the other. The very act of negotiating this type of exchange can benefit the couple by demonstrating a new process of securing change in the relationship, without one of them feeling as though he or she has lost.

This process can be facilitated by asking the couple to generate a list of what they would like more of, or less of, from the other. Upon exchanging and examining each other's lists, they are then asked to attach a weighted value, based on their perspectives, to each of the listed items. For example, as the wife examines the list of wants/desires identified by the husband, she places a numeral, from one to ten, next to each item. It is understood that the numeral one placed next to an item means that it would be easy for her to do, requiring little effort and without giving her a sense of compromising herself too much, while ten would reflect a major effort or sense of compromising herself. Once the spouses have identified their respective values for each item on the other's list, they can then negotiate trade-offs by exchanging the weighted behaviors. The trade-off may consist of packages in which, for example, the wife agrees to exchange two behaviors she weighted at three and four in exchange for a behavior her husband weighted with a value of seven. There are times, however, when the spouse's drinking seems to be out of control to such a degree that this type of exchange is not effective in producing change.

In such a case, the therapist may choose to develop a different type of contract, one which is referred to as the Acid Test or the Marty Mann Test. Marty Mann, a recovering alcoholic herself, founded the National Council on Alcoholism over forty-five years ago. This contract is based upon the notion that loss of control, or the inability to limit one's drinking to reasonable amounts that do not result in harmful consequences or negative circumstances, is a substantial sign of addictive drug use. To develop this contract, the person is asked to identify how many drinks per day they could have before problems occurred. Once a number has been identified, the person is asked to stay within this self-prescribed limit for a period of four to six weeks. To make the contractual period much shorter than this could diminish the hoped-for effect. The rationale for this contract period is that during a period of four to six weeks, most humans will experience significant stressors in their lives, such that if they are problem drinkers, their inability to control their intake will be evidenced. If the person proves unable to control intake during this period, the problem drinker is asked to engage in an assessment of the problem drinking behavior with a person certified to conduct the assessment. During the period of time that the contract is in effect, the other spouse is asked to leave the monitoring of the drinking to the therapist and to the drinking spouse. The hope is that the non-drinking spouse can resolve some of the anxiety attached to the other's drinking and begin to detach emotionally from it, avoiding behaviors that otherwise might provoke the drinking spouse and serve as an excuse to drink.

Some will say that this type of contract cannot work, because the drinking spouse could just become more secretive about drinking and lie. While this is certainly true, the drinker will know whether or not he or she has been true to the contract, and this is another way of "spitting in the soup" of the drinker. The drinker can continue to eat his or her soup, but it probably will not be as tasty or gratifying as it was before. In this respect, the process is another way of making the drinking more costly or less satisfying to the problem drinker. Also, the non-drinking spouse may be overly reactive to the drinking behavior of the other spouse, as a result of having been raised in a home with an alcoholic parent and receiving physical or sexual abuse when the parent was intoxicated. Certainly, it is understandable, but the overly reactive spouse can probably benefit from realizing that although this reaction had survival value in his or her family of origin, this is a different relationship.

## EXTERNALIZING ALCOHOL PROBLEMS

White (1989) has written of helping clients to externalize the problem as a means of presenting a new perspective with enhanced opportunity for new solutions as an outcome. When couples or families are seen that have a major concern about a member's struggles with drugs, externalizing the problem can prove very liberating and helpful to everyone. Those involved with a drug-dependent person are frequently observed to develop an external orientation (Barnard, 1990) that results in their exonerating themselves of any complicity in the problem and chronically blaming and shaming the "problem" person. Simultaneously, the "problem" person is frequently observed to be struggling with chronic feelings of worthlessness and shame (Fossum and Mason, 1986). These feelings prompt him or her to become even more closed to feedback and defensive in response to the blaming from others.

Obviously, these are powerful ingredients that ensure more of the same behavior from all of those involved and make resolution even more remote. By changing the perception and subsequent meanings attached to the "problem" behavior, the potential of these people arriving at new solutions is enhanced.

By identifying the "crux of the problem" as being an addiction that has control of the "problem" person and those involved, the beginnings of formulating a helpful coalition are created to replace the adversarial postures previously occupied by family members. Instead of the family members blaming one another as the "problem," the addiction or "struggle with alcohol/drugs" becomes the focal point. The "problem" person is helped to recognize that he or she is feeding the "real problem," or the addiction, by continuing to ingest drugs, and the other family members are helped to recognize and accept that they feed the "real problem" by adding to the sense of shame for the "problem" person and failing to tend to their own life's progress.

To initiate this process, the clinician must establish the negative consequences of the continued drug use for all involved. For the "problem" person, the negative consequences are minimally the hurt, the feelings of betrayal, and the distancing and anger experienced and manifested by the others in the family. Obviously, beyond this there may be other harmful consequences in the form of work- or school-related problems and/or one's health, not to mention relationship difficulties outside of the family as well. The affected family members experience harmful consequences in the form of feeling angry, discounted, frustrated, incompetent, as well as their own work/school- and health-related problems secondary to being so obsessed with the "problem" person.

Once these harmful consequences are established, and using this as a framework for beginning to externalize the problem as an "enemy" they share in common, collaborative interpersonal relationships can be constructed to replace the current adversarial ones. To enhance the collaborative relationships the therapist says something such as:

> It certainly seems as though all of you have been knocked around by this "beast," and it has tricked you into continuing to cooperate with it being fed or maintained. Like you have just discovered, all of you are being hurt by this both individually and collectively. I'm wondering how you might be able to begin to turn this around and fight it together. For instance, Jack ["problem person"], how might you help your wife and other family members to keep from feeding the "beast" with their anger, feelings of being frustrated and overwhelmed, and not tending to their own business? Similarly, to you [those others reporting being affected by Jack's drug taking], I'm wondering how you might be able to begin to help Jack discontinue his feeding of the "beast." Who might have some ideas that will begin to put you folks back on top of this and promote you beginning to win this war?

With that stated, the therapist needs to be prepared to meet with some continued "yes, buts . . . ," if for no other reason than habit. The clinician who accepts the likelihood of this happening is better prepared to avoid feeling discounted and reacting defensively. Instead, the "yes, buts . . ." must be met with further efforts to underscore how the "beast" has control of them. For instance, in response to the foregoing, let us assume Jack's wife responds with something such as: "But I have been trying for four years to help him and all I get is more hurt, frustration, and resentment from him!" To this, the clinician who is concerned with utilizing this "yes, but" to further enhance the need for collaboration to defeat this "beast" might say:

Exactly! That is a perfect example of the power of the "beast" you are confronted with and evidence of the need for all of you to be working together against it, and to use this moment as a starting point for determining how you can pool all of your resources in a cooperative effort. In the absence of that, unfortunately, the "beast" may leave you folks bloodied and defeated in the streets as it has done with countless others. We all probably know of at least some others, if not many, who have been defeated by this "beast" in the past. If you are to win, there is no time to waste in pooling your resources and pulling together.

By changing the perception of the problem and defining it as a shared enemy and one that affects all involved, the potential for arriving at new and more creative solutions is enhanced. This also serves to begin to establish a sense of all being connected once again, if in no other way than having a shared enemy to now conquer together.

## SECRET DISCLOSED TO THERAPIST

When a client discloses an affair or some other secret, unknown to the other spouse, the therapist's access to this secret can prove very debilitating to the therapeutic process. The therapist who colludes with one spouse in maintaining this secret runs the risk of being effectively paralyzed in the context of conjoint therapy, and of promoting an artificial sense of specialness or grandiosity in the spouse colluded with. Either one of these developments can prove extremely counterproductive to therapy.

To prevent this from occurring, the therapist can clearly state the following ground rule to each of the spouses during intake:

Out of fairness to each of you, and myself, I will not accept phone calls between sessions, or in any other way be party to keeping secrets. It is my experience that secrets shared with the therapist do not prove helpful to therapy, and my potential for being helpful to you in the future becomes seriously impaired, if not destroyed, by allowing secrets to be shared with me. You need to understand that whatever information I become aware of, I will determine when and how it will be shared among all of us. Without this understanding, and an agreement regarding this issue, there is little sense in our proceeding.

Should this agreement not be kept, and information about an affair is communicated to the therapist, it is important to address it directly and stand by the intent of policy set initially, even to the point of terminating therapy. To do otherwise puts the therapist in the position of being so compromised that effectiveness is, at best, questionable.

For this reason, it is important to state the rule at the outset of therapy, so all involved are forewarned of the consequences of attempting to share secrets with the therapist. Hopefully, then, the therapist will not end up in the position of being declared unfair, unethical, and so on when termination is suggested for violating the rule. If the therapist does not make this point clear at the outset, the therapist becomes vulnerable to receiving a phone call between sessions and having a secret revealed, and then having to deal with the issue after the fact, which is always more difficult.

## CLIENT EXPRESSES SEXUAL ATTRACTION TOWARD THERAPIST

Perhaps it is less common among family therapists, because we tend to work with more than one client in the consulting room, but inevitably, over the course of a psychotherapeutic career, a therapist will have several clients reveal they are sexually attracted to him or her. While perhaps flattering, such a revelation can create an unpleasant situation, unless it is handled well. If dealt with poorly, the client's self-esteem may be affected, therapy may become sidetracked, the client may terminate, or a malpractice suit may result.

Handling the revelation effectively consists of a multistep procedure. Listening and communicating understanding of the client's feelings make up the first step. Some clients reveal their attraction in a sincere attempt to further therapy, while others disclose their feelings to distract and de-skill their therapist. Listening serves to help the therapist control reactions and to understand the client's motivation. After listening, a statement of a therapist's professional responsibility regarding sexual involvement with clients is needed to clarify that no sexual interaction will occur even though the therapist is flattered to be considered attractive. To aid the client in regaining composure after what amounts to rejection, it is helpful to explain that the therapeutic relationship often produces such feelings. Finally, the client's attention should be directed either toward him- or herself or toward changing existing intimate relationships.

When a client repeatedly expresses attraction, he or she should be told that this behavior is equivalent to sexual harassment. In such instances, a colleague should be consulted for supervision and support.

## CLIENT QUESTIONS THE THERAPIST'S
## LIFE EXPERIENCE

Occasionally, some clients will question the credibility of the therapist on the basis of insufficient or inadequate life experience. This concern may be voiced in the form of questioning the therapist's apparent youth, status as an unmarried person, or lack of experience in raising children. Whatever the concern, the therapist should keep in mind the value of not reacting defensively to the client's inquiry. Keep in mind that the inquiry may be a legitimate one, and not necessarily an expression of resistance. Regardless of the client's motivation, it is likely that a defensive reaction by the therapist will not benefit the therapeutic relationship. Instead, the therapist should use the following type of response:

> That is a reasonable question on your part. I believe you and I will get along fine, because I also tend to be a wary consumer and like to know something about the product I'm buying before I leap in. You are right in saying I'm [younger than you, have not raised children, etc.], but I do believe I can be of some assistance to you. My training has allowed me to acquire skills and knowledge designed to help you folks determine how you can develop more productive ways of operating, and I know I have been able to be helpful to others in situations similar to yours. In this same respect, I've worked with those who have eating disorders, those who were drug dependent, and those who were diagnosed as being psychotic. While I have never personally encountered any of these experiences, I do believe I have been able to be helpful to these folks.
>
> I'd like for you to let me know how you think I'm doing as we move along, and I feel comfortable that you'll do so, recognizing you had enough foresight and wisdom to ask this question. Clients often have questions such as this but never take the risk of asking. I appreciate your doing so. Also, keep in mind you are the employer here, and I the employee, so you can always terminate our contract should you decide.
>
> Might you have any other questions at this time? God only knows, I ask more than my fair share.

This type of response will generally serve to allay whatever anxieties the clients might have, while also serving to solidify the therapeutic alliance rather than distancing it, as a defensive reaction probably would. Specifically, it also reinforces the clients by praising them for asking questions instead of sitting and ruminating about some issue and not attending to the business at hand. Just as important as the content of the therapist's response is the style in which it is delivered. Interpreting the question as a personal assault on professionalism will probably lead to a style of delivery that will override the desired effect of the response. If the delivery style is haughty or defensive, it could at a minimum confuse the client, if not result in outright antagonism and escalation.

## CLIENT QUESTIONS THE VALUE OF THERAPY

There are times when clients question the value of their therapy. Their apprehension may be expressed directly to the therapist, or it may be offered by one spouse reporting what the other spouse has said between sessions. When a spouse reports what the other has said, it will frequently be offered in the fashion of tattling as if in attempt to secure a more favorable position with the therapist or to belittle the other spouse. When this situation occurs, it is often valuable to try to neutralize the process by saying something such as:

> I'm glad to hear that. I highly regard those clients who question and give consideration to their therapy. Frequently, I find they are the ones who benefit the most. In fact, I too have had some questions about what we have been doing, and perhaps this is a good time for us to discuss our concerns.

While this serves to neutralize the tattler it also can serve as a convenient catalyst to discussing the course and process of therapy, which might otherwise be ignored.

This is a valuable time to question the goals of therapy, and the progress that has occurred in reaching them. Frequently, new goals will emanate from these discussions, as will valuable feedback for the therapist regarding the impact of various interventions that have been initiated so far. This corrective feedback can be applied to therapy with future clients.

A primary concern for the family therapist at these times is to avoid retreating into a defensive posture and counterattacking. The therapist whose ego is too invested in the work of therapy and is too reliant upon client approval is particularly vulnerable. Obviously, this type of behavior will not prove productive for anyone involved.

## COUPLE CANNOT DECIDE WHETHER TO DIVORCE OR STAY MARRIED

Couples remain stuck over the decision of whether to divorce or remain married primarily because they do not have the information required to weigh one alternative over the other. Divorce and marriage seem equally onerous and equally attractive. Only with new information can spouses get off the fence, and it is the therapist's job to provide it. One procedure that helps illuminate the pros and cons of either course is termed *planning the divorce.* The objective of such planning is to stop thinking that has become nonproductive and to dump new information into the dyad. The procedure has several stages.

Even though spouses experience their relationship as being in jeopardy, the therapist must first reframe their hesitancy in making a decision. Words such as these are appropriate:

> Your decision to remain undecided is most definitely a stay-married decision because you are still married. A decision to get divorced is a difficult one that requires a good deal of information you do not currently have. In my experience, our best tack is to map out in detail how you would divorce, along with careful discussion of the possible ramifications and likely results. In no way am I suggesting that you should divorce, but I am asking you to stop being undecided for the moment, to thoroughly examine the alternative to staying married and thinking about divorce.

In the second step, the divorce process is described in detail so that both spouses understand the time lines and the legal procedures involved. An outline of the decisions required such as child custody, dividing assets, relations with in-laws, and the nature of the post-divorce relationship should be discussed. After outlining the decisions, each one should be negotiated with special emphasis on detailing the post-divorce relationship between the spouses. How often are they to be in contact? How can they keep in touch (letter or phone)? Do they want to be friends, acquaintances, lovers, enemies, or what? Is sex OK after divorce? Can they seek counsel from one another? Negotiating these decisions typically requires several sessions.

The simple result of planning the divorce is usually greater clarity about why divorce is an option rather than clarity about working for a more successful marriage. Also, once the partners have a clearer view of the gains and losses that might result from the divorce, motivation for working on the marriage tends to increase and treatment can proceed.

## ONE SPOUSE SECRETLY WISHES TO DIVORCE

When one spouse appears to be dragging his or her feet and resisting the flow and direction of therapy, it is possible that a desire for divorce is being masked. In these cases, the spouse may be in therapy for any of these types of reasons: to appease others and to show an effort at "trying" before divorcing; to attempt to develop a relationship between the spouse and the therapist so the leaving can be easier; or to alleviate a sense of guilt or the fear of the other spouse possibly committing suicide at the time of divorce.

The therapist can confront the resistance and foot dragging directly and appropriately declare the impotence that is present, for example:

> In view of the number of assignments that have not been attempted, or only half-heartedly so, and the missed appointments and ongoing disagreements we have, I am confused about your reported desire to improve this marriage. While I am willing to assume some responsibility and believe that perhaps my notion of how to help does not fit with your notions, we appear to be stuck and not moving at all in the direction you reported wanting to move. I mentioned at the outset of this therapy that I could be of assistance in certain ways but could not do the work for you. At this point, I believe either I cannot be of help to you because we do not fit, or I question the sincerity of your stated goal of wanting to improve the marriage, and wonder if you either want to continue the relationship as it has been or, perhaps, want out of it entirely. Is it possible you are not being entirely candid with either yourself or me?

After having made this declaration, it is important to process it and determine reactions. At these times, a therapist must attempt to monitor his or her own ego investment in the therapy, and avoid becoming stuck and subsequently defensive and/or attacking. Certainly, a defensive posture by the therapist will not prove facilitative to productive processing of this issue.

## EVERYONE SPEAKS AT ONCE

Many authors have commented on dealing with this difficulty. It is a problem most often seen in first sessions, usually as a result of family anxiety. The therapist can often help dispel this anxiety by taking care to direct statements and questions to specific family members, rather than to the entire group. If the family persists, a request from the therapist that all speak for themselves will usually suffice.

When these efforts do not produce the desired result, the therapist can safely assume that a homeostatic communication pattern is used by the family to prevent message sending and receiving, de-skill the therapist, or block the effects of therapy. In this situation, some small object (a pencil, magazine, hat, etc.) can be used as a symbol granting permission to speak, and a family member can speak only while holding the object. As with all rule making in therapy, the therapist needs to explain the rule and why it is being imposed. Such a statement might be:

> Hold it! I cannot hear or even think when everyone speaks at once. Let's try using this pencil to slow things down and agree to a rule. The rule is that the only person who can speak besides me is the one holding the pencil. Whenever I ask a family to follow this rule, we always go through a short time when it seems clumsy, but after a while it will be easy. My job will be to make sure the rule is kept. Now, John, you were saying . . . [gives the pencil to John].

When this procedure is first instituted, the family may react in several ways. Younger children are especially likely to break the rule. Parents, not the therapist, should restate the rule to the child, and the person who was interrupted should be directed by the parents (prompted by the therapist) to continue speaking. When an adult breaks the rule, the therapist should immediately intervene by saying, "Stop!" or some similar remark, along with a visible nonverbal gesture (raising arms) that stops all speaking. When all speaking has stopped, the rule should be restated, and the interrupted person encouraged to continue talking. Again, the therapist's role is to maintain the rule.

Another way for a family to react is for someone other than the speaker to complain that the pencil is being hogged or kept too long. In this instance, the rule must be kept, and the therapist can designate the family member who wants to speak to go next *after* the person holding the pencil has finished. When the speaker has voluntarily finished, the family member feeling slighted can be encouraged by the therapist to disclose any irritation and then continue with another message.

When all attempts to keep the rule fail, there is a final option. More experienced therapists correctly view such maneuvers by a family as a battle for structure, and they will refuse to engage. Not participating in a battle means simply leaving the session and telling the family that when they are ready to follow the rule they can ask the therapist to rejoin them. Such a contingency is best delivered without showing frustration or irritation with the family, although these feelings will most certainly be present. Some therapists are rather lenient about keeping the rule, but many choose to implement this last option very quickly once the rule has been described to the family and been broken. Allowing a family to win a battle for structure blocks therapy, leads the therapist to dislike a family, and contributes to therapist burnout.

The purpose of imposing and keeping the rule is to help the family members learn that they can allow each other to speak their minds without falling apart. The new rule imposed by the therapist also establishes a new norm of interaction that can enhance communication and mobilize family resources to better deal with problems.

## NO ONE SPEAKS

Silent, nondisclosing families and their members are among the most frustrating clients encountered in clinical practice. By definition, such a communication pattern may serve to repress interaction, feelings, and even thoughts. To cope with such clients, clinicians often join the family system by withdrawing and eventually terminating therapy.

To avoid this trap, careful diagnosis must determine whether silence is the result of not knowing what to do in therapy, of a skill deficit, or of maintaining homeostasis. Two good diagnostic indicators are whether the family has been in therapy before and whether its members are adequate in other areas of their lives. For example, if the occupational status of the adults requires adequate interpersonal skills or if the children have friends with whom they are close, an absence of family communication is most likely not due to lack of skill. In the case of the family that has not been in therapy, the family members may need to be instructed that therapy is the place where talking about their thoughts and feelings toward one another is expected. If the adults function at an overall low level, and the children appear to be isolated even from one another, the family members may simply not know how to express themselves. When communication skills are absent, the clinician can have the most impact on the family by teaching. When silence serves to maintain homeostasis, however, other tactics are best used.

Therapists often assume that the client family is colluding to maintain a family secret, and then design treatment to make the secret public. Unfortunately, although maintaining a secret may have initially stimulated the family's silence, long-term silence virtually requires family members to become numb; the effect is that, in fact they have nothing to say to each other or to the therapist.

Whether the family is hiding a secret or has become numb, the procedure to open communication is the same; initially, the therapist must do the talking for the family. The difficult question is: What should be said? In the initial interview, all families, even those described as low-disclosing, will divulge information about their lives and, certainly, information about the critical incidents bringing them into therapy. Through this information gathering, the therapist can come to an understanding of the different stresses and concerns experienced by each family member. This understanding is partly the product of the information about the family environment provided by the family, but it mostly depends on the mind of the therapist, who must imagine the feelings and thoughts of each family member based on their roles. For example, the spouse of an unfaithful partner typically feels betrayed, embarrassed, hurt, and angry; and the parent of a runaway child usually feels angry, embarrassed, guilty, manipulated, taken for granted, and confused. In silent families, these feelings are not communicated and often not even perceived, so it is up to the therapist to state them as if expressed by the family members themselves. The therapist's job in this situation is to break the family rule of silence by guessing what the feelings and thoughts of its members are and stating them openly.

An important part of this procedure is how the thoughts and feelings are delivered. If a child's thoughts and feelings are the focus, the therapist needs to take the role of that child, perhaps standing or kneeling beside the child while speaking for him or her. Adults can be dealt with in the same way. Speaking for any family member, however, calls for high-order empathy. A therapist must take on the role of the individual member spoken for, and, for the sake of credibility, try to make statements that accurately reflect that member's viewpoint, even if guessed at.

If the therapist's guesses are correct, a family member may feel understood and take the risky step of saying, "Yes, that's it!" The therapist's instruction immediately following is to say, "Go on, tell us more," and a few words will come stumbling out. If no one reacts to the member's statement and the interaction dies, the therapist can use the same empathic skill and the same creative guessing to understand other family members' reactions to the disclosure and state them openly.

Speaking for a family is a lot of work, but with prompting and encouragement, a therapist can, over a number of sessions, gradually fade out of the speaking role as the family members become more aware of their thoughts and feelings, and as they come to trust that disclosure will not result in crisis.

## CLIENT RAMBLES ON AND ON

Clients who talk on and on, seemingly ignorant of the rules of human interaction, often pose a real barrier to progress in therapy. Whether the family conspires to encourage the rambling or whether such behavior is engaged in out of habit or due to anxiety, it is the therapist's task to intervene. Most often, a comment that communicates the therapist's feelings of impatience or irritation will change the client's behavior, at least for one session. When other family members are also frustrated by parent or sibling rambling, they can be encouraged to express their own needs to talk and their feelings of not being able to. The situation in which nothing is effective is the most trying and leads therapists to have thoughts of letting the person talk until spent and to consider paradoxical strategies of encouraging more rambling. However, a different approach deserves mention because it works so well.

First, note that the chief difficulty of interacting with nonstop ramblers is how to gain the floor without awkwardly grabbing it. Most people are socialized not to interrupt or speak while someone else is talking; we hesitate to barge in on someone's discourse in order to avoid feeling guilty and insensitive. As therapists, we fear that we may model an awkward interruption for our clients. As a result of not knowing how to interrupt and gain the floor, we permit our clients to continue unchecked. However, a way to interrupt without awkwardness and then take the floor is available.

The procedure consists of two steps which are based on the idea that even the most stubborn of ramblers will stop to listen to a simple reflection or summary of their comments. Consequently, the first step consists of verbally or nonverbally capturing the client's attention and then summarizing the client's thoughts and feelings. Then, before the client has a chance to reply or continue talking, the therapist takes command of the floor by asking a question directed toward another family member or by directing the verbal interaction toward some other topic (the second step). For example, suppose a rambling client, distracted from describing a presenting problem, begins to talk about a pet. The therapist might interrupt with, "Let me see if I understand. You were puzzled by Misty's need to always be next to you." Then without pausing for even an instant, the therapist would direct a question to another family member, "John, how would you like the family to change?" The first step permits the therapist to interrupt smoothly and legitimately, and to communicate caring and understanding while setting the stage for the opportunity to take control of the conversation. The second step redirects the conversation to whatever the therapist chooses. Even though it may need to be implemented over and over again, this procedure helps manage rambling clients by making the therapist less hesitant to interrupt with a procedure of gaining the floor that is diplomatic and effective.

## FAMILY MEMBERS SPEAK FOR ONE ANOTHER

Commonly, the communication patterns of families seeking help prohibit some members from speaking for themselves. Those speaking for others believe that everything is fine, while, in reality, those being spoken for are angry and feel ignored or stifled. When such a problem exists, it is the therapist's job to enable all family members to speak for themselves.

Right from the start of therapy, it is most effective to institute the rule that people are to speak for no one but themselves. In the initial interview, for example, parents may try to speak for children or one spouse for another. When this occurs, the therapist needs to react immediately by saying something like, "I'd like Sally to say what she thinks," rather than permitting the violation to continue. If after several such interruptions, the family does not comply, the therapist must address the problem directly by saying:

> I'm having difficulty learning what Sally thinks about this, so I'd like her to explain it in her own way. I would also like us to agree on a general rule that no one speaks for anyone else unless I ask you to. That way, I think we will all learn more from each other.

Refusing to accommodate a family's usual communication pattern is a powerful, destabilizing tactic. It may take several sessions for those who have been silent to open up.

## CLIENTS SPEAK TO THERAPIST, NOT TO EACH OTHER

Because spouses have difficulty communicating and come to therapy to have their problems solved, more often than not they will direct remarks to the therapist rather than to their partner. This pattern of interaction is common in the initial session.

In later sessions, the therapist who retains the role of listener for both spouses becomes triangled between them. Instead of increasing disclosure, trust, and intimacy between the married partners, session time is spent developing these interpersonal dynamics between the therapist and each spouse. Although some relationship development between the therapist and the spouses is necessary, the emphasis of marital therapy should remain on the partners' relationship, and early in therapy, the partners need to be encouraged to speak to one another.

There are several ways to encourage clients to speak directly to one another without expressly telling them to do so. The first way is to phrase requests specifying who is to be spoken to, for example, "Tell John how you reacted to that"; a client will typically follow through and converse with their partner. If not, a nonverbal gesture pointing to their partner will usually spur compliance. If the client still addresses the therapist, the therapist should repeat the two strategies just mentioned, break eye contact with the spouse who is to speak, and look at the other spouse. If these maneuvers do not work, the therapist can explain that in marital therapy the partners should feel free to interact with one another, and that frequently they will be directed to do so.

A more direct approach to encouraging spouses to interact is to seat them directly facing one another. As with all requests, compliance is more likely if the spouses understand what they are to do and why. For example, if the therapist wants to get a sample of their communication style when discussing a negative issue, the following might be said:

I'd like to get an idea of how the two of you talk together on this issue. Turn your chairs around so you are directly facing one another. Marsha, I'd like you to bring up the topic as you usually would. . . .

Or, in another situation when the therapist wants to make sure the partners are attending to one another so that an important message gets through, the therapist can say the following:

I want to emphasize the importance of that message. Turn your chairs around to directly face each other. Now, say the same thing again.

More often than not, spouses need direction from the therapist to interact with one another in therapy, in part because our social custom is to include others in conversation. The participant responsible for changing this norm is the therapist.

## CLIENTS TAKE POTSHOTS AT EACH OTHER

Therapy is a new experience for many couples and families, and they tend to be on their best behavior initially. As anxiety decreases, however, their *at-home* interaction style will probably emerge. It usually includes put-downs, confrontations, and a host of other interpersonal attacks and defenses that fit under the rubric of verbal potshots. As a family becomes more comfortable in therapy, these behaviors tend to be displayed more frequently in session, if the therapist so permits.

Verbal potshots are short, quickly delivered, hit-and-run statements designed to gain some momentary interpersonal advantage. Name calling, using words such as *never* and *always* in an accusation, and assigning motive (for example, "You just want me to give in so you'll feel superior") are examples of potshots. If the therapist does not take steps to prevent such behavior and does not intervene when potshots first appear, then clients may rightly assume that they are to behave in session just as they do at home. If therapy is to be successful, however, clients must learn to behave differently.

As has been often stated in family therapy texts, the purpose of family therapy is to change the way a family system functions. By definition then, clinicians are successful in this task depending on whether they permit a family to maintain homeostasis. Therapy sessions are the time and place to initiate new behavior that changes homeostasis.

Stopping verbal potshots is a straightforward procedure consisting of two steps. The first consists of acting—doing something immediately to stop interaction. That means keeping careful tabs on what clients are saying and acting quickly once a potshot is delivered (before the receiver of the attack has a chance to respond). It also means that clinicians must overcome their socialization not to interrupt others' conversation. There is nothing wrong with barging into an interaction with the statement, "Hold it, that was a potshot, not allowed in here." Hand and arm waving, standing up, and stretching one's legs out are nonverbal ways to accomplish the same task of stopping or distracting clients from continuing to behave as they have in the past.

Once the interaction is stopped, the next task is to direct the attacker to restate feelings and thoughts in a constructive manner, and for the therapist to discuss why such behavior is harmful to the communication process. To elicit a restatement, the therapist might say, "You definitely have some strong feelings about . . . . What do you mean to say?" The client (a spouse, for example) will usually explain the message to the therapist. Through the use of empathy skills, the therapist can help change the message to one that is less accusative, more revealing, and helpful instead of harmful. Then, the therapist can direct the client to state the new message to the other spouse, along with the statement:

> What you said initially was a potshot. The next time you want to get back at her [him], say what you mean so the message can get through. Potshots only confuse issues, make her [him] defensive, and your message does not get through.

If the therapist gives consistent attention to stopping dysfunctional communication when it occurs in session, clients will learn to stop themselves at home, and the homeostatic patterns of communication they have developed over time can evolve into new and more functional patterns.

## CLARIFYING CLIENTS' UNCLEAR LABELS

Couples and families often come to therapy with difficulties that, in part, are the product of misused or undefined labels. Concepts such as independence, dependence, trust, temper, depression, and many more contribute to communication breakdowns among intimate relationship members.

Throughout therapy, one important task that belongs to the therapist is to help clients communicate with one another more clearly and avoid the traps created by undefined labels. As in any relationship, the therapeutic relationship develops along with the acceptance of certain concepts and labels used to describe important feeling states. Unless these labels are mutually understood by all participants in therapy, the prospect of change may be limited because the lexicon of communication symbols is not shared.

In the first session, especially, the therapist must listen very carefully to the labels clients use. For example, if a wife describes her desire for more independence in her marriage, she should be asked to clarify what the label *independence* means to her. When clients state they are afraid of their partners or another family member, their fears need to be defined. Another example involves the label *trust.* One spouse might say, "I just don't trust her anymore." Responding to these labels, the therapist might ask, "What do you mean by . . . ?"

When asked to clarify their labels, clients are often confused by the therapist's request for a definition. If clients comply and explain the label, communication is aided. When clients balk, remain confused at the request, or define the label with a circular definition (for example, to trust is to trust), either they do not know what they mean or they are maintaining a dysfunctional pattern in the family system. When clients do not know what they mean, conjoint session time or an individual session can be devoted to clarifying the label. When the undefined label plays an integral role in maintaining system dysfunction, the same steps can be taken, but clarification may not be forthcoming. The clinician may first need to change other aspects of family system operation so that a client can perceive an advantage to clarifying an important label.

## GUIDING CLIENT ATTENTION

An important aspect of any form of therapy is the management of client attention. Clients suffering from depression, for instance, focus attention on their feelings and thoughts of gloom, whereas clients with paranoid ideation focus attention on the behavior and intentions of others to confirm their suspicions of betrayal or harm. Similarly, family members tend to blame an identified patient (IP) for family problems and focus their attention on the IP in an attempt to confirm their beliefs.

In addition to other interventions, it is the therapist's job to direct clients' attention toward other aspects of their lives. Consequently, during the therapy session, a depressed client might be asked to list positive events experienced the previous day. The client who accomplished this task is led, at least for a short time not to dwell on or attend to negative thoughts and feelings. In another case, the clinician may attempt to reframe or relabel IP symptoms to reorient family attention away from the IP toward the family system itself. A good argument can be made that all types of effective therapy consist mainly of contriving ways to manage client attention from minute to minute.

Managing client attention requires that the therapist not only maintain an awareness of what clients are attending to from second to second, but also structure sessions so that clients can easily follow the topics of discussion. The therapist must provide an adequate transition between topics. For example, in the following interaction the therapist does not provide the needed transition:

*Therapist:* "John, you seemed to get uncomfortable when Alice became angry just a minute ago."

*John:* "Yeah, well, she gets pretty hot sometimes, and I'm never sure what she's going to do."

*Therapist:* "Sometimes you are afraid of her."

*John:* "Yeah."

*Therapist:* "How was anger expressed in your family?"

*John:* "What?"

In this interchange, the therapist may have had a very salient point to make, but the change in topic from John's feelings to his family of origin was so radical that John got lost. Had the therapist provided a transitional phrase connecting the two topics, John's attention probably would have been directed toward answering the question instead of asking what it was.

The same interaction, with a transition statement, would appear as follows:

*Therapist:* "John, you seemed to get uncomfortable when Alice became angry just a minute ago."

*John:* "Yeah, well, she gets pretty hot sometimes, and I'm never sure what she's going to do."

*Therapist:* "When she gets angry you get scared of her."

*John:* "Yeah."

*Therapist:* "I'd like to sidestep for a moment here to find out where you learned to react to anger that way. How was anger expressed in your family?"

While we may question the effectiveness of such a shift in topic, the inclusion of the transition statement by the therapist efficiently guides John's attention in a direction that the therapist believes will prove beneficial.

Providing transitions is also important at other times. The need for transition words between precession chitchat and the beginning of a session is familiar to all therapists. Moving from a homework report to the main session task also requires a transition. Clients also profit from transition statements (summaries) that tie sessions together. As a result of paying attention to transitions, therapy flows more smoothly, transactions between therapist and client are less ragged, and the potential for understanding is enhanced.

# ► 10

## Out-of-Session Work

Traditionally, psychotherapy was thought to occur when the therapist and client met for sessions. Little consideration was given to the 167 hours between weekly hour-long meetings in the consulting room. In contrast, family therapists suggest, encourage, cajole, recommend, and/or prescribe all sorts of exercises and action that their clients are to complete between sessions. Many family therapists would comfortably assert that what happens out-of-session is at least if not more significant than what occurs in it. Regardless of the emphasis placed on out-of-session work, family therapists commonly integrate out-of-session work with in-session treatment.

### WHAT TO CALL OUT-OF-SESSION WORK

An interesting issue related to therapy homework and assignments is what to call out-of-session work by clients, and what labels to use in describing such activities during therapy sessions. Among some clients, because of their miserable school experience, the mere mention of the words *homework* or *assignment* will prompt an immediate and negative reaction if that is what out-of-session work is called. Other clients ascribe a positive connotation to the same labels, because their school careers were more satisfying. In either case, by determining clients' school experience in the assessment phase of therapy, an appropriate label can be used. Possibly the best tactic, however, is not to use any label at all.

## ASSIGNING OUT-OF-SESSION WORK

There are several important factors that need to be kept in mind when considering what out-of-session work clients might do. The first is whether the clients are capable of carrying out the task. Nothing is gained, and perhaps much is lost, if spouses who cannot control their hostility in session are asked to go out on a date, for example, to refresh the romantic flavor of their relationship. Failure in this instance is likely, because if they could control their hostility, they would. The same reasoning applies to spouses who cannot share feelings with one another in session and are then asked to spend an hour at home discussing their feelings. If they knew how to do so, they would probably not be in therapy. Before couples like those just described are directed to perform such tasks, they need to have their emotional baggage cleared away, and they need to learn how to conduct themselves. Unless symptom exaggeration is the focus of therapy, clients benefit the most from out-of-session tasks that allow them to be successful. To be successful, they must have the requisite skills before undertaking the task.

A second factor involves explaining why out-of-session work is important and what the potential gains from a task might be. As with other procedures, clients are cooperative if they know why they are asked to perform some task. Likewise, homework needs a rationale. Many therapists, however, do not take time to carefully explain how the homework fits into an overall treatment plan, nor do they specify the goals of the task. One or two sentences about the rationale and the goals usually does not suffice. Rather, a clear and persuasive statement is needed.

A third factor is the degree of specificity needed. To reduce the chance of misunderstanding and resistance, clients should know exactly what they are to do. In assigning spouses to talk with one another about some aspect of their relationship, compliance will be more likely if the time and place for the talk is scheduled when the assignment is made. Explanations can get too detailed, of course, but in general, the fewer decisions clients are forced to make about an assignment, the more likely they are to complete it successfully.

## PROCESSING OUT-OF-SESSION WORK

In-session processing of out-of-session tasks is one of the most important aspects of therapy. As stated earlier, the goal is to extend the influence of the therapist and the session into the everyday life of a family. Through post-session assignments, the therapist can enhance control over the awareness of family members and influence the family system toward some intended change. By asking clients about their assignment, the therapist accomplishes several important objectives.

First, but not foremost, asking about out-of-session work is an easy way to begin a session. After a while, the usual opening remark, "Well, . . . ," gets very tiresome. A much more concrete executive remark is, "What happened this week with my recommendation that you spend less time talking about Sue's depression?" Notice that the assignment is restated, implying that the therapist recalls what occurred in the previous session. Post-session notes should always include assignments given to clients so that even with a very heavy caseload, a therapist can communicate more personal interest in clients' progress.

A second reason to ask about homework or assignments at the beginning of a session is to emphasize the importance of out-of-session work by making it the first order of business. In addition, dealing with assignments first ensures that they will not be forgotten. When a therapist assigns a task and then does not ask about it later on, the client can assume that the assignment was not important, and that perhaps other things the therapist says are not important. Spending session time on assignments is a way therapists can establish and maintain credibility.

A third reason is that since assignments often comprise the end of therapy sessions, beginning sessions with a report of the results of out-of-session work provides continuity between sessions and frames each session with related activities. Therapy sessions, like television programs or novels, need beginnings and endings. Although too much routine becomes boring, enough is needed for the therapist and clients to designate therapy as an event separate from other life activities; thus, the importance of framing sessions. Along with effective transitions from session to session comes a sense of direction and accomplishment especially needed in therapy.

The actual processing of homework can take several forms. When a therapist has clearly defined objectives for a particular session (for example, conduct a genogram), a short report by the clients may be all that is necessary. When a session is based on the outcome of an assignment (such as a no-drinking contract, symptom exaggerated), a more extended procedure is in order. Under these circumstances, the therapist will want to know what happened, how family members felt, and what they thought.

The first task in in-depth processing is to get a general overview of what happened. To obtain this information, the clients can be directed to give an overview without specifics. Once the therapist understands what happened in general, specific questions can be asked. In addition to supplying understanding, the questions should help to determine the assignment's outcome, that is, why it met its goals or failed. Clients' replies to the specific questions will create the content for the remainder of the session.

## CLIENTS NEGLECT OR
## CHANGE OUT-OF-SESSION WORK

When clients either change or fail to complete out-of-session work, it is usually the fault of the therapist. Too often, assignments are not adequately explained or too many tasks are assigned. Also, clients are often asked to complete tasks they cannot perform. For example, asking spouses who have never been verbally intimate to talk for ten minutes, three times in the next week, is sure to fail. The results may be anything from a no-show at the next session to three bitter arguments. Similarly, asking parents to be more consistent in keeping family rules for teenagers, when no rules existed before, is also sure to result in more problems. If clients understand exactly what to do, and if they know how to do it, they will usually comply.

When the assignment is understood and clients have the skills to carry it out but do not, or they change it, two interpretations are possible. One is that the relationship system may have been misread by the therapist, and the clients' fear of changing homeostasis may have prevented completing the task. Such "resistance" means the treatment plan may need reformulation. Perhaps the threat of change is too evident, and the pace of therapy needs slowing. It is more likely, however, that no real treatment plan existed, and the task was assigned out of habit or because it was the only task thought of on the spur of the moment. When a treatment plan has been constructed, and multiple instances of changed or incomplete homework occur, a switch from structural to paradoxical methods may be required.

More typically, however, clients who possess the skills to complete tasks but fail, do not understand why they are to do the task. Asking a couple or family to spend more time together, go out on a date, discuss a family rule, or whatever requires they agree that completing the task is important and that it is a relevant part of the treatment process. By implication then, each assignment should be prefaced with a persuasive statement that specifies why the task is being assigned. Also, therapists with heavy caseloads must develop a system that prevents them from forgetting what was assigned or neglecting to process the assignment in the following session. The importance of out-of-session work assignments is supported by actively persuading clients and following up on their work in the next session with time devoted to discussing the outcome.

## WRITTEN TASKS

Success in using written tasks out-of-session requires an understanding about the implicit nature of writing itself. Writing is usually a solitary activity, and although it can be highly emotional at the time of composition, it is primarily an intellectual activity. This means that writing tasks are best suited primarily for clients' intrapersonal issues that they are working on alone.

A second important consideration is the skills-based nature of writing. Tasks such as lists or single words jotted down on scrap paper are significantly different from the personal journal or letters written to parents who have passed away. Clients who have done poorly in school or who hold jobs requiring little writing may balk at such tasks. Care should be taken to match the level of writing skill demanded by the task with that possessed by the client.

A third consideration regarding writing pertains to the complexity of the task. Some writing tasks require a great deal of time because considerable thought is required while others need just a few moments. Asking your client to compose an entire letter to a parent may seem daunting enough to generate considerable foot dragging until you break the task into parts and work to complete each one separately.

As with all out-of-session work, maximizing the likelihood of success at writing tasks is most important. Clients have considerable control over this matter of course, but at least 70 percent of client success comes from wise decisions by a therapist who tailors the writing task to the client's talents and life situation. Where the task extends over multiple sessions, clarifying for the client the purpose of the writing again and again helps motivation. Another important motivator is the sure knowledge that the therapist will ask about the task in the next session and in every session. Listed below are a few ideas for out-of-session tasks that involve writing.

1. Journals—increasing self-awareness in general and in particular

   Daily journal

   Feeling journal

   Dream journal

   Violence journal

2. Baseline recording—indexing the occurrence of a particular behavior or pattern

3. Letters—composing confrontations and disclosing feelings to parents, perpetrators, or partners from a safe distance (sometimes mailed, sometimes not, sometimes burned)

4. Lists—specifying needs, goals, wants

Writing is commonly used in education to help students integrate new material and to augment other modes of learning. With a suitable client family, the same strategy can be implemented in therapy. For instance, toward the end of a session, five minutes can be devoted to having the clients describe in writing the significant portion of the session or summarize the success of the family to date in working on their concerns. This same procedure can work well as a task completed at home. Written comments from either in or out of the session can be shared or used as an aid to discussion.

## TASKS FOR COUPLES AND FAMILIES

When recommending out-of-session tasks to couples and families, a successful outcome is the highest priority. Asking partners who are alienated from one another to go out on a date or recommending that a family take a traveling vacation when members barely can speak to one another is risky. Success may follow, but failure will most likely result accompanied by reduced faith in the therapist's competence and loss of hope for a positive outcome to therapy. How can a therapist make good decisions on out-of-session tasks?

Start where the clients are. Until they can achieve success at unsupervised work on their problems, clients should reserve their problem discussions for therapy sessions. Once their communication skills and their investment in the family are equal to the demands of working at home, they can begin work on a small, inconsequential issue. If they experience success, they can proceed to a more difficult issue but not to their most difficult problems. These concerns should be dealt with in-session. If the most difficult problems can be addressed at home, what the family or couple needs is encouragement and support to continue those discussions so long as they are productive and caring. Therapists dream of such clients.

Be clear and specific about what the clients are to do out-of-session. Therapists often make task recommendations verbally toward the end of a session, but the best strategy is to write them out on paper as a physician writes out a prescription. Clients can reexamine the instructions between sessions. In fact, following clear instructions can be an empowering moment for a family or relationship on a downward spiral flowing from repeated interaction failures. It bears repeating that fuzzy recommendations delivered as an afterthought while clients are walking out the door are usually forgotten, dismissed, or changed to suit a personal agenda. Make sure each person in the system knows what they are to do.

Make the recommendation with processing during the next session in mind. For example, if a parent is asked to count the number of times a child complies with a request, the recording should be on paper with the date and perhaps the time stated with each occurrence. These detailed notes will prove more meaningful when the parent discusses each incident in the next session than a dim recollection of something that happened "several times." Similarly, when couples are asked to practice their communication skills at home, provide check-off feedback forms they can complete after each drill so that in the next session more meaningful analysis can be pursued. Each out-of-session task should be discussed in the following session, and including some mechanism with the task to assist that discussion can make the recommendation more meaningful.

# ► 11

## Referral and Consultation Procedures

Physicians, psychiatrists, attorneys, mediators, financial planners, school counselors, and social workers—just to name a few—make up the community of professionals who possess the skills and knowledge family therapists need to best serve their own clients. Each one can fill a particular client need. For instance, when couples choose to divorce, their therapist should be able to refer them to several attorneys or mediators not only who are competent and honest but who also can supply services within the clients' means. Similarly, when clients need psychiatric evaluation or a physical examination, effective and ethical family therapy requires referral. The same applies to other professionals as well. Successful family therapists strive to develop and maintain a network of professionals who refer to one another to the mutual benefit of all their clients.

### ACCEPTING REFERRALS

Palazzoli-Selvini and her colleagues have stated, "The problem of the referring person in family therapy is one of the most insidious and potentially compromising to the success of treatment" (1980, p. 3). Nevertheless, the importance of the referring person to therapy needs to be considered. Frequently, the referring person may have become intimately involved in the family's organization and operation and, without realizing it, could prove to be a significant homeostatic force in family therapy. Palazzoli-Selvini finds that child psychiatrists, pediatricians, and family physicians commonly become referring persons after treating one family member for a long time and becoming a friend of the family in the process. Consequently, it is important that the family therapist ascertain the role and function of the referring person in the family's life. Often, this can be expedited by inviting the referring person to the first session. During this session, prior involvements and a history can be secured, and, more importantly, future roles, expectations, and means of communicating can be established and agreed upon by all. The referring person's ongoing involvement with the family, assuming this is to be the case, can be identified as the family therapist delineates responsibility and goals for the person's involvement.

If the referring person is a therapist, it is valuable to determine from him or her and from the family what has been attempted that was helpful and what has proven ineffective. This can provide the family therapist valuable information about what might be most beneficial to attempt. Also, it is good to find out why the referral is being made now, as opposed to some other time. For example, is the referral being made out of frustration/anger with the family (another family therapist making the referral because of this family's apparent unwillingness to effect change that appears within their reach), or is the referring person suggesting that the family's needs appear too challenging (the neurologist who has been treating a brain-damaged family member or the child psychologist who has been doing play therapy with the child)? Whatever the reason for the referral, it must be considered in light of the referring person's prior involvement.

Once the referral has been made and therapy is progressing, sending the referring person a letter of thanks that also contains a brief note regarding the family's status is always valuable. Recognize that in some cases, the referring person may be more involved and need to be asked to rejoin therapy at future points, which would lessen the need for this type of letter.

## MAKING REFERRALS

The following constitute situations that can precipitate a referral to another therapist: (1) the therapist or family is relocating, (2) the client(s) presents a unique problem requiring that a different orientation or specialty become clinically involved, or (3) the therapist and/or family determine they are unable to negotiate a viable therapeutic contract.

When the therapist or family is relocating and together they determine there is value in continued therapeutic involvement, a referral will usually be provided by the therapist. If the therapist is relocating, the therapist can usually make a sound referral based upon firsthand knowledge of the colleague to whom the referral is being made. Even in this case there is real value in having at least one session, prior to the original therapist's departure in which the therapist and family meet with the new therapist. Such a meeting provides the opportunity to review prior involvements, goals, and what has and has not been helpful and to discuss future goals and directions. Referring in this fashion tends to diminish the clients' sense of having "something done to them" and their concern for what is being said about them outside of sessions.

When the family is relocating, therapists can either utilize their professional network to identify possible therapists in the family's new locale or help the family by identifying how they might go about locating a competent therapist. A professional network such as that provided by the American Association for Marriage and Family Therapy (AAMFT) or the American Family Therapy Association (AFTA) can be immensely helpful in this regard. Even if personal information is not available about therapists in the family's new locale, membership in organizations such as these can be one criterion they can be encouraged to use. They can also be encouraged to visit therapists who may be suggested to them by coworkers, neighbors, clergy, or the family doctor and determine if they feel comfortable with one of those recommended.

During the last session it is also wise to have clients sign a release-of-information form that authorizes release of clinical notes once they relocate. In fact, we have found it very helpful to use the last session or even two to have the family discuss the essence of what would be related to a new therapist. They are asked to address things such as goals achieved and those not yet achieved but hoped for, what they have done to achieve the goals, how the therapist was most helpful, and what they would have liked more or less of in the therapy. This procedure not only helps to facilitate the transition, but also provides another means of reinforcing the contents and results of their therapeutic process.

There are also those times when the family's problem is outside the professional interest or expertise of the therapist. An example might be the family with an adolescent who has an eating disorder. A therapist who has not been successful with this type of problem in the past and who knows of an area agency or therapist who specializes in treating eating disorders should refer. In fact, faced with this type of situation, we believe the therapist is ethically bound to make a referral.

Other types of specific presenting problems that therapists may regard as sufficiently outside their expertise to necessitate a referral are those families with an alcoholic, with a specific sexual dysfunction, with difficulty adapting to a particular disability such as mental retardation, or with a parent sexually abused as a child who is now the agent of reported incest. While cases such as those just cited may necessitate the referral of the entire family or couple to another therapist, there are some that may suggest a referral of an individual in the family to another therapist or group available in the area. A prime example might be a family in which one of the parents is the child of an alcoholic, and the therapist may want to refer that person to an area group for adult children of alcoholics. The learning that person secures from the group can then be incorporated into the family work.

Most therapists acknowledge that they cannot engage all families or couples productively. While there is always value for the therapist in employing introspection, consultation, and interaction with the family to solicit feedback for learning in this area, there will likely be some people with whom a therapist just does not "connect," and a referral will become necessary. In these cases therapists are ethically responsible for facilitating as effective a referral as can be carried out. Certainly, therapists also have a responsibility for being candid and ensuring that feelings such as anger and frustration are not displaced onto the family.

## INTRODUCING A NEW COTHERAPIST

A cotherapist may be introduced into the therapeutic system or may replace one who is leaving. In either case the occurrence can be a vital occasion as a source of new energy becomes available to the participants.

The transition from one cotherapist to the next is facilitated by having at least one session at which both are present. This provides the family and departing cotherapist an opportunity to say goodbye, and the new cotherapist can participate in the experience and use it as a means of sharing something important with the family prior to initiating the therapeutic relationship. This time can also be used to identify accomplishments for the new member and as an opportunity to underscore and/or revise the therapeutic contract. This change can in fact have a significant impact in revitalizing ongoing therapy.

There are also occasions when the therapist may choose to be joined by a cotherapist. This may be done for a multitude of reasons, such as becoming "stuck" with a family and wanting new input, facilitating the training/supervisory process of a therapist, or choosing as a matter of personal preference to function with a cotherapist when none has been previously available. During the first session with a cotherapist in attendance, there is value in encouraging the couple/family to share their perceptions of prior work. This provides the cotherapist with the opportunity of determining the clients" perceptions of therapy to that point; it also provides the family another occasion to reaffirm publicly what they have accomplished and to reshape the direction of therapy should their review suggest it. This is also a time for the cotherapist to identify his or her style of working and how they hope to be helpful, based upon what was learned from the clients.

During the get acquainted period it is important for the new cotherapist to monitor his or her own ego needs and not be offended should the family members appear to be more attentive to their "old" therapist. Certainly this phenomenon is not an unusual one, and it is best to expect this behavior initially. Should the new cotherapist attempt to overcompensate and push himself or herself on the family, the long-term effects could be detrimental. The original therapist can facilitate this transition by initially being attentive to the cotherapist, addressing him or her frequently, asking for his or her perceptions, and generally demonstrating respect and value. In most cases this will serve as a catalyst for the family's quick acceptance of a new cotherapist.

## INTRODUCING A CONSULTING PROFESSIONAL

There are times when the practicing family therapist may want to introduce a consultant to the therapeutic system. Examples are when (1) a family presents concern for a child's learning problems and a psychologist may be introduced to do an assessment, or (2) the family therapist may feel stuck and want to introduce a consultant for one or two sessions to provide new insight and impetus to the therapy. Naturally, these two reasons may also be combined, as when a family presents itself with a member who is concerned about having been sexually abused as a child, is possibly drug dependent, or has some other problem that would prompt the family therapist to introduce a consultant. With these cases the consultant might be present to provide new information and to be productively provocative to the therapeutic effort. The reasons for introducing a consultant, then, are to provide new information to the therapeutic system and/or a new component to the system that will result, one hopes, in dislodging barriers and promoting renewed movement.

When choosing the consultant, regardless of the reason, it is important for the therapist to decide if the family should be involved in this process. In those cases involving couples or families who present themselves as dependent and reactive in nature, or with those clients who seem only tenuously engaged in the therapeutic process, it seems best to empower them by involving them in making the decision about a consultant. Families that have been involved in therapy and are emotionally engaged and committed to the process need not become involved in the decision-making process. There is value, however, in informing them of the consultant's background and how his or her role is perceived in the treatment plan.

Attributing expert status to the consultant often increases the potential for effecting change. The fact that the consultant is from outside the therapeutic system also provides an increased potential for therapeutic leverage.

The family knows that an "outsider" will not have the same vested interests in something being said as those they might attribute to their regular therapist. This situation also puts the therapist in the unusual position of siding with the family against what the consultant might say; it therefore strengthens the therapeutic alliance while still making important new information available for therapy. For instance, the consultant who says to the family, "I do not see any evidence of you really wanting to change" can be disagreed with, and the ongoing therapist will be in a different position in relation to the family while still promoting their therapeutic movement. As the ongoing therapist disagrees with the now departed consultant, comments can be uttered such as the following:

> I do not agree with him and it irritates me that he did not show more understanding and concern for you folks. *(This tends to emphasize the understanding and concern of the ongoing therapist.)*

> I believe you demonstrate many characteristics reflective of a desire to change, but I wonder if they are evident only to us and may appear disguised to outsiders. *(This statement, among other things, serves to tighten the sense of the therapist and family being together in this.)*

> Do you have some ideas on how you might be disguising your desire to change? *(This question is designed to provoke the family to begin to explore their elements of change and how they may not be fully capitalizing on these resources.)*

Consultants can be a rich source of catalyzing changes with couples and families. Consultants may be experts on some particular issue (alcoholism, incest) or a colleague from down the hall who will provide a much needed new perspective. Regardless, consultation is a resource that is probably not used nearly as often as its value would merit.

# Risk Management Procedures

Risk management is a popular topic at professional conferences today and for good reason. Both practitioners and their clients agree that therapy should be safe and it should be provided in a competent manner. In the past, some sloppy practitioners depended on clients' reluctance to pursue grievances. Although suits by clients are still rare, the frequency is increasing as reflected in the rising cost of psychotherapy liability insurance.

Changes in the structure of the mental health system has also influenced practitioners' concern about risk management. Most states now license or certify marriage and family therapists. As a result, virtually every family therapist practices under either a state ethics code or that of the American Association for Marriage and Family Therapy or both. Third-party payers and practice liability companies also are interested in minimizing risk to their organizations created by the practice of family therapy. Risk management, always part of competent and successful practice, receives more attention today.

Risk-free therapy simply does not exist; we only can minimize and manage the risk we create. The unforeseen is always a threat, of course. Nonetheless, even this type of risk can be minimized by adhering to the common practice guidelines specified in ethics codes that make up the accumulated wisdom of the profession. Additionally, therapists can create an environment in their relations with clients that further reduces risk. The procedures described in this chapter are designed to help with these efforts. At the end of the chapter is the Ethics At-Risk Test, which can serve to alert practitioners to when they are engaging in high-risk behavior.

## DEALING WITH SUICIDE THREATS

Many families have been touched by suicide. Unfortunately, suicide has a dramatic ripple effect; the lives of relatives and friends are seriously damaged in the form of emotional and mental disturbances, failure in life tasks, and repetition of suicide and other forms of self-destructive behavior.

When suicide is mentioned as an option by someone in the family, it must be taken seriously and responded to by the therapist. The activation of the family becomes crucial at this point, and family members should be tapped as resources. For instance, after a family member has identified suicide as an option, other family members can be asked:

> You just heard Jack talk of killing himself as a way out of this. When pushed like he's feeling, it's not easy to think of all possible options. We all know suicide is a permanent solution to what is usually something that will subside or pass. In Jack's shoes, what do you believe are the other options available?

Once the family members offer what they believe to be the variety of options available, the person talking of suicide is asked to respond to the suggestions. Throughout this process the goal has a short-term focus of identifying not only possible options, but also ways in which each family member would be willing to help in this time of crisis. As with the options offered, the family member considering suicide is asked to identify what assistance offered by the family members he or she would like to receive.

Once this process is completed, a contract is negotiated for implementation between the current session and the next. The goal is to create a perception of the circumstances as manageable, to replace the suicidal person's notion of the world as out of control and no longer manageable. It is also important to recognize that a suicidal person's expression may be representative of other family members' thoughts and feelings as well. In this regard, it is valuable to ask each person about his or her experiences with suicidal thinking. Typically, at least one other person will acknowledge suicidal thoughts, and frequently most of the others will. The discovery of universality is often curative by itself. It also sets the tone for future treatment considerations regarding how the family members do not use one another as resources but instead hide and feel alone in despair.

Richman (1986) has identified a set of characteristics of a family in which suicide is a possibility. While most of these characteristics are reflective of dysfunctional families regardless of presenting problem, his observations and treatment ideas are worthy of attention. He identifies the following as characteristics of families with suicidal potential: an inability to accept necessary change, such as separations and mourning; role and interpersonal conflicts; disturbed family structure, such as fragility or prohibition of intimacy outside the family; one-sided intrafamilial relationships, such as scapegoating; affective difficulties, such as a one-sided pattern of aggression or a family depression; communication disturbances; and an intolerance for crises. The interested reader is referred to Richman's book for more detailed treatment considerations.

Many clinicians also ask potentially suicidal clients three questions: Have you attempted suicide before? If you were to kill yourself, how would you do it? Do you have the means (gun, pills, etc.) ready? Because these three questions are the best predictors of suicide, a positive answer to all three may suggest short-term hospitalization. Also, as a result of asking these questions, the therapist can feel more assured that precautions were taken to prevent a suicide.

In a published interview of psychotherapy pioneer Viktor Frankl, Short (1996) chronicles Frankl's experience gathered from working with over twelve thousand suicidal patients during his career from 1928 to 1938. During this period of time, Frankl was director of the Suicide Pavilion at the Steinhof, a psychiatric hospital in Vienna. As director, he was responsible for determining whether or not a patient was ready for discharge. From this ten-year experience, he developed a series of questions that allowed him to assess the condition of a person regarding suicidality in only five minutes.

Frankl describes how he would first ask the patient, "Do you know that it is time for your release?" Inevitably, the patient would respond, "Yes." Frankl would then ask, "What do we do next? Should we keep you here?" In almost every case, the patient would say, "No." He would then go on to ask, "Are you truly free from all intention to commit suicide?" With few exceptions, the patient would deny intent to suicide and ask to go home. Frankl said he had to make sure the patient was sincere and not dissimulating; so in order to better insure no suicidal intent on the part of the patient, he would immediately ask, "Why not suicide?" To this question, patients would respond in one of two ways. The first type of response would be for the patient to sink into his or her chair, unable to look Frankl in the eye or verbally respond. The patient might finally say in a toneless voice something such as "No, no, doctor. I am not going to commit suicide." Frankl believed a patient giving this type of response was still at risk of killing him- or herself. In contrast, the second type of response was when a patient would report that he or she was not at risk because of some kind of duty or responsibility (e.g., "I am needed at work" or "My religion forbids suicide" or "My family is counting on me"). Frankl came to believe this latter type of response indicated that a patient was safe to release from care. He believed these patients would not kill themselves because they had a "why" for living, and he believes that whoever has a "why" will in almost every situation find a "how."

Like Frankl, we also believe there is value in ascertaining whether or not an individual perceives a purpose for his or her continued existence. Perceived purpose is a powerful inoculation against suicide and must be remembered and assessed for when dealing with this population.

## FEELING SEXUALLY ATTRACTED TO A CLIENT

Sexual exploitation of clients by therapists has become a widely publicized concern in both the professional and lay literature. This form of abuse is one that all therapists should particularly avoid in view of the vulnerability typically experienced by clients in the therapist–client relationship. To underscore professional ethics codes, more and more states are legislating and imposing stiff criminal penalties for therapists who choose to exploit clients in this way.

Assuming behavior is generally preceded by a feeling state, therapists are wise to be responsive to feelings of sexual attraction to a client. While these feelings may not culminate in sexual acting out, they certainly could clutter professional objectivity and reduce the potential for being helpful.

Suppose, for instance, that a therapist is attracted to the wife of a couple being seen. If this physical attraction is not addressed, it may lead the therapist to become overly protective of the wife in session, or it may take another form and lead to an attack on her directly and/or to overly identify and side with her husband. Neither of these options will be therapeutic for either of the partners or their therapy. For this reason, it is important for the therapist to have supervision available at times so that attraction feelings can be professionally processed and monitored to ensure the best possible service for the clients.

Along with concern for the clients' welfare, feelings of sexual attraction to clients (particularly if they occur frequently) may be reflective of a dynamic within the therapist that constitutes a psychological blind spot, which will not be resolved without the benefit of supervision and/or therapy.

## FEELING BORED WITH A CASE/SESSION

Therapists, like other people, periodically experience boredom. For this reason, it is important for therapists to be certain that what they interpret as boredom with a case is not emanating from their own world and being displaced onto clients. Assuming there is no reason to believe that what is being experienced as boredom is primarily the therapist's responsibility, there can be value in using these feelings therapeutically. Therapists may use these sensations to ask themselves:

> How have we become stalemated? In what way has our therapeutic system become like their relationship? In what ways am I, or are we, playing it safe and consequently just experiencing sameness with little potential for initiating change? What may I be perceiving in

their relationship that is uncomfortable for me in my own life and subsequently defending against by avoiding a therapeutic confrontation? What needs to be confronted/addressed that I am missing?

These questions can be best addressed with the assistance of a colleague or supervisor facilitating the exploration with the therapist.

Carl Whitaker and some of the Italian family therapists, such as Andolfi, have discussed the utilization of boredom as a therapeutic ally. They suggest presenting the boredom to the couple or family and encouraging them to take initiative to reengage the therapist. This tactic is based upon the supposition that the couple or family feels some sense of allegiance and/or commitment to the therapist and the therapeutic process. Without a sense of attachment, it is reasonable to assume the family would interpret this suggestion from the therapist as rejection or apathy and choose to terminate therapy. When there is a question about the intensity of their commitment, it is advisable to assume some potential ownership in describing the boredom, for instance:

> I've been thinking about our recent session(s). As I have reflected on it, I don't know if it's me or what, but it's been difficult for me to be as attentive as I like to be. It's as though what is being addressed doesn't seem to be vital or have much importance; it's as though we're besieged with boredom. Like I say, perhaps it's just me, I'm not certain and that's the reason I'd like to discuss this with you now. What are your thoughts on this?

At other times, when there is some certainty regarding the therapeutic alliance and the nature of the relationship, it may suffice to simply say, "I find this boring and difficult to maintain an interest. For me, I need a change here to make sure I stay involved the way I want to be."

Regardless of which of these suggestions might be followed, the wise therapist will be responsive to boredom that is experienced and not just attempt to disregard it. To do so could be very dangerous and a big step in the direction of burning out both professionally and personally.

## CLIENT THREATENS TO SUE FOR MALPRACTICE

One of the major fears that clinicians in practice must face is the potential for a malpractice suit. Even though the chances of being sued are slim and the chances of a successful suit even slimmer, we must know how to deal with clients who for whatever reason are angry at their therapist and act out that anger through the threat of malpractice action.

Most typically, clients' feelings of anger are not the product of single instances when a therapist perhaps makes a mistake. Clients most often get angry as a result of a series of events or when issues have had a chance to build. For example, if a therapist allows clients to pay for sessions on a monthly or bimonthly basis, the risk of their getting angry about high therapy bills is much higher than if they paid by the session. Similarly, consider the client who threatens to sue because marital therapy ended in divorce. The divorce may have been a long time coming, with or without therapeutic intervention, and a client may blame a therapist to avoid personal responsibility. Typically, then, client threats to sue are predictable responses that can be foreseen.

Part of our job as therapists is to help clients face their feelings honestly. When clients seem to be withdrawing and letting themselves build toward anger, the therapist must open up discussion about the issue or issues of concern. For example, if a client is behind in paying fees, that issue should be openly discussed, and the sooner the better. Similarly, if a client appears angry, the therapist needs to initiate the discussion of what he or she is angry about. Beginning these discussions most often consists of an opener such as "We need to talk about your paying for the past three sessions" or "I sense you are irritated or angry at me about . . . . I would like to know what's bothering you because I'm getting worried."

The conversation following these openers can be made more productive if the clinician attends to the client's feelings. The important task in these discussions is open disclosure of feelings because open disclosure prevents the client from being forced to sue to get even, that is, to be taken seriously. The therapeutic skill most likely to prevent clients from carrying out a threat of malpractice action is empathic responding in a most Rogerian manner while simultaneously maintaining one's personal and professional integrity.

## MEETING CLIENTS OUTSIDE OF THERAPY

Meeting clients outside of therapy is bound to occur on occasion. However, in smaller communities there will likely be more frequent encounters. Therapists are wise not to promote discussion of issues that are, or have been, part of the therapy. During cross-examination the wise attorney avoids asking a question that could yield a harmful answer. Similarly, on meeting a client in the general community, a therapist could open a Pandora's box of problems by asking questions. The answer may divulge information that places the therapist in a compromised position with regard to other family members and/or may result in the client's detaining the therapist for a long period of time.

On the occasion of these chance meetings it is advisable to keep the conversation as brief and casual as possible. Even while wanting to be sociable, the therapist should model appropriate maintenance of private time and personal boundaries. Should a particular client seem to be pressing for more than what the therapist is willing to offer at that time and context, a comment such as the following generally suffices:

> It appears this is important, but speaking personally, I am not comfortable discussing this type of important information in this setting and under these time constraints. I would be far more comfortable if we were to pursue this issue in our next session. You deserve better than this.

If it is a client seen in the past who is no longer involved in therapy, a similar comment encouraging him or her to call you to arrange another appointment should prove sufficient.

Therapists run the risk of burning out rapidly and beginning to resent their clients if they are not protective of their personal boundaries and are willing to engage clients wherever and whenever they meet. Such therapists might also be wise to reevaluate how they are perceiving themselves as professionals and ask themselves whether they may be attempting to satisfy needs that are not in the best interests of either themselves or their clients.

## CLIENTS CALLING THE THERAPIST AT HOME

Many therapists have an unlisted phone number to prevent clients from calling. For those who find an unlisted phone number too troublesome, the problem of calls from clients can be addressed by identifying certain therapeutic ground rules. Many therapists who use written therapeutic contracts have included clear statements that phone calls to the therapist's home will be billed at the same rate as sessions in the office, with the time rounded off to the closest fifteen minutes. This is obviously one way of eliminating some clients from believing they may use the phone for free therapy. Whether the ground rule is established in writing or verbally shared, it is also imperative to communicate that what might be divulged in phone calls may be brought into therapy by the therapist. This rule can prevent calls from clients who hope to use them to share a secret with the therapist in order to create a notion of having something special with the therapist. The sharing of a secret in this fashion can place the therapist in a situation of feeling (and becoming) therapeutically paralyzed.

There are times, regardless of preventive measures, when a client persists in calling. With such clients it is important to address the issue directly in the next face to face session. Therapists should express their concerns about the phone calls directly and in a nonaccusatory fashion while promoting discussion of the implications of frequent calls. The calls may be a manifestation of the client's insecurity and self-perception of not being as competent as the therapist perceives the client to be—and this should be clarified. Another possible reason is that the client is attempting to test the therapist for caring and/or competence; that is, whether the therapist cares enough to talk on the phone, or whether this therapist really means what is said about no home phone calls. Regardless, persistent phone calls should be addressed directly before the therapist gets angry at the client.

## TOUCHING CLIENTS

During the course of therapy, there are many times when a particularly emotional exchange has occurred and the therapist may want to express feelings by touch. This type of exchange can often prove valuable and affirming to those involved and promote the therapeutic process, but caution should be exercised.

A male client touched by a male therapist may experience a sense of homosexual panic or a much more mild sense of uneasiness. Similarly, for a male therapist to touch a female who has been sexually abused, or is otherwise suspicious of others' intentions, could prove detrimental to the therapeutic process. In working with couples, there also exists the possibility that jealousy may be provoked by the therapist's touching one of the spouses, particularly if the therapist has been taking sides during the session with the spouse who is touched. This sort of incident could prove detrimental to what progress has been previously achieved in the couple's therapy.

Therapists should also be sensitive to the widespread publicity that sexual abuse of clients by therapists has received. For instance, a 1986 study of Wisconsin psychologists, family therapists, psychiatrists, social workers, clergy, and other psychotherapists was widely publicized across the country (Wisconsin Psychological Association, 1987). The results of the survey of 1,559 respondents showed that 310, or 20 percent, had treated clients between 1982 and 1984 who had been involved in a sexual relationship with a previous counselor. The study went on to indicate that 89 percent of the client victims were women and 93 percent of the offending therapists were men. Ninety percent of the respondents to this survey reported believing that the client's welfare had been seriously and negatively affected by the sexual encounter with his/her therapist. Naturally, such publicity about the therapeutic community is likely to further intensify the potential for misinterpreting an otherwise benign and nobly intended hug or touch on the shoulder.

For reasons such as these, the family therapist is best advised to ask permission prior to hugging a client, for instance: "Right now I am really appreciating the amount of honesty and work you have just demonstrated. Would it be all right if I gave you a hug?" This request serves not only to make the therapist's intentions clear, but also to empower clients and demonstrate to them a respect for the ownership of their bodies and physical boundaries. While being responsive to the divergent backgrounds and perceptions clients bring into our offices, this is also a means of exercising the caution that seems so appropriate today.

## SELF-SUPERVISION

After training, the benefit of supervision will not be so available as it was during training. Help from a colleague can prove valuable as a source of "bouncing ideas around" and deriving benefit, but systems-oriented colleagues may also be unavailable. Although there is truth in the old dictum, "It takes two to know one," meaning that the therapist must receive feedback regarding blind spots, reality dictates that we will not always have others available to us. At these times, self-supervision can be helpful in an attempt to examine practices systematically with couples and families.

Frequently, it is helpful to reflect back upon supervised experience received during training in an effort to recall issues that were emphasized with a past supervisor, for instance: "You're attempting to push this family in a direction that reflects your agenda rather than theirs," "You're taking too long for assessment and not intervening to effect some change quickly enough," "You seem to be siding too quickly and too strongly with the adolescent in this family," or "You seem to be caught up in the content of their presentation to the detriment of understanding their process." Reflecting on frequently uttered statements by past supervisors may disclose areas that are still problematic.

Another option is to periodically or, more particularly, when feeling stuck with a specific case, complete a rating scale/questionnaire such as that provided by Piercy, Laird, and Mohammed (1983). Their rating scale consists of ten items within five broad categories of skills deemed important in the function of family therapy. Reviewing this scale with your own practices in mind can focus attention on areas that may be in need of review and/or identify areas being overlooked that are producing an impasse in working with a particular family.

Professional associations such as the American Association for Marriage and Family Therapy (AAMFT) or the American Family Therapy Association (AFTA) have, in the past, established regional clusters, and these groups provide the benefit of closer contact with like-minded colleagues. It is common for these regional groups to be a rich source of peers who are readily available for support and peer supervision. While the benefit of supervision provided by a skilled supervisor cannot be overstated, the above identified practices can help to offset the absence of supervision.

## CLIENTS REJECT/ATTACK ONE COTHERAPIST

This phenomenon will occur at times as a result of simple personality clashes or attempts by the clients to split the cotherapists. A family member may feel attacked by the cotherapy team and choose to react to the cotherapist he or she views as weakest/strongest and most/least vulnerable, or whatever else may govern the choice of target.

At these times it is most valuable for the other cotherapist to remain available to the attacked cotherapist and client as a facilitator to their issue. The available cotherapist can attempt to clarify the concern(s) expressed by the client and ensure that the other cotherapist has effectively heard what was expressed before responding, and so on. In this respect, the available cotherapist can work with the cotherapist–client relationship, much as one would work with spouses who are processing dissonant perceptions of one another, and attempt to achieve some resolution. In this fashion, both cotherapists can effectively model for the couple/family productive means for resolving differences that are probably not characteristic of the family relationships.

Once the session is completed, it is generally valuable for the cotherapists to focus on what occurred and attempt to determine what may have precipitated the attack. This discussion can help them determine what they may have done to contribute to the client's behavior, what its further ramifications may be to the process of therapy, what they can do to avoid attacks in the future, and what should be addressed in the next session. Thus, this is a circumstance that can promote much learning and understanding for the cotherapists rather than simply being an unpleasant incident.

## WHEN THERAPIST'S PROBLEMS INFLUENCE THERAPY

There are obvious times in therapists' lives when it is unlikely they can provide appropriate therapeutic experiences to others. When a therapist is reeling from the death of a loved one, struggling with his or her own divorce, or obsessively consumed with any other life-changing concern, the intrapersonal interference will likely be too great to facilitate effective therapy. Therapists can conduct an internal inventory to determine when issues of this nature are so dramatically present that it would be best to postpone scheduled sessions. At these times the difficulty in concentrating on the clients' concerns is usually self-evident.

There are also more subtle therapist difficulties that may prove counter-productive to therapy. Adequate assessment of these problems requires the use of a consultant. We can often benefit from the feedback of another person to help us more clearly perceive our blind spots. For example, a therapist consistently sides with the parents against their adolescent son, which predictably leads the son to escalate his acting out. This escalating pattern may occur for several sessions, until the therapist gets a consultant who helps to clarify how the therapist is fighting the therapist's own adolescent son through a client family's struggle. With this new awareness the therapist can become more judicious in joining both parents and adolescent; without this awareness, the therapist will continue to be a factor that not only promotes maintenance, but intensifies the pattern the family presents. At such times the consultant may be a colleague, spouse, or some other person who is capable of providing the necessary perspective from outside the therapist's circumscribed self-perceptions.

When therapists find themselves stuck with a particular case and/or are receiving consistent feedback expressing concerns from a family, a consult will also likely prove valuable. Perhaps the therapist is simply overlooking an obvious piece of the family's operation that needs attention, but the therapist may also have become blinded by his or her own intrapersonally motivated distortions. Many therapists have found an ongoing professional support group invaluable in this regard. The fact that the group is an ongoing effort facilitates the members' coming to know one another well enough that valuable case consultation can be provided in regard to these difficult situations. If this type of problem recurs, the therapist might find it beneficial to consider entering therapy to determine the source of repeated distortions or blocks.

## TELLING CLIENTS ABOUT VACATION

Everyone needs a break in the routine of daily work, and family therapists are no different. The structure of therapy practice, however, interferes with that need because the right time for a vacation never seems to present itself. Within a group of clients, some family or another is always at a crucial phase in treatment, or some couple is always just about to make the flight to health. The problem is how to create the needed space in the appointment calendar without feeling irresponsible.

Clients can easily cope even if their therapist is on an extended vacation (more than two weeks) if they are warned well in advance and if they know what to do in a crisis. An upcoming vacation should be first mentioned approximately four sessions (weekly appointment schedule) beforehand and again at each session until the vacation begins. A statement such as "I want to let you know that I'll be out of town for three weeks beginning next month," or something similar, is adequate. Some therapists use the impending break as an intervention by asking clients to predict potential problems and crises and to discuss potential means of resolution. More typically, a long discussion of the upcoming break in sessions is not appropriate because the pace of therapy may be affected and any information regarding whom to call in a crisis may be forgotten.

In the following weeks, clients will need reminding, they will need information about whom to call in an emergency, and they will need to know the date of their next session after the break. Therapists in group practice often give clients the name and phone number of a colleague who has been briefed about the caseload. Those in solo practice may rely on a secretary, an answering service, or an answering machine to convey phone messages from clients needing emergency consultation. With the advent of voice mail systems, maintaining contact with the office while on vacation is becoming easier.

To avoid the difficulties imposed by extended vacations, many therapists take three- or four-day holidays instead. No warning is usually required because appointments can easily be shifted or canceled for one week. True irresponsibility is not realizing the need to take time off in order to avoid getting burned out. Therapy is highly demanding of intellectual and emotional resources, and the burnout cost is equally demanding. We all know therapists who have sacrificed their health, their jobs, and ultimately their own families to duty and service. The cost of not taking time off is high; time off is part of the job.

## DISCUSSING FEES

Fees for services rendered are a fact of life and should be dealt with directly by the family therapist. Many believe that therapists who have fees handled by a receptionist are missing out on a potentially valuable therapeutic opportunity. If the couple/family has insurance that pays for the service, the receptionist can likely handle the necessary paperwork, but there is much value in the therapist's handling those situations in which the clients pay directly for the service.

One way of handling fee payment is to tell the clients that they can pay at the end of every session or after every other session, as they might choose. This option not only gives them the element of choice, it also guards against the generation of bills so large that they create animosity in either the therapist or clients. If an unpaid bill is left to grow, it is not unreasonable to expect that the therapist and clients may begin to experience ill will toward one another, particularly at times of painful but necessary confrontation or when a therapeutic plateau seems to have been reached. Consequently, keeping the bill regularly paid up should be regarded as a preventive measure designed to avoid problems.

When therapists handle their own fees, they are also afforded a direct opportunity to model for clients how to consider oneself important and communicate directly and openly about issues that may be regarded as sensitive by others. In all likelihood, these issues of self-esteem and communication about sensitive material are difficulties for at least some family members. The negotiation of fee payments thus allows the therapist an opportunity to immediately model and begin to address structural issues of therapy. This situation also provides the therapist the opportunity to observe how decisions are made in the family. Do they consult one another, or does one member make the decision unilaterally? Also, who seems to be responsible for the management of money?

Making exceptions in the matter of payment of fees is often a harbinger of erosion of the therapist's effectiveness and the family's sense of engagement in the therapy. Although various reasons might be offered for these occurrences, the important consideration in this regard is to prevent erosion by not becoming lax. Unfortunately, therapists have not attended to this issue as directly as its importance should dictate. It is discussed only rarely in the professional literature and training programs, and it seems to have been given an aura of forbidden mystery. Until therapists value themselves enough to address fees directly, it may be unrealistic to expect more respect from society as a whole.

## FEELING STUCK IN A SESSION

Family therapy is a complex process, and even the most competent therapist does not always know which procedure in a session will prove to be the most beneficial. What has been successful in the past may or may not succeed again, and what has failed before may yield striking gains. A chesslike strategy, in which every move is planned on the basis of many possible countermoves, is an impossible dream in the context of therapy. As a result of this lack of predictability, therapists must expect to feel stumped, confused, and stuck.

More specifically, getting stuck means losing contact with what is happening or becoming overwhelmed with all the options of intervening in the session so that no action is taken. For example, when clients are allowed to drone on and on about a specific issue, therapists often allow their concentration to drift. Then, when the client stops speaking, a momentary silence occurs because the therapist has not kept up with the discussion. It is in this lull that feelings of being stuck can be most pronounced.

Getting unstuck typically requires that the therapist do something different from what he or she has been doing. If, for instance, the therapist is stuck in an empathic responding mode and is unable to think far enough ahead of the client (the client makes short statements) to do anything other than reflect, the simple acts of standing up, changing chairs, or stretching while sitting can provide the opportunity for redirection of the session and a transition to another topic. Becoming unstuck is mostly the product of providing your mind with the opportunity to consider new options. Altering physical position and taking a five-minute break are easily implemented changes that can create such opportunities.

## KEEPING USABLE NOTES

Historically, clinical case notes have been more content oriented than process oriented. Process notes are more specific regarding systemic notions such as the family's rules, roles, evident communication styles, and patterns that appear to be operational. Attending to the organization and structure of a family in notes lends itself to the development of direction, goals, and possible interventions for the therapist. Merely recording the content of who said what and where the session left off ignores such systemic information and may, in fact, get in the way of the therapist's appropriately conceptualizing the family in systemic fashion. We can all be entranced and diverted by stories. Clinical notes that focus on content are typically more reflective of stories than the workings of the people involved.

The therapist who functions with a particular internalized model for conceptualizing families will often find case notes referring to that model particularly useful. For instance, following the model for conceptualizing family functioning presented by Lewis, Beavers, Gossett, and Phillips (1976) lends itself nicely to process-oriented notes that naturally lead to therapeutic directions or goals. This model has specific checkpoints or potential issues built in, such as:

Are parental coalitions present or absent?

Is the family chaotically organized, organized by dominance, or egalitarian?

Are there vague and indistinct boundaries among family members or disengagement that results in members' questioning the sense of being connected?

Are family members verbally invasive of one another?

Can family members manifest a sense of openness to one another's perceptions, or are they impermeable in this respect?

Notes that are geared to a model of this nature will prove to have the most utilitarian value and be most likely to facilitate successful change if included with information such as who attended the session, any out-of-session assignments, or other case management details.

## REPORTING SEXUAL AND PHYSICAL ABUSE

Between 1963 and 1965 all fifty states passed laws requiring the reporting of sexual and physical abuse to the proper authorities. These laws vary from state to state, but typically carry stiff penalties in the form of fines, jail sentences, and/or professional sanctions. Therapists should familiarize themselves with the reporting laws and procedures in their jurisdiction as soon as they settle in a new locale. Learning about the laws is also a means of introducing the therapist to the protective service staff who are in a significant position to make referrals.

In consideration of these laws, it is incumbent upon the practicing therapist to report any incident within twenty-four hours of learning of the abuse, the period usually required by reporting laws. Although there is the concern about breaking confidentiality and the effects on the therapeutic relationship, the laws supersede confidentiality. Also, while the report will likely promote a crisis and result in inhibiting the therapeutic relationship for at least a short time, the resulting crisis can often serve to activate change in an abusive family that would otherwise not occur, or occur only after much time and suffering have passed. In this sense, as antithetical as it may appear, the reporting can often result in tremendous therapeutic value because change is promoted after the initial upheaval. The therapist reporting the abuse may not be in a position to render assistance but may very well serve as the catalyst to "open" the family to the help of others.

Most states allow for the reporting of an abusive situation anonymously, but the family is probably best served by the therapist who tells them that signs of abuse will have to be reported and then attempts to process family reactions. Therapist candor in this situation can serve as a model of effective interpersonal behavior, which is so frequently absent in abusive families. Typically, these families are closed systems pervaded by secrets. In this regard, the therapist's openness and directness is often a new experience and one that can promote the rekindling of a positive therapeutic relationship once the initial trauma has been resolved. Regardless of what might happen, though, the therapist must report and must be prepared for the potential onslaught by the family and/or the therapist's own struggle with the issue of reporting. At these times it is important to remember that this type of crisis may be the only catalyst that can promote change for these families;

it may be necessary to short-circuit the harm that may otherwise occur to the children.

For these reasons, therapists are wise to become acquainted with their area's child protective services staff. Doing so can facilitate the reporting process and ensure the therapist of having more input into treatment recommendations for the family, as well as an opportunity to encourage the protective services staff to acknowledge and implement a systems perspective. In this way, the family therapist can have a positive impact on the larger societal system that deals with abusive families.

# ETHICS "AT-RISK" TEST FOR MARRIAGE AND FAMILY THERAPISTS

Ever wonder how close you are to blundering over the ethics edge and possibly harming your clients, yourself and/or the profession? This test may tell you. Of course, you must answer honestly. Add up your score and compare the total with the key at the end of the test. *(Circle your answers)*

1. Is it true that you have *never* taken an academic course on MFT practice ethics?     No = 0    Yes = 1

2. Honestly, are you *unfamiliar* with some parts of the latest version of the Ethics Code?     No = 0    Yes = 1

3. Do you think the Ethics Code *interferes* somewhat with the quality of your therapy or research?     No = 0    Yes = 1

4. Have you *ever* sent a false bill for therapy to an insurance carrier?     No = 0    Yes = 1

5. Do you feel sexually attracted to any of your *present* clients?     No = 0    Yes = 1

6. Do you fantasize about kissing or touching a *present* client?     No = 0    Yes = 1

7. Do you comment to a *present* client how attractive he or she is or make positive remarks about his or her body?     No = 0    Yes = 1

8. Are you tempted to ask out an ex-client even though two years have not passed since termination?     No = 0    Yes = 1

9. Do you commonly take off your jewelry, remove shoes, loosen your tie, or become more informal during therapy sessions?     No = 0    Yes = 1

10. *Presently* do you meet a client for coffee or meals or for socializing outside of therapy?     No = 0    Yes = 1

11. Has a *present* client given you an expensive gift or frequently gives you inexpensive gifts?     No = 0    Yes = 1

12. Are you stimulated by a *current* client's description of sexual behavior or thoughts?     No = 0    Yes = 1

13. Are you in the midst of a difficult personal or family crisis yourself?     No = 0    Yes = 1

14. During the past two months, have you seen clients while you were hung over or under the influence of drugs, even if only a little?     No = 0    Yes = 1

| 15. | Does your personal financial situation cross your mind when considering whether to terminate therapy or to refer a client? | No = 0 | Yes = 1 |
|-----|---|---|---|
| 16. | Do you feel manipulated by a *current* client such that you are wary of them or are angry and frustrated by them? | No = 0 | Yes = 1 |
| 17. | Do you provide therapy to a *current* student, supervisee, or employee? | No = 0 | Yes = 1 |
| 18. | Have you wanted to talk to a colleague about a *current* case but feared doing so would show your lack of skill or lead to an ethics case against you? | No = 0 | Yes = 1 |
| 19. | Are you behind on case notes? | No = 0 | Yes = 1 |
| 20. | Do you talk about clients with other clients or gossip about clients with colleagues? | No = 0 | Yes = 1 |

0    Excellent, you are nearly risk free.

1–2  Review your practice. Read and follow the Ethics Code.

3–4  Review your practice for problem areas. Consider needed changes.

5–7  Consult a supervisor. You are engaging in high-risk behavior.

8+   Probably you have already harmed clients. Seek therapy and supervision. Come to terms with your situation by making immediate changes.

*Note:* The items making up the Ethics "At-Risk" Test come from the authors' research and ethics committee case experience. Send your comments and questions to Gregory Brock, Ph.D., 315 Funkhouser Building, University of Kentucky, Lexington, KY 40506-0054, USA. You have permission to copy, distribute, and publish the test with credit noted.

# References

Ackerman, N. W. (1958). Toward an integrative therapy of the family. *American Journal of Psychiatry, 8,* 727–733.

Ackerman, R. J. (1983). *Children of alcoholics.* Holmes Beach, FL: Learning Publications.

American Psychiatric Association. (1994). *Diagnostic and statistical manual of mental disorders* (4th ed.). Washington, DC: American Psychiatric Association.

Andersen, T. (1990). *The reflecting team: Dialogues and dialogues about the dialogues.* Kent, UK: Borgmann Publishing, Ltd.

Anderson, C. M., Reiss, D. J., & Hogarty, G. E. (1986). *Schizophrenia and the family: A practitioner's guide to psychoeducation and management.* New York: The Guilford Press.

Anderson, C. M., & Stewart, S. (1983). *Mastering resistance: A practical guide to family therapy.* New York: The Guilford Press.

Atlas, S. L. (1981). *Single parenting: A practical resource guide.* Englewood Cliffs, NJ: Prentice-Hall.

Auld, F., & Murray, E. (1955). Content-analysis studies of psychotherapy. *Psychological Bulletin, 52,* 377–395.

Bach, G., & Wyden, P. (1970). *The intimate enemy: How to fight fair in love and marriage.* New York: William Morrow & Co.

Barnard, C. P. (1990). *Families with an alcoholic member: The invisible patient.* New York: Human Sciences Press.

Barnard, C. P., & Corrales, R. G. (1979). *The theory and technique of family therapy.* Springfield, IL: Charles C. Thomas.

Berenson, D. (1976). Alcohol and the family system. In P. J. Guerin (Ed.), *Family therapy: Theory and practice* (pp. 284–297). New York: Gardner Press.

Berg, I., & Miller, S. (1992). *Working with the problem drinker: A solution-focused approach.* New York: Norton.

Bergin, A. E., & Garfield, S. L. (Eds.). (1994). *Handbook of psychotherapy and behavior change* (4th ed.). New York: Wiley.

Black, C. (1981). *It will never happen to me.* Denver, CO: M.A.C.

Bogus, S. (1993). An integrative treatment model for children's attentional and learning problems. *Family Systems Medicine, 11* (4):385–394.

Bossard, J., & Boll, E. (1950). *Ritual in family living.* Philadelphia: University of Pennsylvania Press.

Boszormenyi-Nagy, I., & Spark, G. (1973). *Invisible loyalties.* New York: Harper & Row.

Bowen, M. (1976). Theory in the practice of psychotherapy. In P. J. Guerin (Ed.), *Family therapy: Theory and practice* (pp. 43–90). New York: Gardner Press.

Boyd-Franklin, N. (1989). *Black families in therapy.* New York: The Guilford Press.

Brock, G., & Sanderson, B. (1984). Social exchange in the initial family therapy interview. *Journal of Marital and Family Therapy, 10,* 317–320.

Cartwright, D. (1966). Analysis of qualitative material. In L. Festinger & D. Katz (Eds.), *Research methods in the behavioral sciences* (pp. 421–470). New York: Holt, Reinhart & Winston.

Combrinck-Graham, L. (1988). Keeping children and families together: A report card. *AFTA Newsletter,* No. 32.

Cowley, G., & Springen, K. (1995). Rewriting life stories. *Newsweek,* Apr. 17, 1995, pp. 70–74.

Cruse, S. W. (1983). *Another chance: Hope and health for the alcoholic family.* Palo Alto, CA: Science and Behavior Books.

Cruse, S. W. (1989). *Another chance: Hope and health for the alcoholic family* (2nd ed.). Palo Alto, CA: Science and Behavior Books.

de Shazer, S. (1982). *Patterns of brief family therapy.* New York: The Guilford Press.

deShazer, S. (1985). *Keys to solutions in brief therapy.* New York: Norton.

deShazer, S. (1991). *Putting difference to work.* New York: Norton.

Epston, D., & White, M. (1995). Termination as a rite of passage: Questioning strategies for a therapy of inclusion. In R. A. Neimeyer & M. J. Mahoney (Eds.), *Constructivism in psychotherapy.* Washington, DC: American Psychological Association.

Ewing, J. A. (1984). Detecting alcoholism: The CAGE questionnaire. *Journal of the American Medical Association, 252,* 14, 1905–1907.

Ewing, J. A., & Rouse, B. A. (1970). *Identifying the hidden alcoholic.* Presented at the 29th International Congress on Alcohol and Drug Dependence, Sydney, Australia, Feb. 3, 1970.

Figley, C. R. (1988). Post-traumatic family therapy. In F. M. Ochberg (Ed.), *Post-traumatic therapy and victims of violence* (pp. 83–109). New York: Brunner/Mazel.

Finkelhor, D. (1979). *Sexually victimized children.* New York: Free Press.

Fossum, M., & Mason, M. J. (1986). *Facing shame: Families in recovery.* New York: Norton Publishers.

Goldman, G. D., & Milman, D. S. (1978). The initial phase of treatment. In G. D. Goldman & D. S. Milman (Eds.), *Psychoanalytic Psychotherapy* (pp. 20–33). Reading, MA: Addison & Wesley.

Good, G., Gilbert, L., & Scher, M. (1990). Gender aware therapy: A synthesis of feminist therapy and knowledge about gender. *Journal of Counseling and Development, 68,* 376–380.

Granvold, D. K., & Tarrant, R. (1983). Structured marital separation as a marital treatment method. *Journal of Marital and Family Therapy, 9,* 189–198.

Gravitz, H. L., & Bowden, J. D. (1985). *Guide to recovery: A book for adult children of alcoholics.* Holmes Beach, FL: Learning Publications.

Gurman, A. (1983). Family therapy research and the "new epistemology." *Journal of Marital and Family Therapy, 9,* 227–234.

Gurman, A., & Kniskern, D. (1986). Research on marital and family therapy: The process and outcome of. In S. Garfield & A. Bergin (Eds.), *Handbook of psychotherapy and behavior change* (3rd ed.). New York: Wiley.

Haley, H. (1976). *Problem solving therapy.* San Francisco, CA: Jossey-Bass.

Haley, J. (1973). *Uncommon therapy.* New York: Ballantine.

Hamburg, S. R. (1983). Reading aloud as an initial assignment in marital therapy. *Journal of Marital and Family Therapy, 9,* 81–88.

Hampson, R. B., & Beavers, W. R. (1996). Family therapy and outcome: Relationships between therapist and family styles. *Contemporary Family Therapy, 18* (3):345–370.

Heilman, R. O. (1973). *Early recognition of alcoholism and other drug dependence.* Center City, MN: Hazelden Institute.

Henggeler, S. W., Bourdin, C. M., & Mann, B. J. (1993). Advances in family therapy: Empirical foundations. *Advances in Clinical Child Psychology, 12,* 207–241.

Henkes, J. (1994). In search of answers: UW-Madison researcher tackles the mystery of Attention Deficit Disorder. *Wisconsin Ideas, 11* (2):13–15.

Hill, R. (1958). Generic features of families under stress. *Social Casework, 49,* 139–150.

Hof, L., & Berman, E. (1986). The sexual genogram. *Journal of Marital and Family Therapy, 12,* 39–47.

Hoffman, L. (1976). Breaking the homeostatic cycle. In P. J. Guerin (Ed.), *Family therapy: Theory and practice* (pp. 501–519). New York: Gardner Press.

Holmes, T. H., & Rahe, R. (1967). The social readjustment rating scale. *Journal of Psychosomatic Research, 11,* 213–218.

Howard, K. I., Lueger, R. J., Mating, M. S., & Martinovich, Z. (1993). A phase model of psychotherapy: Causal mediation of outcome. *Journal of Counseling & Clinical Psychology, 61,* 678–685.

Johnson, V. E. (1973). *I'll quit tomorrow.* New York: Harper & Row.

Keith, D. V. (1980). Family therapy and lithium deficiency. *Journal of Marital and Family Therapy, 6,* 49–54.

Kuehl, B., & Barnard, C. P. (1998). Making the genogram solution based. In T. S. Nelson & T. S. Trepper (Eds.), *101 interventions in family therapy, Vol. 2.* New York: Haworth Press.

Lambert, M. J. (1992). Implications for outcome research for psychotherapy integration. In J. C. Norcross & M. R. Goldstein (Eds.), *Handbook of psychotherapy integration* (pp. 94–129). New York: Basic Books.

Lewis, J. M., Beavers, W. R., Gossett, J. T., & Phillip, V. A. (1976). *No single thread: Psychological health in family systems.* New York: Brunner/Mazel.

MacAndrew, C. (1965). The differentiation of male alcoholic outpatients from nonalcoholic psychiatric patients by means of the MMPI. *Quarterly Journal of Studies on Alcohol, 26,* 238–246.

Mayfield, D. G., McLeod, G., & Hall, P. (1974). The CAGE questionnaire: Validation of a new alcoholism screening instrument. *American Journal of Psychiatry, 131,* 1121–1123.

McCubbin, H. I., & Patterson, J. M. (1982). Family adaptation to crises. In H. McCubbin, A. Cauble, & J. Patterson (Eds.), *Family stress, coping and social support* (pp. 26–47). Springfield, IL: Charles C. Thomas.

McGoldrick, M., Pearce, J., & Giordano, J. (1982). *Ethnicity and family therapy.* New York: The Guilford Press.

Meisel, P., & Kendrick, W. (1985). *Bloomsbury/Freud.* New York: Basic Books.

Minuchin, S. (1974). *Families and family therapy.* Cambridge, MA: Harvard University Press.

Minuchin, S., & Fishman, H. C. (1981). *Family therapy techniques.* Cambridge: Harvard University Press.

Nagy, B. I. (1987). *Foundations of contextual therapy.* New York: Brunner/Mazel.

Napier, A., & Whitaker, C. A. (1978). *The family crucible.* New York: Harper & Row.

Nathan, W. A. (1992). Integrated multimodel therapy of children with attention-deficit hyperactivity disorder. *Bulletin of the Menninger Clinic, 56* (3):283–312.

National Resource Center on Family Based Services. (1988). *An analysis of factors contributing to failure in family based child welfare services in eleven family based agencies: Executive summary.* Iowa City: University of Iowa.

Navran, L. (1973). *Marital diagnostic inventory.* Los Angeles: Western Psychological Services.

Neimeyer, R. A., & Mahoney, M. J. (1995). *Constructivism in psychotherapy.* Washington, DC: American Psychological Association.

O'Brian, C., & Bruggen, P. (1985). Our personal and professional lives: Learning positive connotation and circular questions. *Family Process, 24,* 311–322.

O'Hanlon, W., & Weiner-Davis, M. (1989). *In search of solutions: A new direction in psychotherapy.* New York: Norton.

Oliveri, M., & Reiss, D. (1982). Family styles of construing the social environment: A perspective on variation among nonclinical families. In F. Walsh (Ed.), *Normal family processes* (pp. 94–114). New York: The Guilford Press.

Olson, D. H., & McCubbin, H. I. (1982). Circumplex model of marital and family systems V: Application to family stress and crises intervention. In H. I. McCubbin, A. Cauble, & J. Patterson (Eds.), *Family stress, coping and social support* (pp. 48–72). Springfield, IL: Charles C. Thomas.

Palazzoli-Selvini, M., Boscolo, L., Gianfranco, C., & Prata, G. (1980). The problem of the referring person. *Journal of Marital and Family Therapy, 6,* 3–10.

Paul, N. (1967). The use of empathy in the resolution of grief. *Perspectives in Biology and Medicine, 11,* 153–169.

Peters, S. D., Wyatt, G. E., & Finkelhor, D. (1986). Prevalence. In D. Finkelhor (Ed.), *A sourcebook on child sexual abuse* (pp. 15–59). Beverly Hills, CA: Sage Publications, Inc.

Piercy, F. P., Laird, R. A., & Mohammed, Z. (1983). A family therapist rating scale. *Journal of Marital and Family Therapy, 9,* 49–60.

Pinsof, G., & Wynne, L. (1995). *Family therapy effectiveness: Current research and theory.* Washington DC: American Association for Marriage and Family Therapy.

Reddy, B. (1973). *Alcoholism: A family illness.* Park Ridge, IL: Lutheran General Hospital.

Richman, J. (1986). *Family therapy for suicidal people.* New York: Springer.

Rogers, C. (1951). *Client centered therapy.* Boston: Houghton Mifflin.

Schvaneveldt, J., & Lee, T. (1983). The emergence and practice of ritual in the American family. *Family Perspective, 17,* 137–143.

Selzer, M. L. (1971). The Michigan alcoholism screening test: The quest for a new diagnostic instrument. *American Journal of Psychiatry, 127,* 1653–1658.

Shadish, W. R., Ragsdale, K., Glaser, R. R., & Montgomery, L. M. (1995). The efficacy and effectiveness of marital and family therapy: A perspective from meta-analysis. In G. Pinsof & L. Wynne (Eds.), *Family therapy effectiveness: Current research and theory* (pp. 345–360). Washington, DC: American Association for Marriage and Family Therapy.

Shay, J. (1997). Website on Post Traumatic Stress Disorder [On-line]. Available: http://uhs.bsd.uchicago.edu/~bhsiung/tips/ptsd.html.

Short, D. (1996). Viktor Frankl, M.D., Ph.D. *Milton H. Erickson Foundation Newsletter, 16* (3):1, 18–20.

Smets, A. (1985). [Personal communication.]

Stahmann, R., & Heibert, W. (1977). The initial interview. In R. Stahmann & W. Heibert (Eds.), *Klemer's counseling in marital and sexual problems* (2nd ed.) (pp. 34–49). Baltimore: Williams & Wilkins.

Stanton, M., Todd, T., & Associates (1982). *The family therapy of drug abuse and addiction.* New York: The Guilford Press.

Storm, C., & Minuchin, S. (1993). Creating family friendly organizations: An interview with Salvador Minuchin. *Supervision Bulletin, 3,* 1–2.

Straus, M. A. (1978). Wife beating: How common and why? *Victimology, 2,* 443–458.

Straus, M. A., & Brown, B. W. (1978). *Family measurement techniques.* Minneapolis: University of Minnesota Press.

Strupp, H. H. (1993). The Vanderbilt psychotherapy studies: Synopsis. *Journal of Consulting & Clinical Psychology, 61* (3):431–433.

Strupp, H. H. (1996). The tripartite model and the consumer reports study. *American Psychologist, 51* (10):1017–1024.

Talmon, M. (1990). *Single-session therapy: Maximizing the effect of the first (and often only) therapeutic encounter.* San Francisco: Jossey-Bass.

Taylor-Jones, C. (1997). The effect on the marriage of a child diagnosed with the AD/HD-Tourette Spectrum disorder. *Progress: Family Systems Research & Therapy, 6,* 69–83.

Thurber, J. (1967). *The secret life of Walter Mitty.* New York: Associated Educational Services Corp.

Touliatos, J., Perlmutter, B., & Straus, M. (Eds.). (1990). *Handbook of family measurement techniques.* Newbury Park, CA: Sage Publishers.

Truax, C., & Carkhuff, R. (1967). *Toward effective counseling and psychotherapy.* Chicago: Aldine.

Vaillant, G. (1983). *The natural history of alcoholism.* Cambridge, MA: Harvard University Press.

Walker, L. (1978). The development, implementation, and evaluation of two educational models of family intervention (Doctoral dissertation, the University of Texas at Austin, 1978). *Dissertation Abstracts International, 39,* 2160A.

Walker, L. E. (1979). *The battered woman.* New York: Harper & Row.

Walsh, F. (1982). *Normal family processes.* New York: The Guilford Press.

Watzlawick, P., Weakland, J. H., & Fisch, R. (1974). *Change: Principles of problem formation and problem resolution.* New York: Norton.

Weber, T., McKeever, J., & McDaniel, S. (1985). A beginner's guide to the problem-oriented first family interview. *Family Process, 24,* 357–364.

Wegscheider, S. (1981). *Another chance: Hope and health for the alcoholic family.* Palo Alto, CA: Science & Behavior Books.

Weitzman, J., & Dreen, K. (1982). Wifebeating: A view of the marital dyad. *Social Casework, 63,* 259–265.

White, M. (1989). *The externalizing of the problem and the re-authoring of lives and relationships.* Adelaide, Australia: Dulwich Centre Publishers.

White, M., & Epston, D. (1990). *Narrative means to therapeutic ends.* New York: Norton.

Wisconsin Psychological Association. (1987). *Survey of sexual misconduct by psychotherapists and counselors.* Madison, WI.

Woititz, J. G. (1983). *Adult children of alcoholics.* Hollywood, FL: Health Communications.

Wolin, S. J., Bennett, L. A., Noonan, D. L., & Teitelbaum, M. A. (1980). Disrupted family rituals: A factor in the intergenerational transmission of alcoholism. *Journal of Studies of Alcohol, 41,* 199–213.

Zuk, G. H. (1981). *Family therapy: A triadic-based approach.* New York: Human Sciences Press.

# Author Index

# Subject Index